Flexibility at Work

To all of my family for their support and forbearance

Flexibility at Work

Balancing the interests of employer and employee

PETER REILLY

Gower

Published by
Gower Publishing Limited
Gower House
Croft Road
Aldershot
Hampshire GU11 3HR
England

Gower Publishing Company
131 Main Street
Burlington VT 05401-5600 USA

Peter Reilly has asserted his right under the Copyright, Designs and Patents Act 1988 to be identified as the author of this work.

British Library Cataloguing in Publication Data
Reilly, Peter A. (Peter Andrew), 1952–
   Flexibility at work : balancing the interests of employer
      and employee
   1. Hours of labour, Flexible – Great Britain 2. Manpower
   planning – Great Britain 3. Industrial relations – Great
   Britain
   I. Title
   331.2′572′0941

ISBN 0 566 08259 4

Library of Congress Cataloging-in-Publication Data
Reilly, Peter A, (Peter Andrew), 1952–
   Flexibility at work : balancing the interests of employer and employee / Peter A. Reilly.
      p. cm.
   Includes bibiographical references and index.
   ISBN 0-566-08259-4 (hardback)
      1. Hours of labor, Flexible–Great Britain. I. Title.

HD5109.2.G7 R44 2000
331.25′72′0941–dc21

                                                                00-042973

Typeset in 9 pt Utopia by Acorn Bookwork, Salisbury and printed in Great Britain by
MPG Books Limited, Bodmin.

Contents

List of Figures and Tables

FIGURES

TABLES

Acknowledgements

My thanks go to Stephen Bevan for giving helpful suggestions on the draft text; to Claire Lee and Elaine Sheppard for tracking down references; to Peter Bates for database searches; to Peter Herriot for reading suggestions; to Norman Lamb of Steele and Co. for his advice on legal questions; and to Robbie Gilbert of European Public Policy Advisers for his help with European affairs. Thanks are also due to Merle Read for her careful and sympathetic editing and to the rest of the Gower team for ensuring that the book has seen the light of day.

Any errors or omissions naturally remain my responsibility.

P.R.

Introduction

The word flexibility always seems to be in the news. We hear government ministers commending flexible labour markets to us. We hear of new family-friendly initiatives designed to make working and living easier to combine through more flexible working arrangements. We learn of industrial relations problems where employees resist new work patterns, or of employment tribunal cases concerning the apparent imposition of flexible forms of working.

So there is a lot of talk about flexibility. Is there as much action? And what do the parties mean when they use the term? In truth flexibility is a very flexible concept itself, and can be shaped to fit the needs of the protagonists. It is the contention of this book that such elasticity is a weakness more than a strength. Politicians, business people and trades unionists all argue their case on flexibility without defining what they mean. If the rhetoric was confined to parliament, perhaps this would not matter. But it infects the workplace. The talk gets in the way of doing day-to-day business. A former head of the International Monetary Fund (IMF) suggested that in France the word flexibility is seen as 'almost pornographic' (Whitehead, 1998). Things may not have got this far in the UK, yet the term tends to polarize opinion between those who see it as a necessary prerequisite to survival in the global market and those who see it as a means of eroding the rights of workers. The difference comes in part from a lack of shared understanding of the concept – are we talking about wages adjusting to changing macroeconomic performance or whether Mrs Smith can flex her working hours to look after little Bengy? – and in part from dissimilar views about how the world of work should be organized.

Lack of clarity over the meaning of the term flexibility, its use in a number of different guises, and the various models of the employment relationship used by those involved with work all combine to make this a tricky subject to get to grips with. This is true for academics and journalists, but more critically so for employers and employees. This book is really addressed to them. Ambiguity in a subject, especially one which is surrounded by so much rhetoric, is a recipe for conflict. As some of the illustrations in the book show, there have been strikes, legal disputes and disharmony over flexible work arrangements. There are, however, many other examples of the successful introduction of new work patterns or contracts. The key to success, this book argues, lies in balancing the understandable needs of employers to be efficient and competitive with the equally understandable needs of employees to protect their incomes and lead the lifestyle that suits them. This we call mutual flexibility, to be contrasted with other forms of flexibility where one or the other party benefits to the exclusion of the other.

It is all very well pointing to what in an ideal world ought to be done and giving examples of good practice: what the reader also needs to know is how to go about achieving this nirvana. Of course all organizations are different and I would not wish to offer a blueprint that should be uncritically adopted in all circumstances. Instead, I offer a model of how mutual flexibility might be developed and what preconditions are necessary to its success.

One notable characteristic of the model is that it approaches the issue of flexibility from the point of view of the individual. All too often flexible work arrangements are designed without due consideration given to the individual circumstances of employees. Mutuality can and should be achieved at collective level, but its application has to take account of the needs of people and their own particular lives: Mrs Smith has to look after little Bengy; Mr Brown has his elderly father to consider; Ms

Evans has been left by her partner to bring up the twins all by herself. The employment scene is increasingly diverse. Policies that assume that the organization is composed solely of middle-aged men with a housewife and two kids at home are obviously misconceived. But are organizations really recognizing that the drive to be more efficient is taking place at a time when the needs of the workforce itself are shifting, and shifting in ways that vary by gender, age, ethnic origin, sexual orientation, and above all individual circumstances?

So, put simply, the argument of this book is that the rhetoric on flexibility, the elasticity of the term and the different mental models held by those responsible for defining employment relationships make it harder to achieve success in developing flexible work arrangements. To overcome these difficulties, organizations should strive to get beyond the rhetoric and to find mutually advantageous approaches that cater for the variety of needs of their increasingly diverse workforce.

I hope that readers will be encouraged by the book to see the logic of the argument and feel emboldened to experiment in their own organization in the way that is proposed. I argue that treating employees as suggested here is more than a question of good practice but a mark of a civilized society. I hope that readers, though they find such sentiments acceptable, do not think that the idea of applying them is unrealistically naive. I have used evidence not just from examples of practice but from research to demonstrate the real business benefits of this approach. I have also sketched the changing external environment that is pressing on organizations to take more notice of the views of their employees and respond to their needs. Organizations, I argue, have to take account of the changing demography of the workforce and the social context within which it operates. They also have to consider the political environment, not just legislation emanating from Brussels or Westminster, but the climate within which actions are deemed to be acceptable or not.

Thus I am suggesting that there may be a moral imperative to take mutual flexibility seriously, as well as practical benefits to be derived from so doing in terms of organizational performance and a requirement to respond to the wider external pressures and influences.

We begin by looking at the rhetoric and mental models in Chapter 1. We move on to the changing demographic and labour market context in Chapter 2. The next two chapters explore what the term flexibility encompasses and why organizations are interested in its various manifestations. We then switch to the employees' perspective in Chapter 5: why are they attracted to flexibility? Chapter 6 examines the different types of employment relationship, and Chapter 7 argues for mutual flexibility. Chapter 8 offers a model of how to achieve mutuality in this way, with Chapters 9 and 10 giving examples of where it has worked and the preconditions to success. The next two chapters remind us that there are constraints to success, but give pointers to ways in which balancing the needs of employers and employees can overcome some of the difficulties. In the conclusion we attempt to bring these themes together.

CHAPTER ONE

Mindsets and Models

RHETORIC

'A flexible labour market! When I hear the Labour government using Tory phrases, I shiver just a little. Politicians of all parties urge working people to embrace a new model of employment, where employability replaces security,' said John Edmonds at the 1997 conference of the Trades Union Congress.

'We will keep the flexibility of the present labour market. And it may make some of you shiver, but I tell you in the end it is warmer in the real world,' retorted Tony Blair at the same conference.

These quotations illustrate the divide that separates the British political classes over the term flexibility. There are those who see it as a necessary precondition to success in the global economy, whereas there are others who regard it as a threat to job security and decent working conditions for those in employment. Such is the gulf that exists between these two groups that they communicate by megaphone. The volume is turned up loud, but they do not seem to hear or appreciate their opponents' point of view.

Much of the difficulty stems from the fact that politicians, trades unionists and business leaders start from very different conceptions of flexibility, and attach quite different meanings to the word. The present (2000) Labour government, like its Conservative predecessors, is principally concerned with flexible labour markets at the macro level. Government is interested in how the labour market can quickly adjust to changing economic circumstances. This requires the labour market to alter its size and nature to suit both broad variations resulting from the economic cycle or specific changes in demand within particular sectors or occupational groups. Thus politicians are pleased to see labour costs rise and fall in line with market needs or the movement of labour between regions, industrial sectors, occupations or even employers as the supply/demand balance shifts. While rather more difficult for politicians to stomach, labour market flexibility of this sort also implies the ability of organizations to recruit or dispose of labour as required to suit economic conditions.

William Waldegrave, when chief secretary to the Treasury in 1996, for example, claimed in a speech to American Chambers of Commerce that the move to a flexible labour market was responsible for reducing long-term and structural unemployment, and for evening out regional labour-market differences. This is because, he believed, removing regulation benefits job creation: 'Big government not only destroys freedom, it destroys jobs. Keeping the state in check – and thereby helping the magic of the market to provide jobs – is the best way to avoid a society which is not divided against itself by the cancer of long term unemployment' (quoted in Thomas, 1996). In similar vein Michael Portillo, as Secretary of State for Employment, told an Institute of Personnel and Development (IPD) conference in 1994: 'We must give people the freedom to exercise their skills, the freedom, for example, to work the hours which suit them and their employer, and not the hours the bureaucrats decide are good for them.'

Note the moral tone of this approach: there is a big-government-bad, small-government-good tone to these speeches. This view was more recently echoed, with a practical twist, by Sir Clive Thompson, at the time President of the Confederation of British Industry (CBI), speaking at the British Chambers of Commerce Conference in 1999 (quoted in Rana, 1999). 'More regulated economies tend to have slower growth and higher unemployment. It really doesn't matter whether the regulation comes from Westminster or Brussels – it's all a burden that requires managers to commit time and money they can ill afford'.

Thus the argument put forward by those in favour of a flexible labour market has a number of features. It is

- practical: managers find it harder to manage in a regulated economy
- moral: flexible labour markets provide freedom for people to decide what suits them best
- philosophical: voluntarism is a better approach than statism
- economic: this form of organization produces better performance and lower unemployment.

Support for this approach has also come internationally. The Organization for Economic Cooperation and Development (OECD) and International Monetary Fund have both commended the UK's flexible labour market in contrast to other 'unreformed' situations. They have taken the same view as Waldegrave that flexibility can ease unemployment:

> The widening distribution of working hours, low strike activity, ease of hiring and firing, greater decentralisation of fixing pay and work conditions, and wider wage differentials according to skills and regional variations are clear manifestations of greater labour market flexibility. This on-going process should help to lower aggregate unemployment as the expansion continues. (OECD, 1996b)

In a similar tone the IMF in its 1997 annual report commended certain countries for their efforts, including the UK, but has argued that 'in most European countries there was a need to reform the complex system of regulations, benefits and taxes that discouraged job creation and job search, while safeguarding a reasonable level of social protection and meeting legitimate equity objectives' (International Monetary Fund, 1997).

Moreover, the IMF has claimed that too many labour market interventions in Europe

have been cosmetic and not addressed the root cause of the problem. Indeed, some (like work-sharing schemes) may even have provided added protection to those in work, but perpetuated the exclusion of those out of work. The OECD has also taken countries to task for the negative impact that legislation on employment protection has had on job creation, favouring instead voluntary agreements entered into at enterprise level.

The alternative position adopted by trades unionists, and by some dissenting economists, is that flexibility can be exploitative. These commentators and pressure groups are interested more in the employment consequences of flexible labour market policies than its perceived economic efficiency. John Edmonds at the 1997 TUC Conference rejected the notion that employment protection hinders job growth. Instead, he complained that the term flexibility too often meant 'you're sacked'. He was asserting the need for employment rights against the 'hire and fire' practices of employers 'who are too idle, too blinkered and too misguided to apply the civilised standards that ought to underpin our society and our law'.

Trades unionists believe that the Conservative government created an environment in which this exploitation flourished. John Monks said at the October 1998 IPD Conference: 'The labour market today – far from being characterised by fairness and flexibility – is manifestly unfair and the legislative framework established by the previous government has largely benefited the bad employer'. They objected to Britain being promoted as the 'bargain basement economy of Europe' (Monks, 1996b), with low wages and little regulation.

Trades unionists are equally unconvinced of the economic benefits of the flexible labour market. An analyst at HSBC (the Hong Kong and Shanghai Banking Corporation) commented on the UK's flexible labour market when unemployment was expected to rise in early 1999, given an economic downturn: 'In previous cycles, changes in total employment have taken an average of two or three quarters to respond to changes in activity. If anything the lag may be shorter this time, adding weight to the theory that the labour market has become significantly more flexible in the last 10 to 15 years' (Dharshini David, quoted in Atkinson, 1999). Contrast this City approval with the view of John Monks given at the Jim Conway Memorial Lecture in November 1997: 'In our unstable labour market unemployment falls impressively fast during a recovery but shoots up during a recession'. Monks is talking about the same issue, but is looking at the other side of the coin: the consequences of flexibility, the redundancies, the dismissals, the inequality of incomes and such like.

Moreover, those on the political left believe that the job insecurity and unemployment engendered by flexibility are deleterious to economic performance. They argue that flexibility means that workers do not have the confidence to spend their earnings, fearful as they are that their employment might come to a sudden halt. They think this problem has been compounded by management's failure to develop high-quality product strategies that depend upon having a skilled workforce. The result, as far as they are concerned, is that investment in training and development has been neglected, thereby leaving the workforce underskilled.

In the report of the Commission on Wealth Creation and Social Cohesion (1995), Lord Dahrendorf made a broader point regarding the wider social effects of a flexible labour market. He was concerned that 'an insecure and fractured society' was being created 'with fewer and fewer shared values and common interests'. He was particularly worried about the impact of the exclusion of a class of people and its effects on social cohesion. The Borrie Commission had come to similar conclusions: 'Unregulated markets cannot by themselves deliver a satisfactory combination of economic growth and social cohesion; in fact they deliver the worst of all worlds – low growth and high inequality' (Commission on Social Justice, 1994).

Trades unionists do see that flexibility can provide benefits at the micro- or organizational level. John Monks again, lecturing at the Manchester Business School in June 1998, said:

> Undoubtedly firms and organisations need to be flexible so that they can respond to rapid changes in market conditions. Their staff in turn need to contribute fully to the firm's flexibility, but this is not the same as, and is often the opposite of, the hire and fire we are asked to support.

Monks in particular likes to compare the beneficial effects of flexibility when delivered in the right way with the negative consequences in other people's hands.

> The bald fact is that a terrified workforce will resist change, and businesses that are flexible need to adapt to changing demand quickly and efficiently. Truly flexible workforces are those that feel secure and are confident about coping with changing conditions. In these organisations, staff want to work with the company in meeting changing demands. Contingent on this is the need for good training and development policies. (Monks, 1996a)

However, these more balanced comments are frequently drowned out by the emotional and exaggerated language used by some critics of flexible labour markets, as evidenced by the following illustrative quotations:

● Studs Terkel: under the 'mantra' of flexibility, 'the worker has become a robot and is as dispensable as Kleenex' (quoted in Christy, 1998).
● 'We do not mean the Martini economy flexibility, beloved by so many employers: "You work anywhere, any time, any place, and you even sing as off to work you go"' (Simon Petch, Society of Telecom Executives, TUC Conference 1997).
● Borrie Commission on Social Justice: 'The hire and fire culture of casino capitalism destroys employee loyalty. The search for a

fast buck destroys the trust that is the basis of successful co-operation between firms' (Commission on Social Justice, 1994).

- John Monks in the Jim Conway Memorial Lecture in November 1997 talked of flexibility providing 'cover for backward practices that do no one, other than the worst kind of spiv employer, any good at all.'
- 'I was taught all about flexibility by a previous administration where the Iron Lady created a Plasticine workforce; easy to squeeze, easy to squash and easy to roll into a ball and throw away. I was not taught much about fairness, except by example. They showed me that the "haves" could get as much as they could grab and the "have nots" could get knotted' (Daniel Yates, Chartered Society of Physiotherapy, TUC Conference 1997).
- Larry Elliot, the economics editor of *The Guardian*: 'Flexibility of course means sacking people, driving down wages and cutting welfare benefits' (Elliot, 1999a).
- 'Tony Blair's ideas about flexible working guarantee a poverty that gives the children of the British working people the worst health in western Europe, now on a par with Slovenia and Albania' (Pilger, 1999).

MODELS

One of the reasons for the rhetorical clashes I have described is that those who are speaking have conflicting models in mind. All of us rely on mental maps to guide us in our understanding of the world. Having conceptions of how employment relationships ought to operate is no different. Broadly it seems the UK is offered a choice between American and European labour market models, though some commentators would add the Japanese system, aiming to have the best of both worlds. The models are often distortions of reality: descriptions are partial and incomplete, differences between them are exaggerated – all so as to argue the particular case of the protagonist. From the viewpoint of John Monks, for example, there is the following choice: 'On the one hand there is an essentially Anglo Saxon

model based on hire and fire and short termism. On the other there is a European model based on long termism and social partnership: co-operation by all stakeholders in an enterprise to promote their mutual interests' (Monks, 1996a). Those on the other side of the argument would contrast the economic vitality of the US with the stagnation of the European economies. Adair Turner, former Director General of the CBI, speaking at the 1997 conference of the Trades Union Congress, claimed that 'something is going wrong with Europe's competitiveness, with the way that labour markets work in Europe and with the operation of what is sometimes called "the European model."' He argued 'what is not true is that continental Europe has everything wrong and that the Anglo-Saxons have everything right, [but] the fact is the US has a superior job creation record than continental Europe'.

I will now outline the shape of these models as argued by their supporters.

THE US MODEL

Those who favour the American model like to emphasize the long-running period of economic growth as evidence of the sustainability and superiority of its form of market capitalism. Proponents claim that success is just as visible at the workplace as it is on Wall Street. They point to the buoyancy of job creation – the 40 million jobs generated in the US between 1970 and 1992. This is favourably compared with only 6 million jobs created in the European Union (EU) over the same time (Organization for Economic Cooperation and Development, 1994). Moreover, since 1984 unemployment in the USA has been consistently lower than in the EU, currently standing at around half the European rate (Commission of the European Communities, 1999). One reason for this situation, it is claimed, is the high turnover of jobs, the result especially of the mobility between jobs of young workers in their search for employment. This is evidenced by the fact that the average number of jobs a US worker will have in his or her lifetime is ten, whereas in Germany it is only four.

Similarly, an unemployed person is five times more likely to become re-employed having lost his or her job in the US compared to the UK. It is accepted that there is a cost to this job creation – the frequency of job loss. The same American is three times more likely to become unemployed in the first place than his or her British cousin. But this price is seen as worth paying because of the benefit of having a labour force responsive to changing economic conditions.

Supporters of this model claim that this sort of vigorous and flexible labour market is largely a consequence of the unregulated nature of American business activities. Employers, it is argued, face few restrictions in their ability to hire and fire. Wage determination in the US is said to be pretty decentralized and uncoordinated, and therefore more market driven than in Europe. So wages respond quickly to changes in unemployment. Advocates also point out that American employers face lower employment tax and social contribution costs compared with their European counterparts. For example, US payroll tax rate is roughly half that of Sweden, Italy or France as a percentage of wage costs. Those in favour of the American model claim that such taxes and restrictions have priced low-skilled jobs out of the European market place.

Attitudes to employment in the US are underpinned by an individualistic social philosophy. America is seen as a country of free individuals who are able to achieve whatever they will, unburdened by class or other restrictions. Self-help is the name of the game. People are expected to rescue themselves from unemployment, not rely upon the State to bail them out. Organizations too are unfettered. They are free to establish the form of their relationship with employees without being dictated to by government. Given the strength of the commercial imperative, US companies tend to be interested in schemes of employee participation only if they believe that they will improve organizational efficiency and, ultimately, profitability. Mutuality in employee relations, other than driven by self-interest, is unusual. The State may occasionally intervene,

but largely it is left to the market place to determine the nature of employment relationships.

THE EUROPEAN APPROACH

Advocates of the alternative European continental model say that it too operates a free-market economy, but, by contrast, within the boundaries of protective legislation. Its 'welfare capitalism' provides a safety net for those at the margin of employment. This approach is supported by a corporate system that recognizes the interests of both employer and employee. Organizations accept that they must take cognisance of the social consequences of their actions. Governments play an active role in maintaining employment. This is seen, for example, in reskilling and retraining initiatives, in cutting working hours and in direct intervention to secure jobs.

By comparison with the US, many western European countries regard the State as a reflection of a national community. Its interests may on occasion transcend those of the individual: on this basis regulation is justifiable. The rights of the individual need protection and have to be balanced with the rights of the organization. Given the Napoleonic legacy of codification, employee involvement is built into the legal system. And there is a much wider acceptance that individuals may be at the mercy of economic events over which they have no control.

Supporters would say that the European model produces a reasonable trade-off between economic performance and social cohesion. They point to the social cost of US-style labour market flexibility – its 'supreme flexibility but extreme social conditions', according to Bill Morris, General Secretary of the Transport and General Workers Union (TGWU). They illustrate this by citing the wide income-disparity in the US caused by the extremely low wages at the bottom end of the labour market (the top 10 per cent of US workers earn 4.5 times the bottom 10 per cent, compared with 2.3 times in Germany); social inequality that extends beyond wealth to access to housing and health care; the insecurity of job tenure and even the significant prison population, amounting to some 2 per cent of the US workforce with a further 5 per cent on parole or probation. Indeed some go further in saying that economic efficiency is promoted by equality, or at least that inequality limits economic performance. This form of 'stakeholder' capitalism ensures co-operation between employers and employees in a higher trust environment than found in the US, thereby facilitating greater, not lesser, organizational adaptability. As the European Commissioner for employment and social affairs, Anna Diamantopoulou, has argued: 'We must promote a more inclusive Europe – not only for reasons of social justice, but also because social inclusion is a positive economic factor' (Diamantopoulou, 2000).

THE JAPANESE VARIANT

The Japanese approach to employee relations has, until recently, been seen by some people as an attractive alternative to the hire and fire approach of the US, and one that could also point to a great deal of economic success. It has managed high rates of growth with low unemployment. There are said to be three pillars to the Japanese model:

- lifetime employment
- progression on the basis of seniority
- enterprise unions.

In the Japanese model a clear link is established between stable employment and the motivation and commitment of the workforce. The firm is seen as a community whose members share a common consciousness about its aims, especially its future prosperity. The system extends beyond employment, so that an internal welfare system looks after employees' social needs. At work the employee is guaranteed lifetime employment. This is supported by age- and service-based promotion and pay progression. Training and development are given a high priority, and employees are provided with opportunities to better themselves. Thus, on joining a company, an employee would expect to see how his (it is a predominantly male-oriented system) career would develop over time and how his skills would improve, and at the same time have every aspect of life provided for in an all-encompassing way.

In exchange, workers are expected to be highly adaptable and mobile within the organization. They must remain loyal – resignation is unheard of – until retirement. In addition, for management posts at least, people have to be prepared to work long hours and take few holidays. In other words, employees put themselves at the disposal of management to be used as management sees fit.

What then is the role of the trades union? As part of the post-war bargain between employers and trades unions, the former were allowed by the latter a fair measure of managerial control at the workplace, in exchange for a continuing improvement in terms and conditions. Employee relations were based on a shared and common commitment to the community of the firm. Occupational or sectoral unionism played second fiddle to enterprise unionism. This has meant that, instead of challenging the employers, as we would expect in the West, unions accepted that they were also part of the established order. Proponents of the Japanese model would say that this did not represent incorporation of the unions into the management of the firm, since this misconceives the purpose of the enterprise. Japanese companies are expected to recognize the interests of employees just as much as those of shareholders, so that collective bargaining is more about the distribution of rewards among the workforce than between employees and shareholders. And similarly, if restructuring is required, employees are not to be treated as resources that can simply be dumped, because the company has a responsibility for their future welfare.

Japanese companies emphasize individual responsibility for performance, but also the importance of interdependence and teamworking. Moreover, they stress the value of employee involvement in structuring work and of consensual decision making. A sense of common purpose is thereby generated. As Nissan explained: 'The system of lifetime employment gives employees a sense of security and a feeling of belonging.... It motivates a feeling of unity among employees and a consciousness of sharing the same future as the company' (quoted in Wickens, 1987).

The Japanese employment system is part of a wider culture, where long-term relationships are supported by strong social norms in what has been described as a 'clan' society. High levels of trust between contracting parties, it is claimed, are possible in this situation.

THE TRUTH?

Naturally, the truth is more complicated than the models would suggest. It has to be remembered that these are simplifications of what are in reality more complex pictures. This is especially true for Europe, where the experiences of several countries are conflated into the one model. As the CBI nicely puts it, Europe is a 'patchwork quilt of different practices with uniquely complementary strengths and weaknesses' (Confederation of British Industry, 1997). The active intervention policies of a country like Sweden starkly contrast with, say, those of Spain. France may have high payroll taxes; Denmark does not.

There is also the problem of attribution: how do cause and effect actually work? It may well be correct to point out the sluggish economic performance of EU countries in recent years, but is this due to a lack of flexible labour markets or to overly tight fiscal control? Does employment protection really lead to unnecessary unemployment? Despite its support for flexible labour markets, the OECD recently concluded that it does not (Organization for Economic Cooperation and Development, 1999). This is in line with detailed work done by Stephen Nickell (1997), which found that only a handful of labour market features (for example, generous unemployment benefits with little attempt to push people back to work) are associated with unemployment, and some labour market 'rigidities' could be seen as positively helpful. The same point has been put more graphically by John Monks: 'Those that claim that red tape is strangling economic

growth have failed to produce the murder weapon' (Monks, 1996b).

The models also tend to be a partial description of what is happening. In the Japanese account, for example, Western understanding and interest have tended to concentrate on life in the blue-chip industrial and commercial companies that operate a system of lifetime employment. The other side of Japanese life has been neglected. Their employment model clearly distinguishes between those at the core of economic life, and those at the periphery. Those at the core, as we have seen, have been well looked after, but the demarcation with the periphery can be stark. Temporary and part-time employees have never been part of the core. So women are frequently excluded, as are low-skill and -status workers. These peripheral workers are vulnerable to dismissal when demand drops, given the protection afforded to core workers. Work is also contracted in or out as demand rises and falls. Thus for these peripheral workers the labour market is very flexible and produces for them a rather more precarious existence than it does for those employed at the core, who are expected merely to be adaptable within the confines of the firm (Benson, 1996).

Partiality in description also tends to give the impression of complete consistency: the US is said to have an entirely unregulated labour market, with low taxation and employer freedom to set wages in line with economic performance, in contrast with the restrictions of the European approach. This account not only distorts the variety of European practice but it also ignores aspects of the American situation that do not fit the model. There are minimum-wage laws in the US and wage flexibility is no greater than in Europe. Payroll taxes are lower in the US than Sweden, but they are higher than Portugal, let alone Denmark. Equal opportunities legislation in the US is distinctly more restrictive than in several European countries.

Also, the different countries of Europe make different trade-offs between flexibility and regulation. There may be greater restrictions within Europe compared with the US in terms of flexibility in working time, in the ease of changing employment levels and in the employer's ability to adjust wages. However, this may be compensated for by greater task-flexibility within the workplace (as in Germany), the capacity to alter the national paybill in the light of economic circumstances (as in the Nordic countries) and the promotion of skill development (for example, in the Netherlands, France or Germany).

Nor is the world static. The EU has tried to respond to the lack of economic vitality and persistent unemployment. The European Commission has supported the removal of 'artificial barriers' to job creation. The European continental countries themselves have been trying to deregulate, to allow greater flexibility of labour use and reduced payroll on-costs, in order to stimulate better economic performance and more employment. The business community has been urging governments to reduce the welfare bill and to deregulate. Hans-Olaf Henkel, President of the Bundesverband der Deutschen Industrie (BDI, the German equivalent of the CBI), has called for fewer regulations, lower labour costs and tax incentives in a drive towards greater labour market flexibility. The threat is that if this is not achieved companies in the global market place will 'leave Europe, progressively, and step by step they will move their investments outside of Europe', according to Jean René Fourtou, chairman of Rhône Poulenc (*International Herald Tribune*, 1999).

In 1999 the German government established a series of interlocking committees (called the Alliance for Jobs), chaired by a cabinet member and involving employer representatives, trades unions and academics, to look at the nature of the German social contract in the context of economic change. At the time of writing, plans are afoot to cut corporate taxes and restrain social spending, to the applause of business leaders.

These changes allow Romano Prodi, President of the European Commission, to write:

> Europe is no longer crudely divided between corporatists and free-mar-

keters, between the Anglo-Saxon or continental model, or between advocates or opponents of the welfare state. Few are any longer in denial over the need for tough structural reform, deregulation, flexible labour markets and the modernisation of pension schemes. And many countries no longer shrink from publicly espousing the goal of full employment. (Prodi, 2000)

The Japanese model, too, has been under pressure from declining economic performance, financial instability, new technology, competitive pressures in a global market place and changing social and demographic trends. The response of organizations appears to be a gradual process of adaptation. The core/periphery distinction has been under pressure, blurred by the recognition of some employers that there are those with particular expertise who are likely to be mobile between employers, selling their knowledge as they go. More choice in career paths has therefore to be expected. Incentivization may increasingly come not merely through service with a single company, but through performance in the job. There has seemingly been less challenge to industrial relations. Companies still try to manage change with as little hurt to their employees as possible, using redeployment, including to affiliates, as an alternative to redundancy wherever possible. The Japanese Employers' Federation indeed has been advocating a third way between high levels of continental European unemployment and large income differentials of the Anglo-Saxon variety (Whittaker, 1998). It is interesting to note that the more radical change that has come at Nissan was instigated from outside: a secondee from Renault was responsible for significant downsizing plans.

Finally, there is the issue of whether these concepts are of practical value. Can they be exported, especially in isolated pieces? To what extent are adaptations necessary? Japanese companies setting up abroad have brought with them some aspects of their model. In 1993 a survey of 25 Japanese companies working in the UK found that 20 had some form of lifetime employment on offer to staff (Involvement and Participation Association, 1995). In the wider business community, we have learnt about quality circles, *kaizen* (or continuous improvement) and just-in-time inventory control. Sometimes these transplants have worked well; in other cases there has been an imperfect understanding of the nature of the holistic approach of Japanese management. US ideas have been more pervasive, though whether they have been more successful is a matter of debate. Companies with continental European origins have tended towards greater employee-participation mechanisms and more information provision (Milward et al., 1992), which fits ideas from home, whereas Japanese companies have been inclined to follow the local approach to employee relations (Kessler and Bayliss, 1992).

THE NATIONAL IMPACT

As I have suggested, though there are significant differences between the US and European labour markets, these can be exaggerated. Similarly, there are characteristics of the Japanese model found elsewhere. Nevertheless, these descriptions are forms of shorthand which are used in political argument, whatever the precise truth of the situation. And truth is always difficult to establish in a world of 'lies, damned lies and statistics'!

The importance of the models is that they directly or indirectly influence thinking. In the UK, this has been the case at both national and organizational level.

THATCHERISM

After the Second World War, during the time of Butskellism, the UK was clearly something of a halfway house between Europe and the US, a kind of hybrid. More than in the US, the notion of a mixed economy with both private enterprise and public ownership was generally accepted. The UK had a much more developed welfare state than in the US. Government intervention through Keynesian demand-management was more widely practised. On the other hand, despite the Wilson government's forays into a corporatist approach to managing UK plc, there was less of the continental European tripartite (government, trades union and employer) co-ordination of the economy.

When the Thatcher government came to power in 1979 there was a gradual and then more self-conscious aim to transform the UK economy and its labour relations, much more along the lines of the US under Reagan. The Conservatives tried to do this through creating or sustaining a new value structure. Its emphasis was on entrepreneurial activity, highly responsive to economic signals and operating within limited constraints. This, it was hoped, would produce high wages and low unemployment derived from a productive and competitive economy.

The White Paper *Competitiveness: Helping Business to Win*, published by the Department for Trade and Industry (DTI) in June 1994, set out the terms of the ideal labour market as one in which:

- employment and labour productivity are maximised by efficient matching of supply and demand;
- wages are based on local labour market conditions;
- enterprises are characterised by responsive management, good industrial relations and flexible bargaining systems; and
- freedom from discrimination and rigid demarcations allow individuals to make their full economic contribution.

It was accepted that in this approach there would be a widening difference in wage levels, but this differential was justified in providing a premium for acquiring the skills in demand and giving an incentive to get out of unemployment into work. Flexibility was clearly the order of the day, not just financially through individualized rather than collectively determined pay, but also through increased labour mobility and greater responsiveness in working practices to changing technology or business needs.

In practice these aspirations were supported by reducing the government's role in the labour market (through privatization, eschewing intervention in labour disputes, wages council abolition and so on), applying a 'free-market' philosophy to public services (seen especially in compulsory competitive tendering), curbing the power of trades unions to set wages or control workplace deployment, and allowing employers more freedom to hire and fire through changing legislation on closed shops and dismissals.

The result was described thus in a Department of Employment research report: 'The UK would appear to be in an intermediate position, with some features of its labour market resembling the USA and in some more resembling its EU partners. However, the UK has probably moved closer to a US style labour market since the end of the 1970s' (Beatson, 1995).

Thus the hybrid became more like one parent than the other.

BLAIRISM

The present UK government, as we saw at the start of this chapter, sees the economic necessity of flexible labour markets, and has stressed their worth to its European partners – so much so that French Socialists have described Blair's position as 'Reaganomics with a red rose in its lapel' (Walker, 1999). However, in practice, government attitudes to the employment relationship seem to centre on the notion of partnership within the context of flexibility with security. Even before government a Labour Party pamphlet (1996) talked about organizational success being linked to flexibility, but in circumstances where there were minimum standards and the 'security which underpins new working relationships'. The term partnership has been used to justify new employment legislation and achieve a balance between regulation and freedom of business to pursue its interests. Thus Ian McCartney, then Minister of State at the DTI, launched the Employment Relations Bill in

January 1999, saying: 'We are on the threshold of a renaissance in employment relations. Employers, employees and their trade unions are realising that partnerships in the workplace are a genuine win/win situation for all concerned, and that their advantages for competitiveness and job creation must be exploited to the full' (Department for Trade and Industry, 1999).

Some 18 months earlier, at an Electricity Association conference, McCartney had made similar points about partnership by saying that it involved protecting employee rights and valuing their contribution, while at the same time ensuring that business operated as efficiently as possible. In the context of flexibility, he said that 'we want a framework that provides protection for employees but which allow firms to adapt'. This he called 'flexibility plus'.

This concept is not a million miles away from the 'flexibility with security' that is talked of by the European Commission, so it could be suggested that the UK hybrid, having turned its face more towards its American side during the Conservative years, is now turning its head the other way towards the European model. Yet from the way in which it insists that labour market flexibility is an essential prerequisite to economic success, and that business should not be burdened by regulation, the government also seems to identify strongly with the Anglo-Saxon strain of capitalism. Unlike some continental European countries, it also seems more prepared to embrace globalization. Rather than see it as a threat, the government sees opportunity for enterprise capitalism in a globalized information age. Some would regard this as equivocation on the government's part; others that it is trying to have the best of both worlds in facing both ways at the same time.

ORGANIZATIONAL IMPACT

The models we have considered have influenced thinking in organizations in a number of ways. There has been the direct adoption of some of these ideas as guiding philosophies on how companies ought to be run. There has also been an indirect effect through generating a climate of opinion where some concepts flourished more than others. This has been seen specifically in the way the human resource management approach to people management has stimulated debate and influenced practice.

HUMAN RESOURCE MANAGEMENT

The Conservative government's policies on flexible labour markets coincided, perhaps not entirely by chance, with growing interest in the ideas of human resource management (HRM). These came from the US and concerned how people ought to be managed at work. It is in fact a very broad theory that has appeared in a number of guises (Guest, 1989). Among its features is the desire to:

- integrate people management with business strategy
- encourage employee flexibility, commitment and contribution
- more closely manage and incentivize the performance of employees
- develop employee skills
- facilitate change and innovation
- communicate directly with employees, keeping them informed of business developments
- facilitate a strong organizational culture based on the premise that there is a common purpose between employer and employee.

As can be seen, a flexible and adaptable workforce is a central feature of the HRM vision. In practice some HRM advocates have taken the idea of alignment with business strategy and the notion of a unitary view of employee relations to mean that trades unions are an obstacle to both meeting business requirements and generating a common purpose in an enterprise. They reject the pluralist notion that employees may hold a different perspective of work and that this needs to be represented by trades unions or others. They do not accept that there is an alternative legitimate point of view – a different employee 'voice'. As Ian Beardwell (1998) put

it: 'employers have become concerned with bringing employees into a series of relationships through work reorganization and reallocation (also known as flexibility); renaming the job (partners or associates rather than employees); and new communication systems (team briefings and focus groups)'. HRM in particular has rejected an approach to industrial relations that emphasizes regulation and due legal process, in favour of the management of change within organizations to maximize the contribution of people resources.

The HRM view of people management has been very influential. Its very name, human resources, has widely replaced the traditional personnel management. 'People professionals' have not necessarily swallowed the HRM argument whole: they have picked out parts of the argument that fit their views. And this has been made all the easier by the fact that in practice HRM has not proved to be a single, unified concept, but a variegated approach to people management. As one commentator (Williams, 1993) explains, some versions emphasize the human (by talking of the importance of employee development) part of the equation; others concentrate on resources (emphasizing their utilitarian role as part of the corporate business strategy). A similar distinction has been drawn between soft HRM (concentrating on communication, motivation and leadership) and hard HRM (emphasizing the economic, numerical and calculative aspects) as alternative approaches (Storey, 1989). The hard, resource-based view of HRM sees exploitation as simply that – getting the most out of employees for the benefit of the organization. The soft, human-based approach can be seen as a means of addressing the mutual needs of both employees and employers to maximize skills and potential for the good of all.

These differences in approach and philosophy within HRM thinking have manifested themselves within organizations, especially over their attitude to labour flexibility. These can be conceptualized into two broad schools of thought on flexible working: one that advocates increasing flexible employment in a fundamental shift of relationships at work (the transformation of employment model), and one that emphasizes stability and incremental change (the continuity of employment model). It would be an exaggeration to say that the first represents hard HRM and the latter soft; views on HRM are too imprecise to be that simplistic. But there is clear resonance between the differences in HRM thinking and these philosophies. The alignment may be closer for hard HRM and the transformation model – both see increased flexible employment as likely and desirable. Those that subscribe to the continuity model stress the benefits of a more traditional approach to people management that even soft HRM has dispensed with.

TRANSFORMATION OF EMPLOYMENT

Those who believe in the transformation of employment model contend that if the UK, and their own businesses, are to compete internationally, unnecessary restrictions to the way staff are employed and utilized must be removed. They argue that significant social changes are taking place and that the world of work will be fundamentally altered by new technology. This they believe should be recognized by the use of more varied working patterns, and greater organizational flexibility. They foresee fewer people working in conventional offices and factories, and more home and mobile working. With ever more powerful communication systems, they think there will be a sizeable reduction in administrative work and its transfer to remote processing factories.

At the organizational level those that support this model claim that a harmonious, all-inclusive corporate system, where everybody is employed on integrated terms and conditions, is no longer appropriate, being too expensive to operate in a highly competitive business environment. Instead they see greater segmentation in terms and conditions within the workplace, and greater differentiation between organizations. These differences will be market based, set by the rules of supply and demand.

It will also be a performance-driven culture. Pay will be increasingly determined through personal contribution and, above all, results driven. Reward is also likely to include an element based upon the business success: if the company does well, employees will share in the proceeds.

Those advocating this model make a clear distinction between a core group employed for an extended period and a peripheral workforce, either employed for shorter periods or supplied externally. Thus they see a continuing trend towards outsourcing and further growth in services provided by the self-employed. Thus there will be multiple work relationships, many of them outside the traditional employment contract.

Skills and performance will fix who is included in the core group. As Amin Rajan put it: 'performance will determine who is retained, who is trained and who is de-hired'. The relationship between performance and flexibility is such that an approach to job security means that 'employers perceive all staff as flexible and potentially temporary' (Rajan et al., 1997).

The volatility of employment, the stripping out of managerial bureaucracy, and employee aspiration towards having greater control over work patterns are likely to lead to the emergence of the 'portfolio career' and confirm the end to any notion of lifetime engagement by one organization. As a consequence, loyalty will be less and less offered or expected. Employees will give their allegiance instead to their profession and skill development will become more important to employees than climbing the organizational ladder.

Flexibility and change in the distribution of work can also be anticipated. This is a reaction to the rigid demarcations of the past, and a recognition that to survive organizations must maximize output in the most efficient way. Some, such as William Bridges, one of the American gurus of 'dejobbing', go further, denying that jobs will exist in the future, such is the speed with which tasks will alter and such the requirement for flexible organizational design. Much broader roles will take the place of jobs within project teams working within much more fluid organizational structures than at present.

Employment relationships would have an element of 'win/win' about them. Both parties would derive benefits from their association. Employers would have a responsibility to encourage individuals to develop their skills. Despite the fact that employment is likely to be more transient than in the past, employers would be expected to contribute to the 'employability' of their staff in exchange for the increased flexibility they demand and reduced security they offer. Thus greater honesty and transparency would be seen in relationships when the elements of the employment deal are being set out.

No mention has been made so far of the collective dimension to work. The stress is on individuals and their relationship with their manager. Communication is to be encouraged but through direct contact with employees, not mediated via trades unions or consultative bodies. Unions are seen as dinosaurs from the past, at best an irrelevance to the needs of the present, at worst a hindrance to the legitimate right of managers to manage. It may be accepted that energizing the workforce requires increased employee involvement, but the way to achieve this is seen as by direct dealing with individual employees.

CONTINUITY OF EMPLOYMENT

Those who support the alternative paradigm – the continuity of employment model – claim that, while clearly there have been changes in employment terms and patterns, and indeed the rate of change may be increasing, this is nothing new. Technological advances have occurred before and have been accommodated without radical alteration to working conditions or to employment levels. They regard the anticipated death of the office as much exaggerated. There is nothing to suggest they believe that employers would encourage extensive homeworking. They would not be happy to lose face-to-face contact with their staff, or to allow them the sort of control they would have over their work if they were almost exclusively out of sight. Employees too may moan about commuting or about working in offices or on the factory floor, but will be reluctant to

lose the social interaction of working with colleagues. As to job losses, technology will create work just as it will destroy certain types of employment. They believe that a lot of the talk about the impact of change, be it techno-logical or economic, on work and careers is the result of hype 'peddled by change merchants' and typical of the sort of fads and fashions that appear in management literature.

As a result supporters of this model would argue that employees still want traditional careers, and that few would be attracted to the notion of a portfolio career, even if they were able to develop one. Indeed, they say the new model of employment is based on an 'idealized' concept of employees. Most would not have the emotional capacity to job-hop in this way; in general people tend to find employment that they are comfortable with and meets their needs, then stick to it. This is not to say that career patterns have not changed and will not continue to do so. Fewer people will be employed for a lifetime by one organization, but there has always been, they say, a spectrum of commitment by employers to their employees and vice versa. Certainly in the private sector at least they would argue that companies have rarely guaranteed long-term employment to anyone, either explicitly or implicitly. Nevertheless, they believe it is desirable to have a clear understanding with employees that recognizes uncertainty and emphasizes the need for sustained good performance, both individual and corporate.

Advocates of this model do not support extensive outsourcing, fearing that it will produce an 'anorexic' organization. Similarly they recoil at the core/periphery distinction, finding it an unhelpful and divisive concept. They would argue that it is foolish to fix such a boundary, that the view of what is central to business needs is not immutable but shifts over time both in relation to cost and capacity, for the client and the contractor. They think that the need to ensure a high quality of output and service requires direct control over all important aspects of the value chain, rather than to pass them to a third party to manage. The qualification that control of 'important' activities is required recognizes that there may be some tasks that are better handled by a specialist supplier, but the default is that work is better done in-house. Their wish, if at all possible, is to sustain a long-term employment relationship with their staff. Thus they would reject the use of fixed-period contracts as the standard form of agreement. They would aim to recruit and retain talent because they put an emphasis on experience and the maintenance of the organization's inherent values. All employees are seen as key, and their contribution should be maximized by providing an environment that encourages learning, teamwork and commitment. As one organization contacted to take part in a study of flexible working replied apropos the use of complementary workers, 'Good employers who care about their permanent staff should not contemplate a resourcing policy of this kind' (Corfield Wright, 1996).

At the macro-level, proponents of this model are dubious about the alleged benefits of the American approach to employment. They fear the social consequences of widening disparities of income and the relegation of parts of the labour force to the margins of employment. They are concerned that unrest will result from the creation of an underclass. From the economic point of view it strikes them as dysfunctional to have to pay so much to keep so many in idleness and outside of the consumer society. They feel too that the 'excesses of capitalism' (echoing Ted Heath's objection to the 'unacceptable face of capitalism') hardly help the situation, exemplified by what they regard as the barely justifiable level of some senior executives' pay awards. Thus they would stress the need for internal equity in the treatment of staff. They are attracted to a more consensual approach to labour relations. They see advantages in a broader definition of what constitutes a stakeholder, and support means to encourage the participation of employees in the management of organizations. While not wishing to return to the trades union militancy and obstructionism of the past, they see value in employee representative structures and can see benefits in

dealing with employees on a collective as well as individual basis.

In many ways this model is negative in tone because it is often advocated in opposition to what are regarded as the dubious benefits of the alternative transformation of employment model. The supporters of the continuity of employment model wish to challenge the assumptions made by the transformation school, such as the benefits of externalization and the proposition that conventional careers and lifetime employment are at an end. They reject these ideas both as a description of the world and as a conception of what employment relationships should be like.

EMPLOYER PRACTICE

As the reader will have realized, there are clear echoes of the US model in the description of the transformation of employment approach, with its emphasis on labour market dynamism. Similarly the continuity of employment school is more influenced by the continental European or Japanese models of employee relations.

Some commentators have tried to distinguish between organizations holding these two viewpoints on the basis of objective criteria. It has been proposed that whether employees are seen as a 'resource' or 'cost' depends upon the economics of the business and the nature of the technology. It would seem reasonable to think that fast-moving consumer goods companies, where low skills and high employment costs dominate, would tend towards the transformation model, while those companies with large capital investment, complex skill inputs and long investment horizons would be more likely to embrace a continuity approach.

In fact there are well-known examples that demonstrate the opposite. While Chris Haskins, chairman of Northern Foods, may not see himself as a spokesman for the continuity school, he articulated their viewpoint when he said, in October 1994 at the time of launching the Borrie Commission findings, 'Deregulators claim that the only way to create more jobs is US-style deregulation of the labour market. But deregulation discourages investment in skills and results in low wages and low productivity' – and this from a company which is very much of the fast-moving consumer goods type, at the lower-skills, lower-pay end of the spectrum.

In reality, organizations are formed by their history and their culture as much as by the markets within which they operate. They are influenced too by the views of their senior management. One chief executive may deliberately choose to break with the past, to act upon a new vision of the organization. Other management teams, by contrast, may see the virtue of continuity, even while their competitors adopt alternative strategies, because the ethos of the company is so ingrained. Evidence of this fact comes from the National Health Service (NHS). For example, some NHS trusts have decided to use temporary staff 'to facilitate change', while others employ permanent employees believing that they offer 'stability and commitment' to the organization (Incomes Data Services, 1998). Both sets of organizations face similar issues, but their response is different because of their different management philosophies.

The distinction between the two models is thus fundamentally about values, whether they are embedded in organizational culture or espoused by business leaders. The transformation model emphasizes the needs of the business and regards employee interests as subordinate in the short term; in the longer term, the increased wealth generated from improved competitiveness would, it is claimed, benefit all. The model is thus very market oriented and sees greater differentiation in pay and prospects as the legitimate expression of economic processes at work. It assumes the relationship with employees to be based on transactional contracts, those where there is a simple exchange of effort and reward. It emphasizes the culture of economic exchange, *Gesellschaft*. By contrast, the continuity model sees equity and community of interest as key values. It is a less individualistic approach, and while it accepts market influence, it wishes to moderate its effects. It tends towards relational contracts based on the nature of the relationship between the parties. It is a model of social exchange, of *Gemeinschaft*.

Since we are involved in philosophies of life, it is not surprising that this is a political as much as a practitioner debate. However, though one might think that organizations would be able to ignore the huff and puff of political debate, rhetoric also infects the workplace. Arguments in favour of the particular models are replicated, in somewhat adjusted form, at organizational level. Business leaders are often keen to trumpet the success of flexibility in their company. Like downsizing it is seen as a 'good thing' and beneficial to the share price. Trades unionists are often no better, mimicking the more extreme words of their general secretaries in opposing flexibility come what may.

In practice the divergence in conception between the models is less clear-cut – there are shades of opinion between the extremes, and people are not always consistent in their views; they may have feet in both camps. Nevertheless, whatever the truth or the merits of these models, however muddled their logic, these ideas are held by opinion formers at the workplace. Decision making does not take place in a vacuum; people are affected by their subjective feelings and beliefs, but also by the social and economic context within which they are operating. It is this we will now consider.

CHAPTER TWO

Social and Labour Market Trends

Before turning to the question of flexible work arrangements, it is necessary to consider the context within which the debate about work organization is taking place. There are some profound changes going on in society and specifically in the labour market. These affect an organization's labour supply in terms not just of its size, but also its characteristics (gender, age distribution and so on). Social context also matters in what people are seeking from work – merely money to pay the grocery bills or a chance to develop an interesting career. A single teenage mother with pre-school-age children may have different aspirations from a thirty-something without any dependants. The sort of job opportunities on offer to the workforce affects attitudes to education and training. There is also the wider social effect of income distribution and the risks and rewards of work. These issues are woven together in a complex, interrelated pattern. Here I will give a flavour of some of the issues that form a backdrop to later chapters.

DEMOGRAPHY AND HOUSEHOLDS

AN AGEING AND MORE DIVERSE POPULATION

According to the 1996 National Population Projections, the UK population is projected to increase from 59 million people in 1998 to peak at around 65 million in 2036 before declining. For our purposes, the critical issue within this projection is the ageing of the population (see Figure 2.1). The number below the age of 16 is set to fall by 3 percentage points by 2021. The proportion of those aged over 65 will not rise noticeably until around 2007, at which stage it will grow significantly to the position where in 2021 there will be more than 12 million people aged over 65. The number of people aged over 90 is already increasing. By 2001 there are expected to be over 400 000 people in this age bracket; this figure is projected to rise to 700 000 by 2031. This ageing trend is being caused by increased life expectancy and improved health, especially perinatal health.

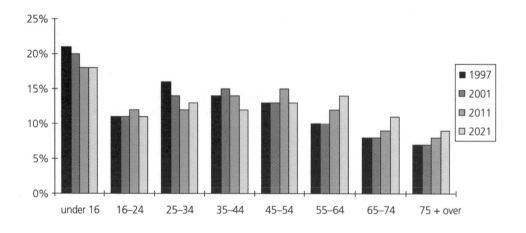

Figure 2.1 The changing UK population profile, 1997–2021 (1996 projection, based on data from the UK Office for National Statistics)

Life expectancy for men has risen from 58 in 1940 to 74 in 1995 and for women from 63 in 1940 to 80 in 1995, and is expected to continue to rise to 79 for men and 84 for women by the middle of the next century.

This increasingly large elderly population, especially the number of very old, will have to be supported, and on occasion cared for, by those at work. Already 6.8 million people, mostly women, perform a 'caring' role and one in six employees are in this situation. Interestingly, 80 per cent of those cared for are over 65.

The ethnic minority population is expected to grow strongly over the next few decades, at a faster rate than the white population. Ethnic minority groups currently make up 6 per cent of the population; by 2030 it will be 8 per cent. This is in part due to the younger age profile of the ethnic minority population in comparison with the white population – one in three people from ethnic minorities is aged under 16, compared with one in five of the white population. As the minority groups are concentrated geographically, in some areas they will represent quite a high density of the population. As their profile is younger than of the white population, there will be a higher percentage active in the labour market. And finally, because people from ethnic minorities have higher staying-on rates in education than whites, they may be better qualified.

Issues concerning equal opportunities for ethnic minorities are becoming an increasingly significant factor in labour management as the workforce becomes more diverse. It cannot be assumed that the needs of members of ethnic minorities will be the same across the board or be concomitant with the white population.

CHANGING HOUSEHOLD AND FAMILY STRUCTURES

There have been some marked trends in changes to household and family formation over the last few decades. In particular there has been a move toward more single households and single-parent families, and later family formation. In 1961 single-parent households represented 11 per cent of all households in Great Britain. By 1998 this proportion had risen to 28 per cent, and is expected to grow to 33 per cent by 2006. This is not just a function of the ageing population or confined to women. In 1971, 3 per cent of men of working age lived alone, but this proportion is expected to increase to 10 per cent by 2001 and to 13 per cent by 2016.

Besides the growth of single persons living alone, the number of single-parent families has also increased. They made up 8 per cent of all families in Great Britain in 1971, and this figure has now risen to 22 per cent. The growth in single households is partly related to changing patterns in marriage. In 1996 there were half the number of marriages in the UK than in 1970. The result is that by 2011 just under half of all adults are expected to be married, compared with around two-thirds in 1981. The average age at which people marry has risen, more noticeably for women, from 23 in 1971 to 27 in 1996. However, cohabiting prior to marriage has risen sharply, from 12 per cent of non-married women in Great Britain aged 18 to 49 in 1981 to 25 per cent in 1997, and people are cohabiting for a longer period. Although most cohabiting couples at present are young, by 2021 almost three-quarters are likely to be over the age of 30.

The pattern in later marriages has been accompanied by a trend towards women starting their family later in life. The average age of women when they have their first child has risen from 24 in 1974 to 28 in 1996. Women are also having fewer children than in the past – the average number of children per family has fallen from 2.0 in 1971 to 1.8 currently. It is expected that a quarter of women born in 1972 will be childless.

The growth in single-parent families is partly explained by the fact that over one in three births occurred outside marriage in 1998, compared to only one in 20 in 1961, and partly explained by the growing divorce rate. The number of divorces trebled between 1968 and 1996. A third of new marriages now end in divorce.

The importance of these changes to family structures lies in the diversity that it represents both in terms of the characteristics of the workforce and the domestic circumstances of these employees. There is no longer a simple pattern on which personnel policies can be based. Many have been predicated on the family comprising two married adults and dependent children. This arrangement of course is still common, but now encompasses less than a quarter of all households, compared with 38 per cent in 1961. Increasingly there are other patterns to be found – couples living together for extended periods; step-children from one marriage sharing a house with children from another; single-parent families; and those living alone. What the people living in these situations think about work and what they want from it may be very different from the traditional conception.

LABOUR MARKET TRENDS

The labour market has also undergone a trans-formation in recent years and will continue to do so over the coming years. The principal features of this change are:

- an increasing but ageing workforce
- the support ratio of those working to those who are inactive is falling
- the growing participation of females in the labour market
- a sectoral shift from manufacturing to ser-vices
- occupational changes and the growing demand for higher skills
- increasing self-employment
- the rise of the small employer
- an increasingly better-educated/trained workforce

We will look at these issues in more detail.

A GROWING, AGEING AND MORE FEMININE WORKFORCE

The labour force is projected to grow over the medium term along with the population. The UK workforce will increase by around three-quarters of a million between 1999 and 2006. Most of this projected growth is accounted for by women, who are expected to make up about half a million out of the increase.

Women comprised 34 per cent of the whole workforce (including the self-employed) in 1971; this figure currently stands at about 43 per cent, and is predicted to rise to 45 per cent by 2006.

This increased female participation in the labour market is due to a number of factors, including:

- later marriage and childbirth
- increased return to work after childbirth: in 1997 two-thirds of women returned to employment after maternity leave compared with half in 1988
- quicker return to work after childbearing/ rearing (the average number of years before returning to work after the birth of the first child was 9.5 in 1950, and even by 1979 this had fallen to 3.5 years)
- higher qualification levels among women in the population
- increased availability of part-time work.

Some women have forsaken their traditional role as mother and housewife in favour of employment, either exclusively or in some form of combination. Nevertheless, rates of female employment still decline with the arrival of children, but nothing like to the extent of the past. About three-quarters of women aged between 16 and 59 without dependent children are economically active, be they married or not. This figure falls to 60 per cent when there are children under 5 to look after, but rises again to nearly 80 per cent by the time the children are over 15.

By contrast, men's participation in the labour market has been falling over the last two decades, mainly because of increased staying-on rates for those of school-leaving age and the withdrawal of older workers owing to early retirement. Thus between 1981 and 1998 the proportion of working-age men in the labour force fell from 90 per cent to 84 per cent. This means that there were at that point some 3 million economically inactive working-age males.

Activity rates for the over 50s are lower both for men and women than for any other age category: 72 per cent of males over 50 are active compared with 93 per cent of 25–49-year-olds. Comparable female rates are 63 per cent and 76 per cent. In 1975, only 7 per cent of males aged between 50 and 64 were inactive. The expectation is that the participation of older male workers in the labour market is likely to decline still further, albeit at a slow pace, while women's activity rate will continue to rise, especially in the 60–64 age group (with the equalization of pension rules).

This is significant when one realizes that the age profile of the labour force as a whole (that is including active and inactive) is expected to become older – the number of 35–59-year-olds in Great Britain is projected to increase by 1.7 million over the period 1997 to 2011, but the numbers aged from 25 to 34 are expected to reduce by 1.3 million (see Figure 2.2). Given the changing pattern of the population as a whole, the ratio of those of working age to those of pension age is predicted to fall – the rate is currently 3.3 workers to 1 non-worker, down from 4 to 1 in the past, and is expected to drop to 2.7 to 1 by 2020. The ageing of the working population is likely to raise more questions about the validity of employment policies that assume that many aged over 50 are well beyond their sell-by date. If employers

do begin to look more seriously at the older worker, they may find that they will have to adjust the employment deal to suit, just as they have had to do with the female workforce. If both genders and all ages of the working population are to find patterns to meet their needs, then even more diversity in employment relationships will probably result.

FROM MANUFACTURING TO SERVICES, FROM BLUE TO WHITE COLLAR

The growth in female part-time work and decline of male manual jobs can partly be explained by the shift from manufacturing to service industries. In 1954 manufacturing employed 34.5 per cent of the UK workforce; by 1997 this proportion had fallen to 16.5 per cent. A similar decline has been seen in primary and utility industries. By contrast, business and miscellaneous services accounted for 8.4 per cent of total employment in 1954, and accounted for 22 per cent of the total by 1997. Non-marketed services have seen a similar rise, from 15.4 per cent to 25.4 per cent, over the same period.

Looking to the future, manufacturing is expected to fall to around 14 per cent of the total workforce by 2006 (Figure 2.3). Further

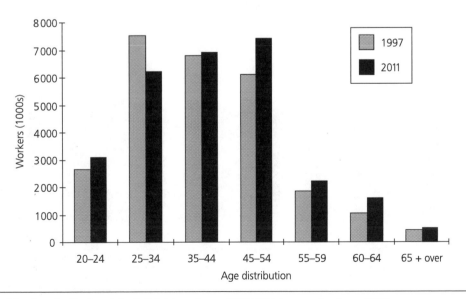

Figure 2.2   Age distribution of the British labour force, 1997–2011 (source: Armitage, 1998)

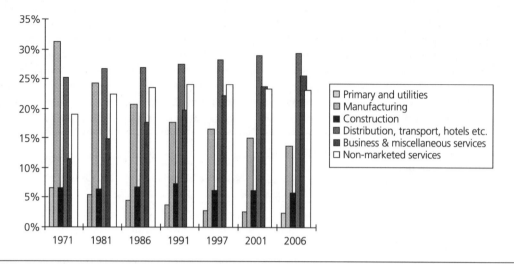

Figure 2.3   Sectoral composition in the UK, 1971–2006 (source: Institute for Economic Research, 1999)

growth is anticipated in the service sector. Specifically, business and miscellaneous services are predicted to grow to 26 per cent of employment by 2006.

The changing industrial pattern of employment has affected and will continue to affect the pattern of the different occupational groups. There has been a steady reduction in skilled and unskilled manual work over the last 25 years. Thus while between 1981 to 1991 there was an overall growth in employment,

plant and machine operatives declined by 440 000, and 'other occupations', mostly unskilled labourers, declined by 300 000. By contrast, there has been a continuing increase in the professional, associate professional and the managerial and administrative occupations.

Although the precise level is impossible to predict, one can be certain that the trend towards higher-skilled (managerial and professional) occupations and a large decrease in manual occupations will continue, with some

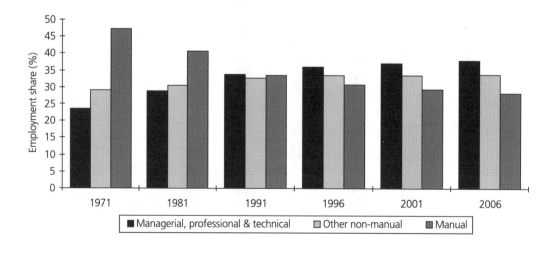

Figure 2.4   Occupational trends in the UK, 1971–2006 (source: Business Strategies Ltd, 1998)

modest growth in non-manual jobs, especially in the personal and protective services area (Figure 2.4). Projections suggest that there will be about a million extra managerial, professional and technical jobs between 1996 and 2006. In addition to increased demand for higher-skilled jobs, there is also a demand for more skills within jobs. In 1998, 68 per cent of employers reported that the skills required for the average worker were increasing, and about a sixth of employers reported a skills gap between what was needed and what was on offer. Computer literacy, customer-handling skills, ability to communicate and practical skills were the skills most felt to be lacking.

The service sector has different work requirements from those of manufacturing, especially in a 24-hour consumer society. This has significant implications for the nature of flexible work arrangements. The occupational shift has more complex effects. In some sectors professional employees are much more likely to be subject to flexible contracts, but also to take advantage of flexible working patterns. Those occupations that are found particularly in the service sector are also prone to work under flexible terms of employment.

THE GROWTH OF SELF-EMPLOYMENT

The self-employed currently make up nearly 13 per cent of the UK workforce in employment. There was a large increase in self-employment during the 1980s and 1990s. This seems to have halted recently, with a fall of over 5 per cent in the number of self-employed between 1996 and 1998.

The Thatcher government extolled the virtues of self-employment because it put workers more directly face to face with the market. For some self-employed there is a strong connection with the flexible labour market in that they are providing services which once were provided in-house. Growth in self-employment has in part therefore been caused by outsourcing and the effects of downsizing. A small proportion of those in self-employment have been forced into it, while a much larger percentage work in sectors (for example, agriculture or construction) where it is a traditional way of working.

THE RISE OF THE SMALL EMPLOYER

The growth in self-employment is one of the factors contributing to an increase in small employers, and their growing importance in employment terms within the labour market. In 1997, 7.5 million people were employed in establishments with fewer than 25 employees, accounting for 33 per cent of the total workforce.

Small companies often have very different patterns of employment compared with large organizations, and frequently different employment relationships as well. As the proportion of people working for small firms rises, so naturally will its impact on working arrangements.

A MORE EDUCATED WORKFORCE

In the UK the impact may yet to be fully felt but there has been a significant increase in the number staying on at school and going into higher education. In percentage terms there has been a 37 per cent increase between 1990 and 1996 in the number of 16–24-year-olds engaged in full-time education. This is due to a much higher staying-on rate in education and training. Almost three-quarters of 16–18-year-olds were involved in education and training in 1998/9, compared with under half in 1985.

Enrolments in tertiary education have consequently risen – from 1.6 million in 1981 to 2.5 million in 1997 in further education colleges, and from 800 000 to 1.8 million in higher education; 27 per cent of 19–20-year-olds were in higher education in 1998/9, compared with 9 per cent in the early 1960s. An increasing proportion of the population is also going on to postgraduate study. In 1998/9 there were over 320 000 enrolments compared to 62 000 in 1969/70.

The result is a better-qualified workforce. Nearly 80 per cent of the population of working age now have some form of qualification, compared to 60 per cent in 1984, and this proportion is higher among 25–34-year-olds at 86 per cent. The growth in higher education has also meant a 65 per cent increase between 1989 and 1997 in the supply of graduates entering employment that has had to be absorbed into the labour market. Within this growth there has been a change in the composition of the 'educated'. Much of the increase in higher education has been accounted for by mature students and female students – in 1995/6 half of first-year undergraduates were aged over 21, and women accounted for just over half of all students in higher education.

Despite the increasing numbers in education, there are still some basic skill deficiencies at the workplace. In a 1998 national literacy and numeracy survey conducted by the Basic Skills Agency, 15 per cent of adults reported low or very low literacy levels and a third had similar problems with numeracy. This is not just a problem with the older worker – one in five 21-year-olds reports difficulties with basic maths, and one in seven reports difficulties with reading and writing.

The last point reminds us that there is a long way still to go if UK education standards are to match those of international competitors. As we increasingly enter the 'knowledge economy', employers will be more demanding and a more educated workforce will be asked to add more value to their work. By the same token, employees may be more exacting, both in terms of requiring more autonomy while at work and in what they expect to get out of their employment.

A BETTER-TRAINED WORKFORCE

Government effort has gone not only into expanding academic education, but also into improving vocational education and training, given its poor record in the UK. Emphasis has been switched from public/industry provision (for example, through the old training boards) to employer responsibility for training. This has been seen in the introduction of National Vocational Qualifications (NVQs) and Investors in People (IiP).

NVQs are intended to increase vocational qualifications in a way that encourages the employee's own responsibility and provides a common, and hence transferable and recogniz-

able, asset. They have been designed to be delivered and assessed in the workplace. IiP was launched in 1991 to produce a national standard of action and excellence, with the aim of getting a better alignment between business goals and the development of employees. However, most of the early achievers have a strong training tradition, and by 1997 only 26 per cent of organizations employing over 200 people were recognised as Investors. It remains to be seen whether the initiative will reach the many employers in the UK with less adequate training provision.

Disappointingly the extent of workplace training is low compared with European competitors. Most employers provide some form of off-the-job training, but this averages only to 3.2 days per employee per annum. Most training relates to health and safety, or induction, though two-thirds say that they offer training on new technology and on management skills.

Employers need a better-trained workforce to undertake jobs to higher-quality standards or when using more complex technology. Employees too have to develop the requisite skills to flourish in the labour market of the future. The government recognizes this and intends to continue to encourage or push employers along the road to achieving a better-equipped labour force.

THE DISADVANTAGED AND EXCLUDED

AFFLUENCE AND WIDENING INCOME DIFFERENTIALS

Society in general is becoming more middle-class in line with the shift in occupational structure. It is also becoming more affluent. The total 'net wealth' of UK households grew by 1 billion pounds between 1987 and 1997. Average total income went up by 38 per cent between 1979 and 1996. Widening home ownership has played its part in wealth acquisition: over two-thirds of dwellings are now owner-occupied. With greater disposable income, consumer possessions have increased too, with the proportion of homes with cars, computers and other household 'essentials' on a steady rise.

However, this account masks a widening of differentials in income and wealth. The top 10 per cent increased their income by 61 per cent over this 1979–1996 period, whereas the poorest 10 per cent saw a 4 per cent cut. Differences in wage increases were even more marked. And the disparity in wealth is more striking still – the richest 10 per cent own half of the 'marketable' wealth of UK households.

Not only is wealth concentrated in certain hands, there is the opposite effect – a concentration of poverty. Evidence in support of there being a marginalized group is not hard to find. Some notable features of divisions within British society include:

- in 18 per cent of households neither partner works
- only 44 per cent of lone mothers work
- over half of single mothers do not have educational qualifications equivalent to O level or higher
- 14 million people live below the unofficial poverty line (half average income) – well over double the 1979 figure of 5 million
- 20 per cent of females earn less than £200 per week, compared with 12 per cent of males
- over 75 per cent of part-time workers earn less than the average hourly wage
- about a third of non-whites are in the poorest 20 per cent of the income distribution, compared with around a fifth of whites
- although the number has fallen in recent years, in 1997 there were still over 100 000 homeless households deemed to be in priority need.

However, some of those at the bottom of the heap do not remain there. It is not a constant pool of the population, shown by the fact that only 16 per cent of men who were in the poorest 10 per cent of the population in 1978 were still there in 1992. Some people drift in and out of employment. But it is true to say that single parents, female single pensioners and those from certain ethnic minorities are most likely to be in this predicament.

UNEMPLOYMENT

The fact of one's being unemployed or not has a profound influence on whether one is part of the disadvantaged minority. After the war the UK unemployment rate (see Figure 2.5) stayed below 3 per cent of the workforce until the early to mid-1970s. Since then it rose steadily to a peak of around 13 per cent in the mid-1980s. The boom of the late 1980s saw unemployment falling. It rose again during the recession of the early 1990s and is now falling back to the levels last seen in the mid-1970s. The January 2000 claimant rate was 4.0 per cent, or 1.16 million people. According to the International Labour Organization (ILO) definition, a further 560 000 were out of work and

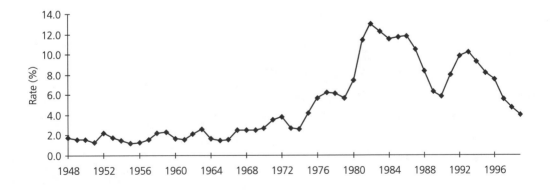

Figure 2.5 UK claimant unemployment rate since 1948 (based on data from the UK Office for National Statistics)

seeking employment. Another 2 million people would like a job but are not actively seeking one. So, in the broadest estimate of those who would like to work but are not doing so, the figure amounts to around 3.7 million people.

Unemployment is concentrated among particular groups in the population. The male unemployment rate is higher than the female rate, especially among young men; those with no qualifications or with disabilities are more likely to be without work, as are those from certain ethnic minorities – particularly black males, and people of Pakistani and Bangladeshi origin.

There are regional variations too in unemployment. The highest rates, based on the spring 1999 ILO count, were to be found in the north-east of England (9.3 per cent), Wales (7.8 per cent) and Northern Ireland (7.6 per cent), and the lowest rates in the south-east (3.8 per cent), east (4.1 per cent) and south-west (4.3 per cent) regions of England (Office for National Statistics, 1999a). Within these areas there are pockets of even higher unemployment and deprivation, especially in the inner cities – places like Newham in London and West Derby in Liverpool.

Do these statistics on unemployment and disadvantage matter to the debate about flexibility? Yes, because, as we shall see later,

some people are forced to accept flexible work arrangements that border on the exploitative. They do so because their circumstances mean they have no choice. While there is an underclass drifting in and out of marginal employment, there will always be individuals vulnerable to unprincipled employers. The figures demonstrate that the risk of exploitation is greatest for certain types of people, living in particular places and in certain labour market conditions.

PRESSURES ON THOSE AT WORK

THE THREAT OF JOB LOSS

There is dispute among commentators about the extent of job insecurity among the British workforce. There are those, often critics of flexible labour markets, who wish to emphasize workers' growing fears of job loss; others (for example, Guest and Conway, 1999) believe that the facts do not support this contention. To some extent it is a question of whether you see the glass half full or half empty: do you concentrate on the majority who feel they are in stable employment, or emphasize the minority who are concerned about their future prospects? There is also an obvious distinction to be drawn between perceptions of insecurity

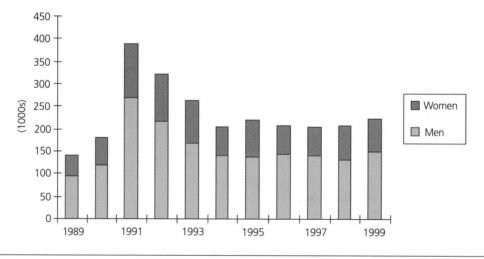

Figure 2.6 People made redundant in the UK within the last three months (source: Office for National Statistics, 1999a)

and the objective risk of job loss. More subtly, there is a difference between those who worry about the consequences of redundancy and those who believe they can get another similar job easily.

So what are the 'facts'? At the objective level, unemployment and redundancy have touched many people over the last twenty years. If one takes the period between 1979 and 1996, 8.7 million people experienced a spell of unemployment (Labour Party, 1996). Although the number of people made redundant has fallen from a peak in 1991, the level is still a lot higher than in 1989. As an indication, 223 000 people were made redundant over a three-month period in the spring of 1999 (Figure 2.6); over the course of a full year that amounts to a lot of people.

But being made unemployed today may have more significant consequences than in the past. In 1995 it took 20 per cent longer for an unemployed person to find work than it did in the 1970s. Thus the numbers of long-term unemployed have been rising – in the 1950s, 80 per cent of unemployment was for less than six months; by the late 1990s the figure was less than 60 per cent. In 1999 the mean duration of unemployment was 25 weeks. Those returning to work can expect to earn less than when previously employed. In 1999 the pay cut averaged 10 per cent. This situation compares unfavourably with that which applied two decades before.

One further objective dimension is job tenure, though this measures job stability rather than job security. Median job tenure fell from 5.8 to 4.6 years between 1975 and 1989, partly because of the increase in female and part-time employment (both of which have higher turnover). The fall is most marked among older workers and less skilled men. By spring 1996 median tenure had recovered after the recession to stand at just over five years. Another way of looking at job tenure is to consider length of service. In 1999 about half of those in full-time work had been with their same employer for five or more years, and just over a third for more than ten years.

As far as perceptions of insecurity are concerned, the most reliable survey evidence (see Guest and Conway, 1999, for a review) suggests that the majority of workers (around three-quarters) are not worried about losing their job. However, one would expect this figure to vary depending upon the state of the economy and the employees' position within their own organization. During the last recession, job security reportedly replaced pay as the primary concern of employees (Gallie et al., 1998). There is evidence, too, that middle-class people have become more fearful of redundancy than in the past. Even if the objective evidence of their risk of redundancy is much lower than for those in less skilled occupations, they may be more concerned. Part of this unease no doubt stems from the fact that redundancies are occurring at unexpected times, to unexpected people and within unexpected organizations. So some household names have been dispensing with loyal and trusted colleagues because of competitive pressures, or even when they are apparently doing well. It is in those organizations with a recent history of turbulence that reported insecurity is highest. Research suggests (Burchell et al., 1999) that the most fearful are those that worry about externally driven risks (merger, closure, downsizing); feel least in control of their working lives; have less faith in their managers; and worry about their ability to get another job if they lose the current one. Those that feel secure exhibit opposite characteristics: in particular they point to their own personal robustness, for example to their performance or capability in the job, or to their capacity to be re-employed.

WORK RICH BUT TIME POOR

For those people in work there are other pressures – long working hours and the need to perform well. Some cope with this intensification of work, others succumb to the effects of stress. Working hours in Britain are the longest in the European Union – the average working week for males in full-time jobs is 45 hours, compared with the EU average of 41, while the female full-time working week is 41 hours, compared with 39 for the EU. Around a quarter of the workforce regularly undertakes paid overtime, and a similar proportion do unpaid extra hours. An Institute of Management survey in 1997 reported that two-fifths of managerial respondents worked at weekends. A Mori poll for the TUC in 1998 (Trades Union Congress, 1998a) found that 43 per cent of men and 32 per cent of women said that they had to work antisocial hours (evenings, nights and weekends). In the same survey similar proportions said that they worked more hours than they liked. Nearly half of respondents to an IPD survey said that they felt under excessive pressure at work at least quite often (Guest and Conway, 1997).

Some 1.3 million people hold down more than one paid job; many more combine paid with unpaid activities. This may be a matter of preference to couple different types of part-time employment – for example, working at a crèche and as a classroom assistant. Or it may be a matter of necessity: the office worker who does taxiing or pub work in the evenings to boost earnings. According to a Royal College of Nursing (RCN) survey 28 per cent of nurses do additional paid work to their main job. Over three-quarters of them said this was to provide extra income (Robinson et al., 1999). In North America holding down a second job is even commoner, involving the professional classes as well. There is a joke that illustrates the American situation: one person says to the other, 'The economy is doing really well – look at all the jobs that are being created'; the second person replies, 'I know. I have three of them' (quoted in Pfeffer, 1998).

Various surveys have described the impact of stress at the workplace (see Office for National Statistics, 1997, 1999c). For example, in 1994 the Health Survey for England found that around 40 per cent of people aged between 35 and 54 reported experiencing more than 'a little' stress at work in the previous four weeks. The British Social Attitudes Survey from 1996 reported that over 40 per cent of respondents regularly came home from work exhausted, and 80 per cent said that at least sometimes they found work stressful. And the Health and Safety Executive announced that stress has become the second most commonly reported cause of working days lost through illness.

One factor associated with increased stress at work may be pressures to be more productive. This includes the speed, effort and volume of work to be completed, because of technological investment, work reorganization or the impact of downsizing. Productivity rates have consequently risen per head as well as by actual output. The prevalence of performance management and performance-related pay also indicates growing pressure to work harder or more effectively. For some workers, but by no means all, there has been greater control over their tasks. At one end of the spectrum are those working in call centres whose behaviour and performance are closely monitored; at the other end of the employment continuum are managers whose work continuously intrudes into their private life. This is summed up by one US manager who reportedly said 'people who work for me should have phones in their bathrooms' (McLean Parks, 1994). The mobile phone seems an adequate substitute for many commuters!

FROM DINKIES TO DIWKIES

In 60 per cent of British households both partners work. Many previous DINKies (double income no kids) have been replaced by DIWKies, that is the double income remains but children have arrived – and if not children, there may be elderly relatives to be cared for. Managing dual careers can be difficult if there are these domestic responsibilities. It can also be costly. The average expenditure on childcare for two children, one of whom is at school, is £6000. Residential care for the elderly costs £18 000 per annum on average. However, only one in six old people ends up in residential care, and on average their stay is for only two years.

Worries about caring for children and relatives may preoccupy those at work. For some these issues prevent them working at all. Four-fifths of non-working mothers say they would work if they had adequate childcare. These problems are obviously most acute for single mothers with pre-school kids.

FINANCING FOR THE FUTURE

In the UK the financial pressures to stay at work derive not just from the fear of redundancy or unemployment, but from a number of wider social and labour market changes, including:

- the value of the state pension, which has fallen from around 25 per cent of average earnings in the 1970s to 16 per cent currently, and is expected to decline at current rates to 9 per cent by 2030. It has been estimated that 80 per cent of the population will receive a total pension of less than £180 per week – the level defined as the minimum for comfort
- the 11 per cent increase between 1986 and 1996 in the number of elderly people in residential care; the numbers looked after in expensive private nursing homes is rising faster still – an 84 per cent increase over the same period
- the cost of tertiary education, with the introduction of student loans to pay for fees
- childcare costs, described above
- high levels of personal debt, grown substantially since 1980.

Taking all these things together, while in employment an individual has to work hard to sustain his/her employment. In the event of redundancy there is the risk of a long period out of work and a lower income on return to work. Given the above financial commitments, this is a matter of some concern. Supporting evidence for this view comes from an Institute of Management survey (1997) which found that financial security, funding retirement and employability were the top three concerns of the managers who responded.

SUMMARY

As we have remarked already, people's reactions to these issues are a mixture of a fair reflection of the objective conditions and a subjective perception of how they are affected by them. This is an important consideration when examining how proposals for change, especially on flexibility, are received. The objective evidence of pressure on individuals to work hard and to sustain an income is clear enough. It is also probable that the experience of the major recessions of the 1980s and 1990s has left a profound mark on people's attitudes to employment. And the presence of an 'underclass' means that some are vulnerable to exploitation, with unscrupulous employers able to insist on unreasonable flexible work arrangements that the desperate have no choice but to accept.

This social and economic review sets the context within which employers are operating, and describes the sort of issues that face those in the labour market. We will return to the points made here as we consider the organizational drivers for flexibility and the way in which employment relationships are formed. But first we must consider in more detail what constitutes the workplace flexibility in which we are interested.

CHAPTER THREE

Types and Incidence of Flexibility

As we saw in Chapter 1, it is the imprecision of the term flexibility which causes much of the difference in understanding between the various parties. It is important therefore to be clear that we know what we mean when we use the word. There are a number of classifications available. Some commentators would include, for example, organizational flexibility or flexibility in attitudes. While not suggesting that these are unimportant issues (and indeed they are referred to at various times in the text), I have decided to concentrate on employer initiatives that directly affect the work employees do or the way in which they are employed. A simple approach therefore divides the various types of flexible work arrangements as follows:

- functional
- numerical
- temporal
- locational
- financial.

The different approaches to flexibility are clustered around common features, be it working time arrangements or numbers deployed. It should be emphasized that this is a conceptual framework. In reality organizations think in terms of solutions to problems rather than of theoretical approaches. There are overlaps between these categories in the benefits they deliver to the organization, so that some types may be complementary in nature. Or it may be that one approach is a substitute for another. Nevertheless, this classification helps unpick some of complexities and makes discussion of the topic easier.

An initial summary of the types of flexibility is given in Table 3.1 to provide a general overview. We will look at each type in turn: what it encompasses, where it is used and how common it is. In the next chapter we will consider why organizations opt for flexible work arrangements in general and why they select a particular type.

Table 3.1 Types of flexible working

Type	Definition/aims	Examples
functional	allows firms to allocate labour across traditional functional boundaries	multi-skilling, cross-functional working, task flexibility
numerical	allows variation in the number of employees or workers used	temporary, seasonal, casual, agency, fixed-term workers, outsourcing
temporal	represents variability of working hours, either in a regular or irregular pattern	part-time, annual hours, shift, overtime, voluntary reduced hours, flexitime, zero hours arrangements
locational	involves using employees outside the normal workplace, including transfer of work to back offices	home, mobile, tele/outworkers
financial	allows paybill to rise and fall in line with corporate performance	gainsharing, profit sharing, variable executive pay schemes, wage cutting deals

FUNCTIONAL FLEXIBILITY

Functional flexibility relates to employers' ability to use labour across functional boundaries. It should give them the freedom to move labour as required to meet business needs.

Proper functional flexibility involves training people to perform work outside of their normal functional area of expertise. In practice the term has blurred into what may be called task flexibility, where employees carry out a wider range of duties than their job title might imply.

Functional flexibility has been particularly associated with manufacturing industry where artificial demarcation lines have often constrained management's ability to transfer staff in an optimum way. This has applied to the boundaries between production and maintenance, and within production and maintenance themselves. Functional flexibility has also been seen in the service sector, where organizations have aimed to provide customers with a one-stop-shop service. This has required employees to be familiar with a range of products or services, rather than just one. So in an insurance company, staff may have to be able to deal with motor and home insurance, claims as well as renewals; in a supermarket a higher-skilled checkout operator may be needed to cover lower-skilled shelf stacking, if the workload necessitates this.

Taking manufacturing therefore as an example, there are many variations in this sort of flexibility:

- full multi-skilled flexibility, where an employee can perform all the tasks required (in production and across the various craft disciplines)
- full flexibility within a functional grouping (for example, within production an employee can operate a machine, pack and load and so on, or an employee may be flexible within the building trades – carpentry, painting, plumbing – but this flexibility does not extend to other maintenance activities)
- limited extensions across functional boundaries (for example, operators performing

minor maintenance, or a mechanical craftsman changing a fuse).

Thus there is flexibility to be obtained within functional activities and between them. Functional flexibility can be upward, downward or horizontal in grade terms: that is, flexibility for a production operative can involve covering the job of an absent senior colleague, carrying out cleaning duties when the plant is down or performing minor maintenance instead of calling out a craftsman. Some forms of teamworking dilute these grade distinctions, so that skilled workers can and do perform semi-skilled work, but they can also tackle some traditional supervisory tasks.

There are no reliable figures on how commonly functional flexibility is used by employers. A quarter of employer respondents to the UK Workplace Employee Relations Survey (WERS) stated in 1998 that there was a lot more task flexibility than five years previously, and a third reported some increase. These figures were higher for production companies: 70 per cent replied that there was more task flexibility.

This is not surprising, given that in many organizations task flexibility has become widespread and unexceptional. The migration

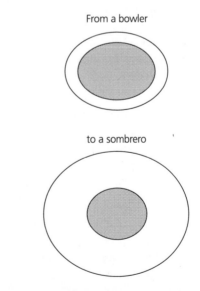

From a bowler

to a sombrero

Figure 3.1 Changing from jobs to roles

from the job, with its highly defined list of responsibilities, to the role, with its broader statement of how to meet business objectives, is indicative of this change. It has been described to me as the move from the bowler to sombrero (Figure 3.1), where the crown of the hat represents the perennial, key part of the job, and the rim the flexible, discretionary part of the job.

NUMERICAL FLEXIBILITY

Numerical flexibility, as the name implies, concerns flexibility around numbers: how organizations vary the numerical input to their work to meet the changing demand for labour. There is a variety of ways of achieving this. It can be done through the use of:

- fixed-term contractors employed for a limited but specified period, often a couple of years
- seasonal or casual labour hired for shorter periods
- temporary staff supplied by an agency
- pools of workers, often ex-employees, who can be called upon at short notice
- self-employed consultants or freelancers who are hired to complete specific pieces of work
- interim managers brought in to cover for extended periods
- outsourcing the whole activity so that the contractor supplies the labour and usually manages the work.

Employing staff on temporary or fixed-term contracts permits the organization to downsize quickly if activities alter or reduce. Consultants, freelancers or interim managers can be brought in for whatever periods of time suits the organization. Using an agency to supply labour gives even more flexibility, because it is the agency that is responsible for managing the consequences of change. The same principle applies to outsourcing. In theory at least it is the service contractor that flexes numbers to meet the client's requirements. This means that numerical flexibility ranges from what has been described as 'spot' contracting through to

long-term transfer of resourcing responsibility.

The distinction between these categories is not always as clear-cut as the theory suggests. The practical difference between fixed-term contracts, temporary, casual or seasonal employees, if they are all employed by the organization, may be merely a question of the length of the contract. Employers may try to impose their own logic to these distinctions. For example, one organization had a classification as follows:

Category	Contract length	Purpose
temporary staff	under 6 months	short-term absence cover
short-term contract	6 to 24 months	specific project
fixed-term contract	3 years	specific work but potential for regular contract

Managers did not find it so easy to make these distinctions; they often blurred in everyday life. For example, the timing of a project was frequently uncertain and labour requirements unclear. Employees hired under one contract might turn out better or worse than expected and have to be moved to another type of contract.

In UK legal terms there is in fact a distinction between those contracts with an end date specified in advance (be it one day or three years later), which is a fixed-term contract, and those that are 'discharged by performance' (the Court of Appeal in *Wiltshire County Council* v. *Natfhe and Guy* [1980] IRLR), where the end of the contract is determined by the completion of a task, for example the construction of a factory. In the former, if the contract is for a fixed term then its expiry counts as dismissal, and if it is not renewed the employee could claim unfair dismissal (assuming he or she has sufficient service). Where a completion of a task is involved, the question of dismissal does not arise. Interestingly, the EU directive on the employment of 'fixed-term workers' (see p. 85) lumps these two groups together in its definition, so that whether the contract relates to an event, date or task it falls within the terms of the directive.

Agency staff are different from the company's own temporary staff simply because they are employed by someone else (or self-employed), but they may be used in exactly the same way. Again managers may find in practice the distinction between these categories technical rather than practical. Similarly, self-employed consultants or freelancers, if they are doing operational work (as opposed to giving advice), may again in reality differ only through the absence of a contractual tie from short-term contractors or temporary workers.

'Bank' contracts are another variation on this theme. Staff are available on a list to be called in as required. The individual is only employed when he or she works, and he or she has the right to refuse work. The bank concept is familiar in nursing. Interestingly, in a survey for the RCN, only 3 per cent of nurses worked for a bank as their primary job, though this was three times the level of agency employees, but 17 per cent of respondents had a second job with a bank (Robinson et al., 1999).

Company employment registers are a similar concept. NatWest, for example, had about 1 300 individuals on an employment register, made up of ex-employees and those on career breaks. These people can be used to provide an internal resourcing service, offering cover for absent staff at all organizational levels (Overell, 1997a).

Contracting out or outsourcing (we use the terms interchangeably) should be clearly different from the other forms of numerical flexibility in that it describes the situation 'where an organisation passes the provision of a service or execution of a task previously undertaken in house to a third party to perform on its behalf' (Reilly and Tamkin, 1997). But in practice there are halfway houses between using an agency to supply labour and full outsourcing. If an activity is performed on the contractor's own premises with its own staff, for example providing a mainframe computer service, then the outsourcing is clear. If the activity is at the client's place of work, but is discrete and only performed by the contractor, for example a catering operation, again it is undoubtedly outsourced. What if the labour supplied to perform a particular task comes entirely from an agency yet is managed by the organization's own supervision: is that outsourcing? Examples of this sort of situation are found in call centres where the management and running of the centre are clearly in the hands of the client, but the telephone operators are all supplied by an agency. This may seem an academic point, but its purpose is to emphasize that there are a multitude of ways for an organization to flex its labour through varying the number of workers at its disposal. (This is illustrated below in Figure 3.5.)

The number of those employed in the UK on fixed-term or temporary contracts amounts to below 4 per cent of employees (Office for National Statistics, 1999a). Those engaged in seasonal or casual work, or employed on a non-permanent basis in any other way, amount to less than 3 per cent of employees, somewhat more during the summer months. Some 250 000 people work for employment agencies according to the Labour Force Survey (ibid.). The number of those self-employed consultants or freelancers used by organizations to flex employment numbers is unknown, though WERS suggests that 12 per cent of organizations use freelancers. It is claimed that there are 10 000 interim managers, half self-employed and half hired via agencies (Goss and Bridson, 1998).

In the 1998 WERS a fifth of organizations reported using agency temporary staff, mostly to cover work done by permanent employees. For 80 per cent of respondents, however, this involved four or fewer people. Short-term fixed-period contracts seem to be more common than longer-term ones, according to WERS: 26 per cent of the sample employed fixed-term contractors on contracts of less than a year, 16 per cent on contracts of more than a year. Again the reported density of fixed-term contractors employed in organizations was low. In a survey of temporary workers, 40 per cent of those whose contract length was specified expected their employment to last at least 12 months (Tremlett and Collins, 1999).

It is argued that the incidence of temporary working rises with an economic upswing and falls with recession. European research suggests that for each 1 per cent gain in GDP, there is a 4 to 5 per cent increase in the number of agency workers (Bakkenist, 1998). There is evidence from Cranfield (Brewster et al., 1996) that the economic cycle affects the numbers of fixed-term contractors employed. Work at the Institute for Employment Studies (Atkinson et al., 1996) supports the view that there is a relationship between the level of temporary workers deployed and the performance of the economy. The logic is that greater economic activity means that organizations use more temporary workers, especially where there is any uncertainty about the extent and length of any business improvement. The latter point is borne out by the fact that those organizations where business demand is very

uncertain tend to use a higher proportion of temporary workers (ibid.).

Figure 3.2 illustrates the rise and fall of the two broad types of temporary work and emphasizes the complexity of the relationship between them and economic performance. From 1984, as output rose, so did the number of short-term temporary staff. As the UK went into recession the level of temporary employment fell, albeit after a delay. When the country came out of recession there was pronounced growth in fixed-term contracts rather than other types of temporary work, especially between 1992 and 1996. Indeed, nearly half the full-time jobs created during this period were temporary ones. The rate of increase then eased as economic performance deteriorated.

Temporary work is somewhat commoner for females than males, and is disproportionately found in part-time work. It tends to be more of a feature in the employment of young people than older. Casual and seasonal work, in particular, is more prevalent in the 16 to 24 age

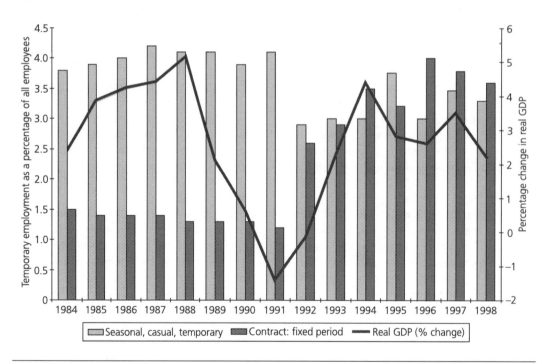

Figure 3.2 The link between economic growth and temporary working (based on data from the UK Office for National Statistics)

category. Fixed-term contractors have a more even age distribution. Of those employed on fixed-term contracts, 13.5 per cent are in professional occupations and 25 per cent are graduates. They are found particularly in education (where contracts are often tied around funding), health and public administration.

Employed casuals are not usually professionals. A noticeable number are in the personal protection occupational group. Seasonal work is traditionally found in agriculture, wholesale and retail trades, and hotels and restaurants.

Not surprisingly, clerical/secretarial employees are well represented among agency workers. Manufacturing and business services each employ about a fifth of the agency population.

The precise extent of outsourcing is not known. The most representative study, the Workplace Employee Relations Survey of 1998, reported that a quarter of organizations had contracted out work over the last five years. These tended to be the bigger organizations. Interestingly, 40 per cent of those outsourcing were in the non-commercial sector and a third contracted out because of compulsory competitive tendering. Of course this means that the vast majority do not report any recent contracting out. There is some evidence that outsourcing rises during recessionary periods and is associated with employment contraction (Brewster et al., 1996). This is very plausible, given that, as we shall see later, cost saving is frequently the principal driver to contracting work out.

Outsourcing has been very much concentrated in ancillary activities. The most popular outsourced activities are building maintenance (60 per cent of organizations in WERS) and cleaning (55 per cent). Transportation is subcontracted by about a third of organizations. There is less evidence, despite the anecdotal reports in management magazines, to demonstrate high penetration into other areas. Training (36 per cent) is much the most common human resource (HR) activity to be undertaken externally. Payroll is outsourced by a fifth of respondents and recruitment by only 11 per cent. Information technology is outsourced again by a fifth of the WERS respondents. Other areas of outsourcing not reported by WERS include car-fleet management and various types of engineering work.

TEMPORAL FLEXIBILITY

Temporal flexibility involves varying working hours to achieve a more effective deployment of labour to meet business requirements. There are a whole host of types of work patterns that permit this. Some of these are long-standing work arrangements (for example, overtime, shift working or part-time working); others appear at least to be more novel (for example, flexitime, flexible working weeks, annual hours or zero hours contracts). Another way of classifying temporal flexibility is to view the extent to which the pattern of hours is fixed or flexible. Table 3.2 illustrates the differences.

OVERTIME

Overtime, which may be paid or unpaid, is

Table 3.2 Types of temporal flexibility

< Unstructured		Structured >
overtime zero hours contracts variable hours contracts voluntary reduced hours	flexitime annual hours contracts short-time working	shift working part-time working job sharing flexible working weeks term-time contracts

Adapted from Reilly (1997c)

unstructured in that it should be used to deal with additional, unexpected tasks which need to be completed over the short term. This means existing employees are asked to work longer hours than the standard contractual requirements. Of course in practice overtime may become institutionalized either to satisfy employee wage aspirations or so that the employer can limit the number of those employed.

As one might expect, paid overtime in the UK is more common among manual employees in sectors such as mining, construction and transportation (Office for National Statistics, 1999a). The average number of paid overtime hours is nine per week (if one excludes periods of less than an hour), but the spread ranges fairly evenly from 1 hour per week to over 11 hours per week. This means over a million people were working in excess of 10 hours' paid overtime per week in the spring of 1999. Unpaid overtime has the opposite labour force characteristics – it is undertaken particularly by managers and professionals, especially in the education sector. The numerical pattern of unpaid overtime is similar to paid.

ZERO HOURS CONTRACTS

These are unstructured in a different way. Although the employee is given a contract of employment, no hours are specified within it, but he or she is expected to work when requested. So the employee only works when asked to by the employer. This gives the organization complete flexibility to vary hours of labour input to suit work demands. According to WERS, less than 4 per cent of employers report using zero hours contracts, amounting to less than 1 per cent of the employed workforce, according to the Labour Force Survey. Employees are spread across a number of sectors with retailing having the largest proportion, but even here it represents a very modest percentage. Interestingly, over a fifth of those on zero hours contracts work in the personal protection occupational group (Office for National Statistics, 1999a).

VARIABLE HOURS CONTRACTS

These are similar to zero hours contracts, but they specify a minimum number of working hours per week or a range of hours but with no guaranteed level. Tesco (Industrial Relations Services, 1996b) introduced a pattern of flexible hours for some of its UK employees in 1996. There are a designated number of core hours (10–16 per week) with the possibility that they might increase up to 31 per week on request. This arrangement gives employees a minimum income, unlike zero hours contracts. There is further protection in having a minimum shift length, 24 hours' call-out notice and 12 hours' rest period. Employees can also refuse to work the extra hours if they give their manager sufficient warning of their unavailability. However, this is deemed to be acceptable only if it happens now and again.

VOLUNTARY REDUCED HOURS

These contracts are more popular in the US than the UK. The idea is that employees can choose to reduce their working week, and their pay, for a period of time to assist with domestic duties or to undertake some private activity. In practice the time off varies considerably both in the duration of the period and in the amount of working time reduced. Often it is a very informal arrangement, say a short period of part-time working for paternity reasons. It can involve extended unpaid time off, for example to travel. Sometimes there are more formal arrangements, but these are usually much more akin to career breaks in that a complete separation from work is involved. Abbey National, for example, allows breaks of between six months and five years to satisfactory performers with three years' service (Stredwick and Ellis, 1998). Barclays has 'responsibility' breaks for up to six months to undertake caring duties (Arkin, 1997). Lily Industries (Daycare Trust, 1998) offers more flexibility: reduced hours can either be in a block or every week for a limited period. The new legal right in Britain to time off without pay for paternity leave might spark off more of these arrangements.

A variant of voluntary reduced hours is where an employee works full-time but only gets paid for part of the week because the difference is credited as leave to be taken as required.

FLEXITIME

Flexitime is a halfway house in terms of structure in that it permits variation in working hours, but within restrictions. Often organizations permit variation only outside core hours (usually four hours, for example 10 a.m. to noon and 2 p.m. to 4 p.m.) within a certain 'bandwidth' of a working day (commonly 10 hours). In other words, flexitime principally allows changes to starting or finishing times. There are other restrictions relating to the requirement to stay within a maximum and minimum number of hours within an overall accounting period, typically a month. However, the balance of hours from period to period can be carried over – often a day or day and a half surplus. Deficits may be less, more like half a day to a day. In some systems, spare hours can be added together to make a day or two's flexileave. Flexitime can provide further flexibility where the core hours are reduced. This is to be found particularly on Fridays, where the working day and core time may be cut by an hour or so. Management of the system is increasingly achieved via swipe cards that allow comprehensive monitoring.

CASE IN POINT

Tucker Fasteners' flexitime system has core hours between 0930 and 1530, with a lunch break of between 30 minutes and 2 hours. Employees can accrue up to 10 hours per month or run a debit of equal size, though this is discouraged. Credits can be exchanged for up to a maximum of one day's leave per month (Trades Union Congress, 1998b).

Flexitime is very much associated with white-collar employment, particularly clerical or professional. It is much less common among manual workers, and management grades are sometimes excluded from schemes in the private sector. A third of all employees enjoying flexitime are to be found in public administration, where a significant 40 per cent of the workforce is covered, compared with just under 10 per cent of employees in the whole UK labour force – a figure which has remained pretty constant over recent years.

ANNUAL HOURS CONTRACTS

These, as the name implies, allow the variation of actual working time within an annual total of contractual hours. To take the example of NatWest Bank (Whitehead, 1999a), this figure amounts to 1589 hours for a typical employee (a calculation of 35 hours × 52 weeks, less 231 hours to account for holidays). There is usually a basic set pattern of work, although there may be a seasonal variation. Some groups of staff have extra hours added to their total because of anticipated additional working – a sort of built-in overtime. They may receive a cash compensation for this, or increased time off in a future rota. Within the broad annual contract, however, there may be shorter accounting periods with specified maximum or minimum hours to avoid excessively long periods of working. It is these restrictions, which might apply to a week and/or a month, that make annual hours contracts a semi-structured form of temporal flexibility.

Annual hours contracts have had a lot of media attention over recent years, and there have been newsworthy deals reported (for example, at Rover cars; see Wheatley, 1999), but, as it involves less than 3 per cent of the workforce (Office for National Statistics, 1999a), or 6 per cent of employers (Workplace Employee Relations Survey, 1998), it is not as common (or growing) as one might expect. A quarter of all those covered by annual hours contracts work in the education sector. Somewhat less than a fifth are in manufacturing, where it tends to be associated with work of a very seasonal nature (for example, in food production) and where continuous production is necessary.

SHORT-TIME WORKING

This is a kind of poor man's version of annual hours contracts. Employees' hours and pay are cut when demand drops, with the expectation that the workload will pick up again after a limited period. Figures are not collected regularly on the use of short-time working: what evidence there is (Beatson, 1995) suggests that it is uncommon in the UK. It is used from time to time in manufacturing industry – one thinks of car plants going onto short-time working when demand for vehicles falls.

SHIFTS

Although there is a variety of shift-working patterns, some with exotic titles like 'reverse continental', each is precisely structured to meet service or production requirements that extend beyond the normal working day. Continuous rotating shifts are the most like this and are used either where the cost of starting and stopping the production process is prohibitive or where capital utilization needs to be maximized. Discontinuous shifts may be used for batch production. Split shifts or specific weekday/weekend working afford some flexibility to adjust working hours at shorter notice by lengthening individual shifts or adding shifts.

Two-shift systems are twice as common as three-shift. A fifth of UK employees work shifts at least some of the time, with 16.5 per cent usually contracted to operate in this way. A quarter of regular shift workers are employed in manufacturing, a similar proportion in health; 12 per cent of shift workers are employed in transport, storage and communication, with somewhat less in wholesale and retail trades. The latter has a higher percentage (15 per cent) of occasional shift workers. More men than women work regular shifts in the ratio of 6:4. Around a third of all plant operatives and those working in the personal protection sector work regular shifts; a quarter of professional/technical staff and 15 per cent of craft workers do likewise (Office for National Statistics, 1999a).

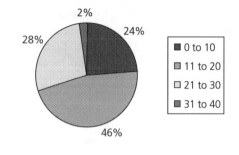

Figure 3.3 Normal weekly hours for part-time employees in the UK (source: Office for National Statistics, 1999a)

PART-TIME WORKING

Organizations vary in how they categorize part-time working. Some specify a maximum number of hours, others merely indicate any number less than standard. Figure 3.3 shows the UK distribution of part-time hours per week. The mean is 17 hours per week. In all cases changing the number, or even pattern, of hours is a contractual variation and so does not happen frequently, which is why we describe it as a structured form of temporal flexibility.

Sometimes part-time workers operate a job-share arrangement. In other words, usually two people cover the one job, sometimes with an overlap day. A little less than 1 per cent of employees share jobs, though this rises to 3 per cent of women with dependent children.

There has been a significant growth in part-time employment since the war (see Figure 3.4). This was especially noticeable between 1992 and 1996, when around half the jobs created were part-time. Since then full-time numbers have grown more strongly than part-time, so that the proportion of part-timers has steadied at 25 per cent of employees. More than 80 per cent of part-timers are women and over 40 per cent of women work part-time. The pattern of part-time working varies with age. A third of part-timers are under 24, most of whom are likely to be students. Around another third are over 55. Men tend to be well represented in both these categories, as they

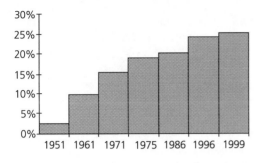

Figure 3.4 Growth of number of part-time employees in the UK (based on data from the UK Office for National Statistics)

take on part-time work on entering employment for the first time or as they near retirement. Women also work part-time in the middle years of employment, especially in combination with child/eldercare responsibilities.

Part-time workers are found more in small firms (fewer than 25 employees), hotels/restaurants and retail establishments, and in education, health and community work; 56 per cent of sales people are part-timers, as are around half of those in personal protection occupations. A bit less than a third of secretarial and clerical workers work on part-time contracts.

FLEXIBLE WORKING WEEKS

These describe the compression of normal hours into, for example, a nine-day fortnight or a four-and-a-half-day week. Sometimes there is employee flexibility to choose the free half day or day off; more usually it is the employer who decides when to close the office or factory. Often this is done on Fridays to minimize disruption, especially in manufacturing. Over 70 per cent of these arrangements occur in manufacturing, but even here they involve only 7 per cent of the workforce.

TERM-TIME CONTRACTS

These refer to school or college terms. In other words people work only during the academic period; the rest of the time is leave. Where this is not the organizational norm, staff are paid equally throughout the year, with standard

holiday entitlement; the extra time off over and above this is treated as unpaid leave. Over a third of those working in the education sector are employed on term-time contracts, 84 per cent of all cases in the labour force as a whole. Where interest exists outside the education sector, it is to meet employee choice rather than organizational demand. Again this is largely in the public sector, but some service activities (banks and hotels) offer term-time contracts. They are favoured by women, especially those with dependent children, compared with men. A variation to term-time contracts is 'part year' contracts, which do not necessarily follow educational terms. It is an option open to employees in the UK civil service.

As we have seen, certain forms of temporal flexibility are more associated with certain sectors. Manufacturing uses a wide variety of working-hour arrangements – shift, annual hours, overtime, flexitime, variable working weeks – but they together involve only 17 per cent of those employed in the sector. The public sector too is a significant user of flexible work arrangements, though not precisely the same pattern, with relatively greater use of flexitime, part-time working (less so in the civil service), annual hours, and term-time contracts (in education) and job sharing (in health). Retail is a notable user too of annual hours contracts, part-time employment, job sharing,

Table 3.3 Frequency of different types of temporal flexible working arrangement

Type of flexible arrangement	Percentage of total employees
paid overtime	25
shift working (regular)	16.5
part-time working	25.1
flexitime	9.5
flexible working week/fortnight	1.9
annualized hours	2.7
term-time contracts	4.0
zero hours contracts	0.5

Source: Office for National Statistics (1999a)

variable working weeks and zero hours contracts.

Frequency of use is summarized in Table 3.3. Note that there are no figures available for some of the types of flexible work arrangement we have described.

LOCATIONAL FLEXIBILITY

Locational flexibility allows work to be carried out away from the traditional workplace by using mobile or partly home-based staff, full outworkers or teleworkers. Relocation of work to back offices or to specialist satellite centres or even outsourcing an activity to a contractor's premises have also been considered variants on this approach. As this definition suggests, locational flexibility is something of a catch-all concept, and there are significant differences between the various types of arrangement that fall within its compass.

Relocating work to another site, even another country, does not necessarily imply any greater flexibility. At the time of transferring the work, this may appear to be so. For example, in place of telephone switchboards at numerous sites, the introduction of a single operation from one (outsourced) location may have various cost-saving benefits which might be attributed to locational flexibility, but once the move has been made any further flexibility is likely to be derived from other forms – functional, temporal or numerical.

Providing rather more flexibility are telecentres, which may offer employees communication facilities close to where they live or where their clients are based, thereby reducing commuting times and costs for the employee, and lower accommodation costs for the employer.

CASE IN POINT

Surrey County Council opened a pilot telecentre in Epsom in 1996, aimed at providing a working base for employees living within five to ten miles and peripatetic workers passing through the area, and offering an alternative to homeworking (Industrial Relations Services, 1999).

Looking at locationally flexible workers, there is another hotchpotch of different types. These include:

- homeworkers
- outworkers
- tele-homeworkers
- peripatetic freelance workers
- multi-site workers
- mobile workers.

The main constituent part of those designated homeworkers is family members who are engaged in supporting the family business from their own premises. Again this has nothing to do with our definition of flexibility. But there are some who work from home for employers based elsewhere: they may do routine clerical work, such as typing or data entry. This category blurs into that of outworkers, who take in work from others. Some of these workers are self-employed, others are formally on the books of remote employers. They have traditionally been employed in the textile industry, making up clothes at home using family-owned machines.

Tele-homeworkers are homeworkers who specifically use the telephone or computer as the principal means of working, for example to sell a product or to provide help-line assistance. As an illustration, the London Borough of Enfield recruited home-based workers to carry out the database management for its revenue support section. Those recruited were employees of the council, but worked from home (Incomes Data Services, 1994).

Freelancers are self-employed and work for numerous clients rather than a single employer. They offer organizations numerical flexibility (see p. 30) as well as locational flexibility.

Multi-centre workers, as the name implies, work in a number of locations. This may involve alternating between office and home, or varying the office used. One Canadian bank offers employees the chance to work part of the week not at their usual branch, but at one more convenient to themselves. This category overlaps that of mobile workers, be they in sales or service support, who are peripatetic and use home as their base. Such staff are often issued with portable equipment (such as laptop computers, pagers, mobile phones, portable fax machines, and so on), and work effectively from home, car, client's office or wherever they happen to be.

These mobile or multi-centre workers often use a hot-desking system at work, where shared facilities at the office are provided to use when they touch base. Digital was one of the pioneers of hot-desking. This came about somewhat by accident in 1990 when their Basingstoke office was partially burnt down. On rebuilding, management decided to accommodate a larger number of staff but with fewer workstations. Staff could use them as required, being able to plug in wherever space was available (Murphy, 1996). Now more organizations, especially on greenfield sites (for example, British Airways' Waterside site) or during renovation (for example, British Telecom's Newgate Street), build in hot-desking possibilities.

Some organizations try to separate out the different types of locationally flexible worker. Hertfordshire County Council Social Services, following an analysis of work patterns, divided its workforce into mobile workers (who spent over half their time away from base) and homeworkers (who worked more than half their time from home). When either group came to work they hot-desked (Industrial Relations Services, 1999).

Given the definitional problems, it is hard to quantify the extent of locational flexibility, except to say that, despite the publicity, teleworking is not yet of great significance in numerical terms. According to the 1991 census, 2.5 per cent of the UK workforce were homeworkers, a mixture of the traditional self- or family-employed and teleworkers. (There was no separate definition for the latter.) More recent information from the Labour Force Survey (Office for National Statistics, 1999a) suggests that about 1.5 per cent of employees work at home and another 3 per cent use home as a base from which to work. Perhaps two-thirds of this population are teleworkers in

the sense that they are dependent on information technology to do their work. Less than 10 per cent of WERS respondents say they employ homeworkers in any numbers.

Broadly speaking, mobile workers tend to be the more skilled employees, engaged in professional or sales work, including higher-technology activities. They tend to be male, middle-aged and, for those involved in high-technology work, concentrated in the south-east of England. They are found in a number of sectors, especially manufacturing, retail, business services, construction and health/social work.

Nearly all homeworkers or outworkers are women. Those of the traditional kind are married with children, and in their twenties and thirties. They are generally low earners, working fewer hours per week than workers in general, so as to earn extra money but still be able to look after their children. Female homeworkers are particularly to be found in secretarial and clerical jobs, and to a lesser extent in craft occupations. Craft work and sales activities account for over half of male homeworkers' occupations (Felstead, 1996, and Felstead and Jewson, 1996). These homeworkers are thus disproportionately to be found in manufacturing and business services. Those who are tele-homeworkers, not surprisingly, have a higher-level occupational profile.

FINANCIAL FLEXIBILITY

The purpose of financial flexibility is to allow employers to increase and decrease wages in line with internal labour market factors (recruitment or retention issues), external economic conditions (labour market tightness leading to shortages, or the opposite) or with business performance (productivity or profitability). This can be seen to a limited extent with profit-related pay or gainsharing – the level of payment depending on the financial success of the organization, be that defined as straight profit or some other measure of successful performance. However, the proportion of money involved in UK profit-sharing schemes is generally small, and they have been used more to secure tax benefits than obtain flexibility. There is little evidence that profit sharing has been used successfully to adjust the wage bill to protect employment during difficult trading times – perhaps because the sums of money are indeed too small.

Before they were phased out, approved cash-based profit-sharing schemes involved around 4.5 million people, with pay-outs of £800 at maximum. There were in addition 1 250 tax-approved share schemes. Broader gainsharing approaches are as yet uncommon.

In theory, too, variable pay schemes, where a percentage of an executive's salary is at risk, dependent upon business performance, is another example of financial flexibility. Performance-related pay is sometimes quoted as a form of financial flexibility (Sparrow, 1997). Yet for many firms it is merely a means of changing the distribution of the pot of money (to reward high performers differentially) rather than altering the size of the pot, and the link between executive pay and corporate performance has according to critics been rather tenuous.

Decentralizing pay is also alleged to be a means of facilitating financial flexibility because it means that decisions are made closer to the influences of the market. However, while this may be a reasonable theory, the locus of decision making is only important if it impacts in the way suggested. The actual evidence is mixed (Beatson, 1995). Centralized pay bargaining may reflect economic and labour market conditions just as well as localized pay bargaining, because the negotiators may have a greater appreciation of labour market conditions than those with only an establishment or enterprise perspective.

A more clear-cut example of financial flexibility occurs where basic wages are adjusted to reflect company circumstances. Thus wages are cut during a company downturn. However, in the UK at least, these examples are pretty rare or the sums of money involved are fairly small (Barrell, 1994). Where they do occur, they are more likely to be one-off events in response to exceptional economic circumstances than a continuing policy.

A CONTINUUM OF RESOURCING OPTIONS

What the above summary of the forms of flexibility should have shown is that there is a multiplicity of types of flexibility (indeed there are other less common variations not listed here). The categories often blur between them. Figure 3.5 tries to capture the interrelationship between them, with the exception of financial flexibility. On the left-hand side there is the traditional employee who is hired on a regular contract, to work full-time, completing a restricted range of tasks, in an operationally integrated activity, at a main location. As one moves across the picture, there is increased flexibility. So self-employment replaces a contract of employment, or working for a

	less ◀——— Flexibility ———▶ *more*				
Employment status	regular	fixed-term contract	casual	agency temp	consultant
Ownership structure	integrated	insourced	subsidiary		outsourced
Location	main site	back office	mobile		home
Working hours	full-time	part-time	variable hours		zero hours
Work organization	mono-functional	task-flexible			multi-functional

Figure 3.5 A continuum of types of flexibility

third party replaces working for the client organization. Greater flexibility is seen in working hours, activities and location. As the diagram shows, there are lots of intervening stages.

Another point which might strike the reader of this chapter is that the incidence of many of these forms of flexibility is not as great as one might expect. Many writers in the early and mid-1990s seemed confident of the growth of flexible work arrangements. Both those on the free-market right, who extolled the virtues of the flexible labour market, and those that opposed these developments expected to see the continuing rise in all kinds of flexibility but especially in the use of temporary contracts. In fact it is the 'traditional' types of flexibility – shift working, overtime and part-time working – that still dominate.

This leads us to ask in more detail why it is that employers choose the particular forms of flexibility they do.

CHAPTER FOUR

Why Employers Use Flexibility

We have described the various types of flexibility and indicated how they have developed. The statistics shown are a reflection of the current organizational landscape in the UK, but this is an ever-changing picture. In this chapter we will look more closely at the reasons why employers are interested in flexible work arrangements. Before going into detail with respect to the different facets of flexibility, it would perhaps be helpful to paint the broader canvas of why the subject has featured so much on the corporate agenda.

THE BIG PICTURE

Growth in interest and practice in flexible work arrangements has occurred because of a number of factors. Some reflect changing labour market conditions, for example:

- high levels of unemployment
- the increasing number of women in the labour market
- the growth in the service sector.

Some are organizationally driven, for example:

- cost-cutting imperatives
- more competitive product markets
- technological innovation.

Others are the result of the impact of the external environment:

- government encouragement
- union weakness.

We will look at these issues in turn.

LABOUR MARKET FACTORS

Organizations have been able to change working practices, hire different types of people or alter contractual arrangements because over much of the last twenty years it has been a buyer's labour market. In other words, employers have been able to choose whom they wanted to employ and on what basis. Evidence of the slackness of the labour market since 1974 is to be seen in the relatively high rates of unemployment shown in Figure 2.5. Of course there have been periods when the labour market has been tighter, especially in particular sectors (for example, finance in the late 1980s) or occupations (for example, information technology specialists). Generally, however, organizations have been able to adjust resourcing policies to meet their business needs.

While there has been organizational pull towards flexibility, there has also been a concomitant push in the labour market in favour of flexible work arrangements. This has been largely driven by increasing female participation in the labour force, which has been fostered by the growing variety of working patterns on offer. As we saw in the last chapter, by and large female employees are more likely to work to more flexible patterns, especially those involving part-time structures. They are more likely to be engaged in temporary contractual arrangements or to work via agencies.

There is also the effect, described in Chapter 2, of the sectoral shift from primary and manufacturing industry to services to be considered. The service sector tends to employ more women because the sort of skills required and the terms of work seem to suit women better than men. So it was inevitable that certain forms of flexible work arrangements would become more common simply because of these macro-trends. This is certainly true for part-time working, but, interestingly, research suggests that it is employer choice that has led to greater use of other forms of temporal flexibility and to the employment of temporary workers (Beatson, 1995, and Casey et al., 1997).

ORGANIZATIONAL FACTORS

Organizations have been under a number of pressures, the response to which has in part been to turn to flexible work arrangements. The key issue that has faced companies in the private sector has been the requirement to cut costs and to compete successfully in a way that brings acceptable shareholder returns. Over the last thirty years the UK stock exchange has expected an average 9.8 per cent per annum rate of return. This is over three times higher than Japan and 50 per cent higher than in Germany (Hutton, 1995). These pressures may be continuous or may be stimulated by a specific event. It is said that British Airways looked at flexibility more seriously after the Gulf War, because the latter significantly affected its profitability. The arrival of Wal-Mart on the UK retailing scene may have a similar effect. The owners of utilities such as water, gas, electricity and telecommunications are stimulated by each regulatory decision to find new ways of working more efficiently and more flexibly.

A critical contextual issue has been the increasing demands of customers. This has been true in terms of quality and speed of service, and in terms of access. People want their services provided at a time suitable to them, not at the convenience of the producer. Parcel Force, for example, can now deliver packages in the evening when people are at home rather than in normal working hours. Television repair staff employed by Granada now work from home on flexible schedules so that they can respond more easily to customer preferences for evening visits. You can order your foreign currency or check the balance of your bank account 24 hours a day. There are new drop-in medical centres, intended to suit those who find it inconvenient to make an appointment with their GP in normal surgery hours.

These trends have been facilitated by information technology and innovation in communication. This is prevalent both at home and work. Increasingly wide swathes of the population are becoming computer familiar, if not fully literate. Modern software is considerably more user friendly than in the past. Costs of machines and connections are falling in real terms. Electronic mail allows fast and easy data transmission. Local area networks (LANs) permit intranet connections within organizations, facilitating message and information transfer. Intranets, for example, can allow employees and managers not only to access details of HR policies, but also to update personnel records. 'Groupware', for example Lotus Notes, permits electronic discussion. Upgraded telephony lets telephone numbers move with the person, as of course do mobile phones. Automated call distribution systems allow calls to be routed to various locations, both office and home. The Internet gives access to all sorts of databases that can be accessed from any workstation, providing information, opportunities for learning and entertainment. E-commerce will soon replace many traditional methods of interaction, especially in financial services and retailing. Electronic data interchange (EDI), because it avoids the rekeying of data, is becoming common as a means of ordering and supplying services. Point of sale (POS) information, through cash registers or barcodes, permit retailers to track their sales to the minute. Stocks and the pattern of what, when and how many goods have been sold can be more easily monitored. Production activities have been revolutionized by process control systems, allowing much more precise monitoring and easy adjustment to optimize performance. Computer-aided design has transformed much engineering and similar design work.

The growing speed and cheapness of information transfer allows activities to be undertaken remotely, whether this be through call centres, offshore data processing or externally based software development. Computing power has provided on-desk expert systems or robotics in the factory. It has produced a world in which 'natural resources are buyable, technology copyable, ... and production processes separable' (Thurlow, 1994).

Sometimes flexibility has been facilitated by technology. Computerized systems can allow precise knowledge about stocks and sales to be combined with personnel information systems to optimize scheduling, not just of goods, but of people. For example, the MD Foods annualized hours roster uses a computer system to track employee hours and link it to demand (Kodz et al., 1998). Telework naturally relies on a communications infrastructure. Computerization has had the effect of deskilling some jobs to make them more routine, as has been true of some call-centre operations. This makes it easier to use temporary staff. Capital investment in equipment has also reduced the need for investment in employee development. At the other end of the spectrum, some jobs have become more complex, with a greater knowledge component or the need to handle more sophisticated equipment. Here it is harder to use untrained and inexperienced workers, as it takes them too long to get up to speed.

The response of organizations to these trends in the management of their own resources has been to downsize the workforce in order to save money; to simplify and speed decision-making through de-layering; to devolve responsibility from the corporate centre to operating units in order to improve responsiveness to business opportunities; to emphasize and focus on the quality of service or production; to re-engineer the organization through an understanding of the linkage between key processes; to restructure on the basis of matrix systems, semi-autonomous business groups; to move from traditional command and control hierarchies, ill suited to the flexibilities required of this modern world, to amoeba-like forms; to create team structures empowered to take their own decisions within their area of expertise; to use just-in-time (JIT) techniques of production and scheduling to reduce inventory costs in themselves and increase responsiveness and flexibility in supply; and, in the softer area of attitudes, behaviour and values, to engender some form of cultural transformation to reflect the new environment within which organizations are operating.

All this adds up to organizations allowing themselves greater flexibility in structure, processes and systems to adjust quickly and flexibly to changing work demands.

In relation to how organizations have responded externally, we have seen a growth in business acquisition and disposal to maximize shareholder return; frequent examples of joint ventures, cross-business partnering or alliances between companies in order to acquire or share expertise, financial resources, or access to markets or technology. Since 1994 it has been estimated that each year the value of mergers and acquisitions worldwide has exceeded $500 billion. In 1998 the total reached over $2 250 billion (Treanor, 1998). Some of the deals between multinationals involve vast sums of money and have major employment consequences. Astra and Zeneca concluded a $42 billion union; Deutsche Bank and Bankers Trust have spent $1 billion in the restructuring that followed their tie-up; Exxon and Mobil cut 12 000 jobs as part of an estimated $5 billion savings in their merger plan; and the BP and Amoco merger aimed to reduce costs by $2 billion (Leigh, 1999).

GOVERNMENT PRESSURES

Public sector organizations in the UK have had the same pressures to increase efficiency and deliver better customer value, but they have also been working within the framework set for them by government. Under the Conservatives there was the introduction of the market mechanism to substantial areas of the public sector. The aim was to cut costs and increase efficiency. Thus the government created internal markets where these had not previously existed (for example, in the NHS). Through market testing they required public services to be compared on cost with the private sector, and via compulsory competitive tendering (CCT) a significant number of activities were outsourced. So some parts of the public sector were pushed into considering forms of flexibility that in other circumstances would not have been on the agenda. Local government especially faced both the requirement for CCT and the need to slash costs radically. Moreover, privatization brought about the transfer of large chunks of the public sector to the private sector.

Although the present Labour government has not gone so far down this track, in its different way it has pressed for efficiency in public services and pragmatically determined whether public or private money should be the source of funding for those activities currently state run. Thus there has been pressure to use the private finance initiative (PFI) to fund hospital building, and the proposed partial sell-off of publicly owned assets, like the air traffic control system. Labour has abandoned CCT and replaced it by the concept of *best value* – pressing the public sector to find ways of delivering services more efficiently.

WANING TRADES UNION POWER

Government-initiated and organizationally driven change has been easier to accomplish with the decline in the power of trades unions over recent years. Trades union membership in Great Britain has fallen from a peak of 13.3 million in 1979 to 7.1 million by 1998. As a proportion of the employed workforce, the drop is from 53 per cent to around 29 per cent in 1998 (Office for National Statistics, 1998). The percentage of employees covered by collective bargaining also fell from around two-thirds in the mid-1980s to about a third by 1997. The number of days lost through strikes has steadily fallen since the 1970s. In the year to December 1999, 231 000 days were lost, compared to an annual average over the period 1985–1995 of 2.6 million (Office for National Statistics). The closed shop, including the pre-entry sort which sustained the trade demarcations that were reported earlier (Chapter 3), has been outlawed.

Union density has suffered from alterations in industrial structure, particularly the decline in manufacturing and growth in small businesses. Union power has been undermined through legislation, symbolic defeats (such as the miners' strike), persistently high unemployment, and the internationalism of business as firms have been prepared to relocate activities to cut costs and avoid industrial strife. Especially in the early 1990s, union weakness allowed many companies to de-recognize unions, removing their representational position. The social trends described in Chapter 2 have, moreover, made employees less prepared to risk strikes because they have more to lose financially as their liabilities and responsibilities have grown.

A STRATEGIC RESPONSE?

Thus the main determinants of organizations' resourcing policies have inclined them towards flexibility or facilitated the introduction of more flexible work patterns:

- technological change has made flexible work arrangements easier or necessary
- competitive pressures and consumer demands have required organizations to be more adaptable and faster on their feet
- labour market conditions have largely given employers the ability to hire and fire as required from a workforce more inclined to be flexible
- institutional constraints on change, from the likes of trades unions, have been limited and some companies have deliberately challenged cultural norms to effect organizational change.

All this is within the context of a government, labour market and economic policy favourable to flexibility. With these sorts of pressures and drivers for change, one might expect that organizations would develop coherent and planned responses. In the area of flexibility, one might expect to see a strategic push that would take the new business requirements and try to find the best match in terms of the number, type and organization of resources. A description of this sort of analytical decision making can be seen in the case in point on the next page.

In fact, research indicates (Hunter et al., 1993; Bresnen and Fowler, 1994; Perry, 1992) that the move to more flexible forms of employment has been largely ad hoc and opportunistic in nature, rather than being part of a conscious strategy.

In one sense this is surprising. Strategy, one

CASE IN POINT

A structured approach to decision making is to be found in transaction-cost economics (Williamson, 1979). This provides a model of how to decide whether to perform a task internally or externally. It suggests that management would examine the relative costs of managing transactions and comparing the costs of production or service. On this basis companies would choose the 'most economical governance structure'. The key aspects of transactions are the

- degree of uncertainty in the market
- frequency of the transaction
- specificity of the activity or investment (in terms of location, equipment, skills or knowledge).

On the basis of this analysis, outsourcing would be favoured where transactions are not specific, irrespective of how frequently they are performed or the degree of uncertainty, whereas companies would decide to retain activities in-house where transactions are very specific, occur frequently and are subject to a high level of uncertainty.

---

might reasonably suppose, concerns among other things the scope of an organization's activities, the resources required to undertake them and the way in which they are organized (Johnson, 1987). On this basis the move to flexible work arrangements would be a strategic decision. This would seem to apply to aspects of all types of flexibility, but especially to significant changes in contractual requirements (for example, a widespread adoption of part-time, shift or temporary contracts), to restructuring of work organization (to be found in functional flexibility) and to changes in who carries out the work and where (which would include outsourcing and locational flexibility).

What in practice seems to be the case is that there is much variation by organization, by sector and, to some extent, by the occupation involved. There is variation too by type of flexible arrangement.

Broadly speaking one can categorize the organizational responses into three sorts:

- the ideological purposive
- the rational strategic
- the ad hoc pragmatic.

THE IDEOLOGICAL PURPOSIVE

There are those who see the shift towards flexibility as part of organizational re-engineering, aimed at responding to the sort of new world of work and business described in Chapter 1. They are adherents to the transformation of employment model and are attracted to the US labour market approach. They see a fast-changing, global business environment which is characterized by high levels of uncertainty. The appropriate response to this is, at a macro-level, to have a fully flexible labour market, like the Americans', and, at the organizational level, to maximize the company's agility to meet new and different challenges.

So what in practice does this mean? At one end of the spectrum it involves the move to a virtual, modular or minimalist organization. Size of the organization is restricted as much as possible; very few people are directly employed. The company works with a series of loose and temporary networks, assembled to perform specific tasks as required. They can be added or withdrawn 'with the flexibility of switching parts in a child's Lego set' (Tully, 1993). These networks may well spread across the globe seeking the best location on the basis of expertise and price. This means substantial outsourcing because, by definition, performing activities internally is seen as more expensive than carrying out work externally. This is because the cost of completing work internally is insufficiently market sensitive, risks inflexibility of response and tends to lead to bureaucratic inertia.

Nike, Reebok, Dell and Cisco are exemplars of the modular corporation. Nike owns but one factory and Reebok none, as all their manufacturing work is subcontracted. Dell, similarly, does not manufacture: it buys in ready-made kit which it assembles at two leased plants. Its customer supply is also outsourced. Instead Dell concentrates on sales and service back-up – the areas it sees as providing competitive advantage. The chief executive of Cisco described his company's approach: 'Of 32 plants worldwide, only two are our own. We have a virtual global plant. The majority of our products are built and shipped to customers without a single Cisco person touching them' (Murphy, 2000).

In the public sector there have also been moves to create minimalist organizations. This may have been prompted initially by compulsory competitive tendering, but may have gone beyond what was statutorily required. One London borough considered the externalization of all its services, except central purchasing (Purcell and Purcell, 1998). A change in political power stopped further development, indicating that the move had more to do with political philosophy than with practical problem solving – a true case of the ideological purposive.

In these examples we see a situation developing in a way anticipated by Atkinson (1984) when he described changing contractual patterns: 'the displacement of employment relationships by commercial relationships through subcontracting, the displacement of implicitly permanent employment by explicitly temporary employment, usually with an accompanying change in employment contract, and the displacement of employment by self-employment'.

High degrees of flexibility within the workforce would also be expected in organizations driven by an ideological purposive approach. Functional flexibility is assumed because work is no longer divided into jobs; people perform broadly based roles. Attitudes to the way tasks are performed are very customer focused. This means working hours are likely to be flexible, and probably long! And as this is a high-tech world, hot-desking, teleworking and mobility in general are also

characteristic. As far as remuneration is concerned, financial flexibility is likely to be seen in the large proportion of pay dependent on business success through profit-related bonuses and gainsharing schemes.

The one-time CoSteel plant at Sheerness exhibited some of these characteristics. CoSteel de-recognized its trades unions. It adopted a philosophy that was based on a unitarist view of the world. It sought competitive advantage from its employees through 'compliant patterns of behaviour'. It, however, aimed for employee job satisfaction and provided single status terms and conditions. Gainsharing and profit-related pay formed part of the remuneration package. Pay did not vary according to hours worked or change of rotational role. Staff were fully flexible and mobile and were expected to develop and improve skills (Billot, 1996).

Not all those who are ideologically in favour of flexibility are so thoroughgoing in their approach. There are some senior executives who require only limited application of the model, but, as distinct from our other categories, they seek flexibility as a matter of principle not on the basis of any cost–benefit analysis. So, for example, one company chief executive instructed that all new recruits should be hired on fixed-term contracts; another declared that a third of the workforce must be temporary staff of one sort or another. As far as one could tell, neither of these managers had thought of the pluses and minuses of such an approach: it was a matter of policy that a degree of flexibility was a good thing in itself.

THE RATIONAL STRATEGIC

The difference between this category and the one above is that those who are ideologically convinced of the need for flexibility adopt it often thoroughly and systematically, and certainly as a matter of principle. Those whom we describe as falling into the rational strategic category are likely to take decisions more in an analytical manner, perhaps on a case-by-case basis, yet nevertheless within a strategic context.

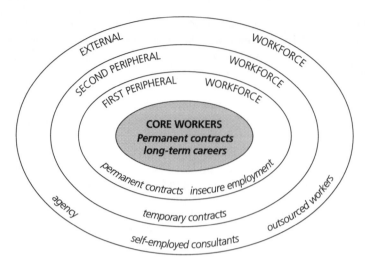

Figure 4.1 The core/periphery model (adapted from Atkinson, 1984)

A model that some of this group adopts is that of the flexible firm. Developed by Atkinson (1984) and Atkinson and Meager (1986) in the mid-1980s, it describes the distinction between the core, peripheral and external workforces. Each is visualized as rings of a circle moving from the central core (see Figure 4.1). The external workforce represents the outsourced activity or work undertaken by agency employees, self-employed consultants or freelancers. This, together with the peripheral group, can be adjusted in size to meet changing market demands. The characteristics of peripheral workers may be that they:

- have low or generalized skill requirements
- have internally focused responsibilities
- are easily found in the external labour market
- are set well-defined or limited tasks
- have jobs that are easily separated from other work.

The core employees would be employed on regular contracts and would have their skills and careers developed for the benefit of the organization. They would be expected to demonstrate a high degree of flexibility, in return for which they would be offered skill

CASE IN POINT

The oil industry in Aberdeen is an example of a core/periphery approach at work. The nature of the economics of the sector means that activity rises and falls with the oil price, or varies in nature. The field operators have responded by keeping a core of permanent staff, while at the same time drafting in temporary staff if the workload demands extra labour. Many of the activities are also outsourced.

Indeed, there is a hierarchy from the primary oil companies, like Shell or BP Amoco, which contract the field operators through to a series of subcontractors that undertake specific tasks (like drilling, transport and construction) and themselves might subcontract even more particular duties (for example, shot-blasting) to small specialist firms. As an industry commentator put it, this

resourcing model 'allows risk to be spread in a high fixed cost industry with volatile product–market conditions' (Gasteen and Sewell, 1994). Evidence of this point came during the oil price crash of 1986 when the oil majors furiously cut costs and the field operators cut wages and reduced peripheral labour, both directly contracted or via the subsidiary contractors.

development and career prospects. Peripheral workers, by contrast, would be engaged either on permanent contracts, but with no long-term expectation of employment, or on temporary contracts. They would receive only job-related training necessary to perform their specific tasks. They would act as a buffer for permanent employees. They would take the strain if numbers had to be reduced, thereby protecting the core workforce. This, in theory, encourages the core employees to be more flexible and adaptable because of the job security offered to them.

Underpinning this employment model is the assumption that organizations distinguish between activities that are core from those that are peripheral. It also assumes that those performing core tasks have the attributes the organization wishes to retain, and, conversely, that those engaged in peripheral activities are not the sort of people the organization wants to keep long term. Deciding on what constitutes core work may be determined by considering the activities that are seen as providing the source of its competitive advantage and those that are not. Another approach is to establish the organization's core competencies or capabilities, and to ensure that these are protected, allowing the non-essential to be outsourced, if appropriate.

To make decisions of this sort organizations might use some form of decision-making

model, such as that shown for decisions regarding outsourcing in Figure 4.2. Here, the organization decides what should be retained on the basis of the importance and availability of skills. Those activities where the required skills are neither specialized nor hard to come by would be clear candidates for outsourcing, and vice versa. Specialist skills not regularly used would probably be bought in. Some companies would externalize work from the top-right quadrant. Indeed, those organizations that describe the core very narrowly come close to the ideological purposive approach.

THE AD HOC PRAGMATIC

Anecdotal evidence, and the research reported earlier, suggests that this is the most common way in which decisions on flexible work arrangements are made. Here judgements are tactical rather than the result of strategic thought, with little relationship to a business or resourcing overview. The emphasis is often on cost control over the short term. There is little attempt to consider the longer-term implications, just a reflex response 'to get the business through a crisis or to secure a transition' (Hunter et al., 1993). This is not surprising, given the pressure to maximize return on investment described earlier. On these grounds alone, activities have been outsourced, work relocated, temporary staff employed and agencies used for supplying all sorts of people.

Another characteristic of this group is that they suffer from the disease of imitation. They are susceptible to fads and fashions. They are liable to pick up ideas peddled by consultants or business gurus. They are receptive to what they read in the press or see on television. They are even affected by what they hear on the golf course! Under the influence of these ideas, managers may (rightly) feel that they can earn 'brownie points' back at the office if they propose flexible solutions.

My respondent at one major UK company, when asked why an activity had been contracted out, told me that the director responsible had felt exposed because he had not yet outsourced any work and believed that it was important to be seen to do so by his

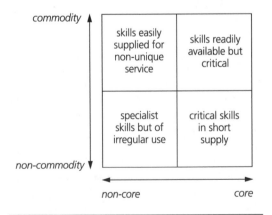

Figure 4.2   An outsourcing decision tool (source: Reilly and Tamkin, 1997)

board colleagues. Similar evidence has been found in information technology outsourcing: 'IT managers may initiate outsourcing decisions for the purpose of enhancing their credibility ... by showing ... senior management that they are corporate players' (Lacity et al., 1994).

Some have argued that the absence of the strategic adoption of flexible work arrangements indicates the absence of a conscious move to a new flexible model of employment. This point of view has been put (see especially Pollert, 1991) in order to demolish the position described earlier that is encapsulated in the transformation of employment model.

The search for 'strategic intent' in employers' decision making does assume itself a certain rationalist model of strategic thinking. The assumption that organizations scan their environment, identify options, select a course of action and then execute their plans has come in for significant criticism over recent years (Mintzberg, 1994). Instead it is suggested that strategy, rather than being developed in a purposive way from top management, occurs unintentionally, through small incremental steps, often taken at operational level, as the organization 'feels' its way towards a new position. The strategy then becomes evident in a post hoc rationalization of what has happened. In this view, strategy and tactics become blurred. What has been called emergent strategy recognizes that changes both within and outside the organization can divert the intended strategy from its chosen path.

In the context of how most organizations seem to operate, this appears to be a plausible view. One should not forget that many firms have limited management resources that tend to concentrate on the day-to-day operations. They have little capacity for change, and perhaps limited interest in it. Usually the status quo is pretty firmly embedded, and to alter direction much resistance has to be overcome. Instead the organization responds to pressures, rather than challenges the world. And it does so in a way which the outsider would find pretty incoherent – certainly, there

would be little evidence of 'joined up' management.

SPECIFIC REASONING

We have considered the reasons why interest in flexibility has developed in a broad context; now we turn to a more detailed examination of the reasons why specific forms of flexibility are adopted. In general, flexibility is introduced at the workplace to:

- provide a better match between labour inputs and work requirements
- act as a hedge against change, especially the need to downsize
- respond to changes in work methods, including technological innovation
- provide cost savings
- respond to new (leaner) organizational structures
- improve quality of service or to meet customer needs
- solve labour supply problems or to attract certain types of employee
- transform the organizational culture, for example by being more responsive to customers or more aware of costs
- encourage labour turnover, thereby being more sensitive to external labour market conditions.

However, the precise combination of reasons varies according to the type of flexibility, so we will look at each of the types in turn.

FUNCTIONAL FLEXIBILITY

The origins of the concept of functional flexibility lie in manufacturing industry where organizations sought to break down barriers that existed within craft trades and between these trades and those who worked in production. A maintenance electrician would not adjust a bolt on a pipe; a mechanical craftsman would not isolate a piece of equipment. Neither of them was trained to assist production, and the operators, for their part, would not take on any craft duties. These demarcations were in many cases reinforced and supported by trades unions that wished to protect their interests, as much between each union group as between themselves and management. So they controlled entry into work and union membership via closed shops. The docks, Fleet Street printing, and shipbuilding were notorious examples of this phenomenon. An extreme personal experience of trying to change these attitudes came when I was leading a team that sought to improve productivity at a loss-making plant. The suggestion that anyone other than the 'cherry picker' driver might operate the vehicle produced the response that if they did they would be 'found in the long grass', and the idea that a plant operator might change a light bulb led to a walkout from the meeting by the electricians.

Change in work organization has been more easily accepted in the service sector, including financial services (O'Reilly, 1992), than in manufacturing, because there has been a greater tradition of staff moving from activity to activity. But attitudes even in manufacturing have changed. On the negative side, employees have had to be more accommodating in the face of plant closures, redundancies and waning trades union power. Technological change has forced people to change behaviours. Organizations both in manufacturing and the service sector have been pushing to improve productivity by reducing costs and maximizing output. More positively, improved terms and conditions have been on offer to those who have chosen to develop or add to their skill base. An example is given in the case in point below.

Functional flexibility can offer the opportunity to achieve these objectives in a number of ways. Cost savings can be obtained because fewer people may need to be employed. The use of all-rounders rather than employing many different specialists may offer the chance of reduced headcount, as deployment can be more flexible and the organization does not have to recruit for each of the specialisms separately. Efficiency can also come from not having to suffer as much downtime. On a production plant this may mean minor maintenance being performed there and then by an operator with the necessary skills, rather than having to wait for specialist support. British Airports Authority at Glasgow Airport can offer a similar example. It suffered from an average 53 hours of downtime when equipment failed, partly because of the need to wait for more than one trade to attend a problem. Now, through multi-skilling, response and repair times have fallen such that downtime is averaging 4 hours per incident (Pollock, 2000). More efficient resourcing can be achieved by

CASE IN POINT

A petrochemical company moved to a greenfield site for operational reasons, with the bonus of leaving behind its traditional labour relations. These were characterized by mutual union and company antagonism; the requirement to negotiate every change in work practices, however minor; and a history of demarcation disputes within and between maintenance craftsmen and production operators. Management was determined not to recognize trades unions because it could not see how it could reach the levels of efficiency it required within this sort of conflictual environment. Instead it wanted to create staff technicians, who would be 'all-singing, all-dancing' craftsmen/operators. They would be trained to operate the plant and to perform the basics of all the principal maintenance activities. Thus experienced mechanical technicians were recruited and then trained in process technology (for plant operations) and in instrument and electrical work. By rotating through production and maintenance shifts, the technician grew in competence in plant operations, retained his or her mechanical skills whenever he or she was the shift expert, and grew familiar with the other areas of maintenance, as and when required.

being able to use labour more flexibly when the workload is slack. When production is halted for the annual overhaul, operators may be asked to do painting or housekeeping tasks. In a service centre the adviser may be able to deal with a range of customer queries rather than having to waste time by having to consult a colleague with the necessary expertise. If call volumes are high in one area, staff can be switched from another to assist. Greater efficiency can also be found among professional staff (as shown in the NHS case in point).

CASE IN POINT

Nottingham City Hospital found that it has become more efficient by multi-skilling its 240 theatre staff. This meant cutting across professional boundaries. According to Jenny Warner, consultant anaesthetist: 'Before the changes, we would often have the right number of staff, but not the right mix of skills, so we had to cancel operations. Now it is a lot easier to fill gaps and we don't cancel lists as often because we can find someone either to scrub or to assist the anaesthetist, as staff do both on a regular basis. Throughput is smoother, there is more flexibility, we have more motivated teams and lower staff turnover.' (Johnson, 1999b)

These points are illustrated by Lands' End, the mail-order clothing company: 'We have cross trained a lot of our employees so that we can juggle them around. If the phones are going mad, we can pull people from other areas to help with calls or send them to the distribution centre to help with the packing' (Industrial Society, 1998).

To try to break down unjustifiable barriers has been one driver to functional flexibility; another pressure for change has been improvement to the quality of customer service. This has involved organizations' providing customers with a one-stop-shop response. Especially in financial services there has been a tendency to gather together different aspects of the service into the hands of a single person.

This makes life easier for the customer, who can have all his or her queries dealt with by the same person, rather than being passed from one contact to the next. Part of the impetus for this change has been improved technology: service personnel can use a computer to assist in accessing and dealing with a customer's records and even employ an expert system to answer the more difficult queries.

NUMERICAL FLEXIBILITY

The advantages to employers in using numerical flexibility vary depending upon whether we are talking about temporary/agency labour or outsourcing. In both cases, though, they allow the level of labour input to adjust in line with the workload. This is achieved by varying the numbers of people utilized (rather than the hours of those employed, as in temporal flexibility). Easier upsizing and downsizing is thereby permitted to manage future uncertainty without the employee relations and financial implications of making 'permanent' staff redundant. Numerical flexibility can also be used simply to cut headcount or the burden of costs. It can sometimes offer cheaper labour if agency or outsourced workers are paid less than would be possible if they were on the internal payroll. A survey in Manchester, for example, found that 60 per cent of agency workers were paid less than their permanent equivalents (Navarro, 1996). Although there is a mark-up to be paid for the supplier's profit, this may not be so substantial in long-term supply deals. Where the resourcing responsibility is passed to a third party, the organization's fixed-cost exposure is also reduced.

Looking specifically at the reasons for using temporary or agency labour, survey evidence (Atkinson et al., 1996) suggests the following motivations, listed in order of importance:

- matching staff numbers to peaks in demand
- short-term cover for holiday or sick leave
- dealing with one-off tasks
- cover for maternity leave
- cover for staff changes
- providing specialist skills
- giving a trial for a permanent job.

The Workplace Employee Relations Survey (1998) produced a similar response, but distinguished between the types of temporary worker and their use. It suggested that 60 per cent of employers use agency staff for cover reasons and 40 per cent for matching peaks in demand. Fixed-term contractors are employed to handle increases in workload (35 per cent), as trial employment (22 per cent) and to make use of specialist skills (17 per cent). Agency temporary staff are more likely to replace permanent staff than fixed-term contractors; the latter are an additional resource in nearly two-thirds of cases.

As we will see, numerical flexibility can overlap with temporal flexibility to cover absence, be it for holidays, maternity leave, sickness or vacancies caused by resignation, transfer and so on. This is sometimes referred to as 'stop gap resourcing' (Goss and Bridson, 1998). The solution to the problem depends upon the expected length of the absence. If it is short term, existing employees may manage by working longer hours or different patterns of hours. If this is not possible, agency staff may be hired, especially if the skill needs are generic – one thinks of the ubiquitous secretarial temp – or the tasks are simple to perform. Call-in lists are also used to bring in casual staff because they may be cheaper than employing an agency, in that no charges have to be paid to a third party. Packaging firms, shops and hotels all have lists of local contacts whom they call in for short-notice problems.

Employment registers can be more sophisticated, as the case in point indicates. Here organizations use former staff to provide support, often for longer periods and more complicated tasks than the above call-in lists. Such people have the advantage of organizational and work knowledge, and are familiar with the corporate culture. These arrangements may suit women that have for the time being at least given up work to have children but are able to manage short spells back at their former employer, or they may be attractive to older workers who left under an early retirement scheme yet need extra cash. However, some organizations have reservations about re-

CASE IN POINT

Cable and Wireless started an in-house placement agency in 1995, called Flexible Resource Ltd. It is an independent subsidiary of the main company and is required to break even, but not generate profits. It has well over 7 000 self-employed people listed on its database. Because of its financial position, it charges out people at half the commercial rate, and so is attractive to Cable and Wireless managers. Moreover, it knows both its customers and its people well. It provides the latter with support and allows them participation in the company pension scheme as non-permanent employees. (Walker, 1996)

employing staff in receipt of any redundancy compensation beyond the statutory minimum.

The longer the absence and the more specialist the skill requirements, the more likely an employer will employ its own temporary staff. For example, a hospital or general practice might use an agency to supply a locum doctor for a short-term replacement, but they might prefer to employ someone themselves (for example, a known contact) when an extended period of cover is required.

The same principles apply to dealing with workload fluctuation. Short-term peaks may be covered by overtime, but where existing resources cannot be stretched to cover the need, because of its volume or extended period, temporary labour may be drafted in from an agency or directly hired. Freelancers are sometimes used for routine clerical (such as overflow copy-typing) or analytical work. Thus employers bring in extra labour to deal with high volumes of post at Christmas, of customers during the sales, of enquiries when a new product is launched, of analysis during a major project, and so on. It may be that the volume cannot be contained within normal working hours: here regular employees may concentrate on the key hours, with temporary staff covering the off-peak times. This frequently happens in the retail sector, and in the hotel and catering industry. So, for example, student temporary staff are used to add or replace regulars at weekends, depending upon whether the demand rises or falls, or just changes in nature.

Some organizations have converted an informal practice of this kind into a formal policy, especially where demand is very seasonal. These organizations may in the past have handled demand fluctuations by taking on and laying off staff. Now they set their manning at the level of minimum demand and then top up with temporary staff when the workload rises. For example, one organization took on 2 000 employees every summer, cutting back to 40 every winter. This practice has been replaced by having their extra staff on four-year fixed-term contracts, with their working hours restricted to the summer months. Here the organization has accepted the routine use of temporary staff to supplement those on 'permanent' contracts.

Numerical flexibility allows the organization to downsize and upsize as the business needs change. However, it may not be easy to turn this general proposition into resourcing policy. It can be difficult to estimate the minimum labour requirement (size and nature of skills) accurately enough to avoid both any slack for the regular employees and excessive fluctuation in temporary numbers. This decision is easier if the pattern of demand is reasonably predictable (even if it rises and falls) or where the time horizons are well defined. What is more difficult is where there is a high degree of uncertainty as to the duration, volume, or volatility of future work requirements.

Using temporary staff may be appropriate during a period of uncertainty. However, if the workload seems set to be at a persistently higher level, the employer might then recruit some people on 'permanent' contracts: see the case in point.

Another reason for the use of temporary staff is to complete one-off specific tasks. These may require particular skills that are infrequently used or do not form part of the normal work requirements. One thinks of resourcing projects, be they establishing a new IT infrastructure, setting up a new form of service delivery or building a new plant, or non-

CASE IN POINT

A metal manufacturing company had an increase in demand. The initial response was to introduce evening and weekend overtime. The latter proved to be unpopular, and so temporary staff were hired. As these increased work requirements were sustained some of the temporary staff were taken on as permanent, and new staff (including those previously made redundant) were employed to man a weekend shift. (Casey et al., 1997)

routine activities such as graphic design, editing, translation or computer programming. Fixed-term contractors are particularly suited to the former situation; freelancers for the one-off technical tasks.

There may be occasions where it is not so much the task that is specific as the fact that the organization wants an outsider to perform it. A consultant might be brought in to provide expert advice or an interim manager to facilitate change, especially if some kind of cultural transformation is envisaged. Some organizations use temporary staff when they are testing out a new business idea. Rather than commit permanent employees at the outset, they see how well the new operation works before settling on their long-term resourcing approach. There may be difficulties in specifying the length of the project or being absolutely clear on the skills to be retained for the future rather than discontinued at the end of the project.

Numerical flexibility is additionally used in circumstances that have nothing to do with flexing supply to meet variable demand. Employing all new starters on fixed-term contracts may not be a means of adjusting labour supply, rather it is signal that the employees have to prove themselves before being offered a regular contract. It may also reflect fears that managers will not properly appraise the new recruits unless there is a conscious decision to be made on long-term engagement.

Organizations that have tight headcount

controls often find themselves with numerous agency/temporary staff not for reasons of flexibility, but because managers are trying to avoid manpower controls. Companies encourage this behaviour by ignoring those not directly employed (self-employed or agency employed) in the headcount. Some even go further by counting only employees on regular contracts, leaving fixed-term contractors as 'freeloaders'.

So, to summarize, agency, temporary or fixed-term contract staff are used to cover short-term gaps in what has been described as 'dyna-rod' resourcing (Wilsher, 1996), to bring in skills, to hedge against uncertainty, to provide probationary employment or merely to get round manpower establishment rules.

Turning to the reasons why organizations outsource, there are similarities but also differences to the rationale for having temporary workers. Outsourcing may be chosen (Reilly and Tamkin, 1997) because it can provide:

- cost savings
- a switch from fixed to variable costs
- improved service by the use of a specialist supplier
- more efficient service due to a fixed-price commercial contract
- greater flexibility in meeting fluctuating supply and demand
- reduced exposure to cost, regulations, employee relations problems, management responsibilities
- better focus on the core business by freeing up managerial time
- avoidance of headcount-based manpower controls.

Especially where ancillary services are concerned the cost focus has predominated. This is because catering, cleaning, security, building maintenance and so on are seen as activities where a better price can be obtained externally. This may be because the contractor can achieve economies of scale, higher labour productivity, more efficient deployment of labour and, at least once free of the constraint to maintain pay rates under transfer of undertakings legislation, lower payroll costs. Indeed

WERS found that nearly half of its respondents contracted out to save money.

Another advantage of outsourcing is that the costs move into the variable column from the fixed. The cost base is thereby lowered. This is particularly important in areas such as IT, given its high capital requirements, or where financial resources need to be released for other more important activities (part of the reason for the public finance initiative, as seen currently in the building of hospitals).

Using outsourcing to improve the quality of service might perhaps be seen to be as important as achieving cost reduction. In fact, only 20 per cent of the respondents to WERS chose this as a reason for contracting out. However, service may be particularly important when considering activities that are more integral to the success of the business, such as IT systems or recruitment. Benefits of externalization can come from using a contractor that is a specialist supplier with access to skills, technology, product or market expertise unavailable to the client. The contractor may be able to improve the speed and consistency of service by exploiting their advantages in size or geographical spread, for example in distribution services.

These advantages offered by the contractor should allow the client organization to increase or decrease the volume of activities in line with business needs without having to deal with the labour consequences. It reduces their exposure to adverse publicity and costs if there is a need to downsize. It means that the organization does not have to worry about changes to regulation and legal requirements. Some organizations have outsourced to get rid of employee relations problems, especially in situations where changes to reduce the cost of high wages or inflexibility of deployment are required.

Some organizations (20 per cent in WERS) choose to outsource non-essential activities in order to concentrate on the core business. This may be because they favour the flexible-firm model reported earlier. It may, more pragmatically, be due to a feeling that managerial competence has become too thinly spread and involved in areas of low strategic importance. Management time may have got tied up in irksome industrial relations problems or in complex technical questions.

Finally, in many organizations managers have been under pressure to cut manpower. Through outsourcing this can be done as employees cease to be on the payroll, even if the cost of providing the service is not avoided.

TEMPORAL FLEXIBILITY

At its most general level, temporal flexibility allows organizations to obtain a better match between service patterns or production schedules and employee input. This may be a case of a simple alignment of getting work done at the time it is needed, as seen in JIT production. It can be to match customer needs, for example when a member of the public contacts the organization for some form of service. It can be to fit in with the work pattern of another organization to which an organization supplies services. It may be that working hours have to fit around equipment's availability for use. Greater efficiency through 'sweating the assets' can be obtained by using plant or premises over a more extended period. Overtime especially is also used to ensure that work is completed on time to meet customer requirements and avoid late-delivery penalties.

In other words, temporal flexibility should achieve a better alignment between work requirements and employees' working hours. Through this means costs can be reduced and productivity improved. The trick is to fix working hours to meet business demand. This may be difficult if demand is very variable. If normal hours are set too low then extra labour may have to be drafted in; if hours are too generous, then employees will be idle or inefficiently utilized. Rigid patterns, be they of standard hours, guaranteed overtime or fixed shifts, may not correspond with the work flow, so flexible working hours may be the solution.

The 'temporal' level for which a response is required is indicated by the mechanism chosen. Thus the solution to variation of work requirements can be described as follows:

Temporal variation	Possible solution
whole year	annual hours contracts
parts of the year	term-time contracts
week	variable working weeks or part-time patterns
day	part-time patterns, zero hours contracts or overtime working

As we have seen, some forms of temporal flexibility have relatively fixed patterns, others are less structured. Where the workload variation is stable one of the more structured methods can be used. Thus, for example, in a retail outlet, if it is always true that custom is at its peak on Saturdays, then part-time staff can be employed to cover that day. In hotels where peak activities coincide with meal times, split shifts are used. If at a distribution centre the workload peaks on the arrival of a vehicle, employees may have to be paid overtime on the occasions when this occurs at the end of the normal working day.

Annual hours contracts, in motor manufacturing for example, recognize that production varies during the year in response to sales peaks and troughs. Companies can therefore have one pattern of long hours working at a certain time of year to be balanced by reduced hours during quieter periods of operation. Moreover, in the Rover case (Whitehead, 1999d), up to 200 hours of credit or debit could be carried forward from year to year to give extra effort when new models were in production.

In call centres or similar operations, annual hours contracts can be valuable in managing the volatility of demand. Call volumes may vary by hour of day, day of week or week during the year. Staffing has to respond so that there are people available to handle enquiries or transactions when required, but are not idly sitting around waiting for the next call. Figure 4.3, taken from a utility-company call centre, illustrates the fluctuation week by week. In fact, there is a similar amount of variation hour by hour.

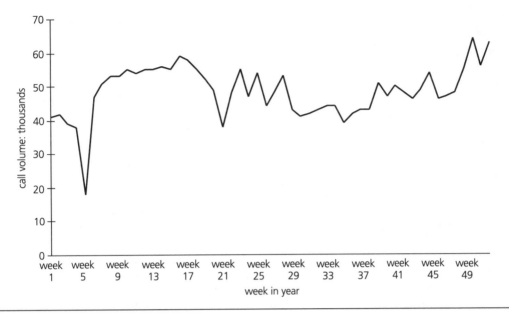

Figure 4.3   An example of the demand pattern in a call centre

Short-time working can be used with fluctuating demand where the oscillations are relatively wide; it is not as efficient as annual hours because it is common to pay overtime rates during the boom periods.

Temporal flexibility can be used for other reasons. When production or service schedules as a matter of routine extend beyond a normal working day, such as on continuous process plants or emergency cover arrangements, shift arrangements may be necessary to ensure that workers are fit to perform their tasks. In other words, they need to be safe and productive, still able to provide high-quality output. This has become more of a pressing issue with the introduction of the Working Time Regulations. This puts limitations on working hours, both their duration in any one period and the intervals between periods of work. This will have implications for both shifts and overtime. Work patterns can be designed to deal with these issues by packaging activities into reasonable units of time. As the personnel manager of a supermarket put it: part-timers make it easier for the business to cover these extended opening hours since they provide 'flexible chunks of time, divisible into hours' (quoted in

Neathey and Hurstfield, 1995). As the example shown illustrates, if the work arrangements are well made then productivity should rise.

CASE IN POINT

By introducing annual hours contracts a UK cheese producer reduced working time from peaks reaching 80 hours per week to an average 39. Despite the fewer hours worked, productivity soared and output volumes grew. Earnings also rose by 9 per cent and holidays were increased.

There may be an indirect cost saving sought by employers through temporal flexibility. They may choose a type of contractual arrangement where not only do hours match work requirements, but also where employment is intrinsically cheaper – employing someone below the national insurance threshold in a variable hours contract, for example, or on a part-time basis where fewer hours have to be remunerated. The flexibility provided by the work pattern could also be at a lower cost. Those on part-time or variable hours contracts can often be asked to work extra hours without the employer having to pay premium rates. Instead informal arrangements allow employees to take compensatory time off when work is quieter. In variable hours contracts, benefits offered may be based on the standard basic working week, not on the average number of hours worked. Annual hours contracts may allow the overall pay bill to reduce both by cutting overtime at premium rates and by reducing the need to use additional temporary staff to cover work peaks.

Another benefit of temporal flexibility, particularly associated with annual hours systems, is the facilitation of training and development. In manufacturing operations it is often difficult to release employees for training because of tight manning. Annual hours contracts make this easier because 'reserve hours' can be used for this purpose, or in the calculation of prime hours an allowance can be similarly made. While there is still a cost to be borne, it is buried in the calculations rather than explicit in the paying out of overtime at premium rates.

Providing benefit to employees is another reason to introduce some types of temporal flexibility. We will discuss this point further in Chapter 5, but we can note here that variable working weeks, flexitime, part- or term-time working, job sharing and even some forms of zero hours contracts are often chosen to help employees meet domestic responsibilities or personal preferences. Employers may do this as a benefit, to emphasize equal opportunities policies or simply in order to attract employees. Being flexible over working hours may provide the employer with a bigger pool of potential recruits, giving more choice with a higher prospect of securing the right sort of recruit. This is especially true if the working hours that need to be covered are extensive (as for supermarkets) and there are different groups in the labour force interested in different patterns – students may prefer evening or weekend work; parents of school-age children may want day shifts.

If the employee is satisfied with the hours, lower sickness absence and higher retention may result. This has been seen especially with annual hours systems. One introduced by MD Foods cut absence from an average 9–10 per cent to 3.5–5 per cent (Arkin, 1998). ICI found their absence rate fell from 7 per cent to 4 per cent per annum on the introduction of annual hours (Stredwick and Ellis, 1998). This is because employees do not wish to use their 'reserve hours', so there is peer-group pressure to attend work. Moreover, productivity can be higher. There is no incentive to stretch out work to obtain premium rate overtime, rather the opposite: reserve hours may be eaten into to respond to increases in demand.

Finally, temporal flexibility can be used as cover for unexpected absences. Zero hours contracts are employed to deal with this problem. Overtime can be used in the same way. Annual hours also allow organizations to call in extra staff as required. If this falls within their contractual limit, then the employee is obliged to attend work. Longer-term absences are usually dealt with through drafting in temporary staff of one sort or another.

LOCATIONAL FLEXIBILITY

For employers the principal driver towards locational flexibility is reduced costs. Through moving work out of the office and into the home, organizations can cut the space needed in buildings, thereby lowering overhead charges and reducing ancillary or support costs in the office or factory. British Telecom (BT) claimed in 1999 that the average cost of a desk is £10000 per annum in London, £6000 in the UK as a whole. Moreover, it said that if 10 per cent of its employees worked from home it could save £134 million in costs. Hence the interest, at the higher technology end of the spectrum, in hot-desking and the like: compared with traditional arrangements, fewer workstations (desk, cabinet, telephone and computer) are necessary, because they are shared by mobile employees who work from home or the car as much as from the office. Whether these savings are realized depends upon the possibility of vacating or transforming the use of an entire building or parts of it.

Telecentres can also provide lower-cost solutions to office space. Digital closed a conventional office in Newmarket with 100 staff employed there. It was replaced by a telecentre with somewhat fewer staff, but, significantly, only nine workstations. These supported a community that also worked from home or was mobile between client offices. By this means running costs were cut by a third (Murphy, 1996).

Costs may also be saved through lower wages. Some low-skill homeworkers are probably paid less than their factory equivalents. Teleworkers may also be employed in areas of the country with lower pay rates, thereby reducing the wage bill compared with operating in a city like London.

Higher productivity is reported to result from teleworking. In the Employment Department's *Teleworking in Britain* survey (Huws, 1994), 47 per cent of employers of teleworkers said that they were more productive than comparable office-based workers, compared with only 5 per cent who thought that they were less so. Schemes report 10–20 per cent productivity gains (Industrial Relations Services, 1999). While such figures need to be treated with care, there seems to be evidence that homeworkers concentrate better, because there are fewer distractions, and work longer as well as more productive hours. There is less time wasted in travelling; instead time is spent working. As the UK Automobile Association found, homeworkers may be prepared to work shorter shifts than office workers because they do not have to add on any commuting time (ibid.).

Homeworking can also reduce turnover and absenteeism. A survey for the Employment Department (Huws, 1994) found that 31 per cent of managers rated teleworkers as better in terms of absenteeism than office workers, and 26 per cent thought that turnover was lower for teleworkers. Offering homeworking may enable the organization to attract staff that are normally excluded from the workforce. This is especially true of disabled workers but may also apply to single parents or others where childcare arrangements are problematic.

Homeworking can then be seen to benefit equal opportunities policies.

CASE IN POINT

Sainsbury's corporate IT staff are allowed to work from home for a maximum of three days per week. Their home is equipped with a computer (lap or desktop), two telephone lines (for voice and data) and a combined fax machine, scanner and printer. Teams are left to sort out how they manage staffing the office, and they make sure that face-to-face communication is adequate. The system has been well received. Turnover has fallen, returns from maternity leave are better and productivity has improved (Industrial Relations Services, 1999).

Locational flexibility of the traditional sort may also provide benefits through allowing organizations to increase or decrease production as required. Homeworkers may be paid by output rather than time. If the organization wishes to change output levels, it is within its power to do so. The same principle applies to home-based telephone operations.

There is a further benefit to be obtained from locational flexibility – widely dispersed customers may be more easily serviced by dispersed employees. Some companies have for many years had their sales force based at home. Now a whole range of service providers are following suit. This may involve a more cost-effective approach, and at the same time they may be able to provide a faster response to customer needs.

FINANCIAL FLEXIBILITY

In the perfect world, employers would be able to see their wage bill rise and fall in line with business activity. Numerical flexibility permits this by varying the quantum of workers and temporal flexibility allows this by aligning working time to demand, so that in times of low activity employees are working reduced hours. Financial flexibility aims to alter the pay bill of those who are in employment to suit the exigencies of the business situation. This as we have seen can be done through gainsharing, profit sharing and variable-pay systems, but these schemes provide only a very limited form of flexibility. Those that involve the whole workforce and relate to significant sums of money are rare.

Financial flexibility can also reflect changing labour market conditions in the pay rates offered. In the UK there is no strong evidence (Beatson, 1995) that organizations' pay-rates are more susceptible to changing supply and demand than in the past. If it does occur it is often in a relatively crude way, such that annual pay settlements reflect the tightness or otherwise of the labour market and that premiums may be paid to occupational groups in specific demand. Certainly, wages of those employed within organizations do not fluctuate much, if at all, with the state of the labour market.

The few examples of some significance where this has happened are to be found in continental Europe, especially Germany. Hoechst, Bayer and BASF obtained acceptance from their trades unions that wages could be reduced by up to 10 per cent in difficult periods (Sparrow, 1997). A similar case occurred in 1993, also in Germany, when the unions representing Volkswagen workers accepted a 'pay for jobs' deal, which cut pay by 11–15 per cent but in exchange reduced working hours.

COMPLEMENTARITY VERSUS SUBSTITUTION

Table 4.1 tries to summarize the different benefits that the various forms of flexibility offer. It shows that several of our theoretical types of flexibility can be used to solve the

Table 4.1 Determining the right flexible option for employers

Drivers for flexibility	Possible solution	Benefits
reducing costs	outsourcing variable hours patterns temps/agency labour remote working multi-skilling	efficiency of supplier alignment with work patterns lower wages reduced overheads downtime cut/improved efficiency
improving quality/service	outsourcing variable hours patterns cross-functional working	expertise of supplier better scheduling seamless service
increasing productivity	multi-skilling variable hours patterns	end to demarcation alignment with work patterns
hedging against change	outsourcing temps/agency/contractors gain- or profit sharing	ability to terminate/alter contract ease of adjusting employee numbers up/down paybill rises and falls with corporate performance
meeting supply needs	variable hours patterns remote working temping	employee domestic needs met employee lifestyle suited variety of work offered

Adapted from Reilly (1997c)

same problem; sometimes these methods are used in combination. If costs are to be cut, part-time working (temporal flexibility) may be extended at the same time as more use made of agency workers (numerical flexibility). Research suggests that functional flexibility of regular employees may be combined with subcontracting and additional temporary resources to optimize manufacturing performance (Ackroyd and Procter, 1998). Sometimes different routes to the same goal are chosen. Labour costs may be reduced through more effective use of labour (for example, by functional flexibility) or by using inherently cheaper labour (for example, by switching to agency workers). However, it is also equally possible that one type of flexibility is used to substitute for another. To cover extended working hours, an organization might choose to use short-term agency workers rather than its own employees working overtime. The Japanese model explicitly eschews numerical flexibility in order to encourage functional flexibility.

There seem to be some certain combinations of flexible work arrangements that are more common than others. As Table 4.2 indicates, the traditional pattern of full-time work on a regular contract on fixed hours is still by far the most common combination, but it is nevertheless in the minority. Over a third of employees have variable hours work arrangements. Part-time working is split between fixed and variable hours in the same way as full-time, with the former having nearly double the

frequency of the latter. The proportion on temporary contracts is naturally small.

What affects the decision of individual organizations to introduce particular forms of flexibility? There are some organizational characteristics that incline towards introducing flexible work arrangements. These include:

- highly variable and/or unpredictable pattern of demand for products or services
- very short periods before stock runs out
- provision of goods and services across a substantial part of the day or week
- continuous nature of production
- easily separable work, organizationally or technologically
- presence of jobs with low-level skill requirements where little training is necessary or where there is limited capacity to train
- work at a lower-quality standard.

Thus those organizations where the nature of what they do requires constant adjustment to meet customer needs or extends beyond the normal nine-to-five day are likely to use some form of flexible work arrangement, as are those manufacturing companies where it is imperative that production is sustained through rotating shifts and through on-call arrangements. Functional flexibility is also designed to sustain production by ensuring that staff are trained to cope with problems rather than having to wait for colleagues with the relevant expertise. If stock levels are kept deliberately low, then there is no protective buffer should demand surge: in this situation either extra

Table 4.2 Frequency of different patterns of flexible contract

full-time employees on regular contracts, fixed weekly hours	44.5%
full-time employees on regular contracts, variable weekly hours	26.4%
part-time employees on regular contracts, fixed weekly hours	14.2%
part-time employees on regular contracts, variable weekly hours	8.1%
full-time temporary staff, fixed weekly hours	2.2%
full-time temporary staff, variable weekly hours	1.4%
part-time temporary staff, fixed weekly hours	1.7%
part-time temporary staff, variable weekly hours	1.4%

Note: 'variable weekly hours' includes any non-standard pattern of working, including shift working; 'fixed weekly hours' is any other pattern. Source: Office for National Statistics (1999a)

hours will need to be worked or extra staff drafted in. Where work is easily defined as separate from the main activities, then outsourcing is possible. The use of outworkers is permitted when work is not highly complex and can be easily packaged. Jobs with low skill requirements or not needing organizationally specific knowledge are easier to fill from the external labour market, so agency staff can be drafted in at short notice to cover them or they can be passed out to third parties. Similarly, if quality standards are not a key issue, then the risk of using unfamiliar staff is not as great. If training is necessary, the organization has to have the capacity to cope with an influx of new people.

Supply considerations also affect the type of flexible work arrangements employed. Certain labour market conditions encourage particular forms of flexibility. High unemployment and a slack labour market allow employers more scope to flex their workforce. A predominantly female labour supply might pressure the employer into offering part-time or variable hours. If shift or overtime working is necessary, it may be easier to attract male workers, especially if there has been a local tradition of non-standard working hours.

As this chapter has shown, some types of flexibility involve altering the number of staff deployed, by accessing other suppliers of labour (sometimes referred to as external flexibility); other forms of flexibility concern how organizations vary the amount of their own labour they use by altering work schedules or patterns (known as internal flexibility). Certain organizations seem to have a preference for exploiting the external labour market, whereas others try to optimize their internal labour market. A number of commentators have produced typologies of organizations most likely to use flexible work arrangements and whether they are inclined to use the internal or external variety. However, organizations do not always neatly fit the categories ascribed to them. A fast-moving consumer goods (FMCG) company with varied work demands may be managed more like a capital-intensive business, or vice versa. While exogenous factors are important, so too are endogenous. Organizational behaviour is not only set by the external environment within which it operates. As we saw in Chapter 1, such factors as culture and ideology (which may be of historical origin, or the product of the current management) also play their part. There is strong evidence to suggest that organizations' employee relations policies and practices affect their attitude to flexibility. The attitude of mail-order company Freemans to the treatment of atypical workers has been said to reflect both its history (the egalitarian views of the founding fathers) and necessity (the patterns of work encourage the use of flexible labour). Its call centre near Sheffield shows both the moral and the pragmatic imperatives at work. High-quality treatment of employees and excellent working conditions have led to very low wastage levels in a sector that tends to suffer from high turnover (North, 1996).

Moreover, many organizations are often too diverse to categorize them as single entities. This is self-evidently true for conglomerates, but even within the same business, requirements vary enormously; for example, an organization may need to use staff on full-time regular contracts for some activities, but be content with a high turnover of temporary staff in other work areas.

The trouble with determinist models is that organizations believe them: we are an FMCG company so we must have high levels of temporal and numerical flexibility, making extensive use of the external labour market; we are a manufacturing organization with demarcations between production and maintenance staff, so functional flexibility must be sought. Table 4.1 should indicate that there are various reasons to adopt flexible work arrangements, and many solutions. It is up to the organization to choose the most appropriate.

CHAPTER FIVE

Employee Interest in Flexibility

It is a key theme of this book that employees have a considerable interest in flexibility at work – it is not just a matter for employers. Naturally, the focus for workers is different than that for management, and is profoundly affected by the social trends described in Chapter 2.

Employees seek flexibility for a wide range of reasons that vary depending upon the particular type of flexibility. The principal reasons include:

- to acquire skills
- to meet domestic responsibilities
- to reduce employment costs or stress
- to facilitate lifestyle preferences
- to maximize earnings
- to improve career opportunities
- to secure employment
- to test suitability of an employer.

Rather than consider employee interest under the headings we used for employers, we will take each one of these reasons and examine it in more detail.

SKILL ACQUISITION

Some employees have always sought to better themselves through education and training; at the present time, becoming more skilled is both easier and more necessary. It is easier because, as was pointed out earlier, employers are seeking continuously to upskill their workforce. This is to meet the pincer movement of constant pressure from competitors and customers. Particularly as the UK moves away from low-skill, low-value activities towards the knowledge economy, innovation based on a highly skilled workforce will be increasingly necessary. So employees will be pushed by their employers to gain skills. This is manifest in assessment via competency frameworks, be they company specific or occupa-

tionally based, through competency-based pay systems and through development processes that require the demonstration of specified competencies.

Moreover, it will be easier for employees to add to their skill base because there is growing support from government to do so. We have already seen the expansion of tertiary education and recognition for vocational attainment through NVQs. Now there are new initiatives, like learning accounts and the University for Industry, to provide further encouragement and improve the quality of UK plc's labour force. The government's aim with the UfI concept is to create new types of learning opportunities for people who have left the learning system, and to deliver these in a way that fits the needs and lifestyles of individuals. So traditional learning locations have been rejected in favour of sports and shopping centres.

For employees it will be all the more necessary to add skills, not just because employers want it, and are literally prepared to pay for it, but because external labour market conditions demand it. Employability is an overworked expression, but its core meaning is plain: in a turbulent economy employees must make themselves resilient to deal with what life throws at them. This means developing skills that not just the current employer requires but also potential organizations of the future. How much the rhetoric of employability emanating from senior management is really only a fig leaf to cover the reality of downsizing is open to question; what is not in doubt is the imperative for employees to upskill.

What does this mean in the context of flexibility? It means that employees would be foolish to ignore the possibilities that functional flexibility offers. This is not just in the narrow sense that a mechanical technician might obtain a knowledge of instrument engineering or an insurance clerk could learn about both renewals and claims in order to be able to do their current job better. It is also in the wider labour market sense that should the employee want or have to move on, he or she has a broader basis of knowledge and skills to offer. The employee has also demonstrated the willingness and capacity to learn, behavioural traits which some employers value more than mere knowledge. As we noted earlier, trades unions have tried to limit the use of this form of skill development, fearing that the end of demarcations would mean the end of employment for many people. Now individuals cannot afford not to add to their curriculum vitae, both to retain employment and to give themselves employability in the external labour market.

Upskilling is facilitated not only via functional flexibility: temporary work can also allow individuals to broaden their skills and knowledge. A survey of those working in the UK television industry made clear that making contacts and obtaining a range of experience were two of the prime virtues of a freelance lifestyle (British Film Institute, 1999). Others engage in temporary work in order to give themselves the time and space to study. Money to live on comes from bouts of employment, but time is made available to attend classes or study at home. This is likely to appeal to mature students, but, given the cost of tuition fees and/or living expenses, the traditional student population may be keener than ever to work to fund their education.

CASE IN POINT

A second-year computer-engineering student works at a food-processing factory doing weekend shifts. 'I looked for jobs in information technology but I needed to pay bills. My mum's sick so I send money back to her as well. I make up for the time by studying late into the night and drinking lots of coffee. On the whole, students accept that they have to work as well as study as everything costs so much.' (Williams, 1999).

MEETING DOMESTIC RESPONSIBILITIES

Helping to meet domestic responsibilities is probably the single most important reason why employees like flexibility. It is the combination of having to work and perform a caring role that makes this such a significant issue. Chapter 2 set out how the social environment impacted on the needs of employees. We described the substantial number of dual income households in the UK, many of which have responsibility for looking after children or elderly relatives. We saw the growing financial burdens (such as pension provision, university fees, private residential accommodation for the elderly, and so on) that rest upon individuals rather than the state. We emphasized that there are an increasing number of educated and career-oriented women who want to stay in employment rather than look after the kids at home. It is for these reasons that people try to square the circle of caring as well as working, instead of resolving such problems by one of the partners giving up his or her job. Of course there are examples of downshifting where one partner withdraws from employment, but there are always the countervailing pressures to stay at work, not least that in a materialistic society there is the requirement to earn and keep up with the Joneses.

Besides the dual working household, there is the growing number of single-parent families that have to resolve the dilemma of earning a living and caring for a family. What is more the current government is trying to induce single parents to move off state benefits and into work as the best way of reducing benefit expenditure and getting families out of poverty.

So how do employees with domestic responsibilities manage to combine work with caring? Some can afford full-time nannies or nurseries. Some can pay for elderly relatives to live in private nursing homes. Some make use of workplace nurseries or day-care centres for the elderly. Others do not have these options because financially they are not equipped to meet the charges. The figures quoted in Chapter 2 for child and eldercare are significant when you consider that average UK earnings amount to about £20 919 per annum for a full-time employee (Office for National Statistics, 1999b).

Some people choose to try to have the best of both worlds and balance caring and working. This balance is most often achieved through women working part-time; both carers and part-time workers are usually women. As an administrative officer at Bristol City Council said in an interview: 'Working a four day week enables me to have extra time to look after my elderly mother without having to eat into my holiday entitlement. It has been a real help. I feel much more able to cope' (Walsh, 1999a).

Term-time working obviously suits parents with school-age children, and some parents no doubt opt for employment as, say, a school assistant for this reason. Flexitime, particularly where both partners can use it, may allow one of the parents to see their children to school in the morning, and the other to receive them home at night. It may give employees the time to sort out domestic emergencies, such as finding someone to care for a sick child. Where flexitime allows any excess hours worked to be banked, the extra leave permitted may be used during school holidays. A Mori poll for the TUC in 1998 (Trades Union Congress, 1998a) found that flexitime was by far the preferred option in flexing location or hours, with over 40 per cent of both men and women choosing it. The benefits are explained by a representative of Unison, the public services union, at Harlow District Council:

> Prior to the flexitime agreement, staff were often having to take a half day off to go to the doctor's or if they had a problem getting the kids to school. They would feel guilty about being late or suddenly taking time off. All that has changed now and the pressure on staff, particularly on carers, has disappeared. They now choose the hours which fit in better with the rest of their lives and do not have to feel guilty. (Trades Union Congress, 1998b)

Zero hours contracts or bank arrangements can provide similar benefits. Some nurses opt for night-shift working in order to be available for their children during the day.

Working from home is also sought by some to ease their domestic problems. An elderly relative can be looked after more easily if there is someone at home most of the time rather than away at work for considerable periods. Children can be taken to school and collected again if a parent is working at home. Participation in school events becomes possible and part-time workers especially can engage in voluntary activities. Survey evidence suggests (Huws, 1996) that where men work from home there is a breakdown in the traditional division of labour between the sexes, as men take on more caring and domestic responsibilities in these circumstances.

CASE IN POINT

A single mother with a small child works as a client liaison manager for a small-business consultancy. She deals with clients, especially when her consultant colleagues are out on visits. She takes calls at home; often these have been re-routed from the consultants' own home numbers.

Of course, potential conflict can exist between the requirement to complete work activities and caring needs. It is not easy to work if there are screaming kids in the background or an elderly parent in need of constant attention. However, some forms of homeworking allow tasks to be completed at any time of day or point in the week. So by this means work can be fitted in around domestic responsibilities.

In one experiment in homeworking at Wiltshire County Council, interviews conducted by Analytica found that employees enjoyed the release from the constant noise and interruptions of an open-plan office environment, while the quiet of the home made it easier to concentrate, was also more relaxing and provided confidentiality for telephone calls (Huws, 1999).

Locational flexibility may also assist family arrangements where mobility is restricted. If one of the partners is tied to a specific place, this could hamper the career of the other, if he or she is expected to move by his or her employer. To an extent at least, working at home or peripatetically from home can in some occupations solve these difficulties. Indeed, this book is being written at home, over 100 miles from the office, because of spousal employment in the home locality!

So there is evidence that family-friendly employment practices in general enable employees to handle the potential conflict between home and work more effectively (Dench et al., 2000).

REDUCED COSTS AND STRESS

Locational flexibility offers employees the chance to reduce costs and ease stress. Working from home can save on the cost of travel to work and avoid the stress of commuting, be it sitting in a traffic jam or standing in an overcrowded train. Using a local telecentre may achieve similar benefits. Back in 1994 BT estimated that homeworking saved employees £900 per year in reduced commuting and clothing costs. They also calculated the average commuting time to be 45 minutes each way, so working from home one day per week would save an individual 10 days per year in lost time.

Another way in which organizations can help their employees make working arrangements easier to manage is by adjusting working times. Telecom Science Ltd in Airdrie, for example, allows job sharers to work two days one week and three the next, rather than 2.5 days per week. Travelling time and costs are reduced, as five rather than six trips to work are made per fortnight (Trades Union Congress, 1998b).

The long-hours culture is seen by many as a cause of familial problems. Some organizations in the UK have tried to address the issue by altering working times or making them more flexible. One manufacturing organization declared that Friday afternoon should be taken off whenever possible, and Birds Eye Foods declared a 3 p.m. finish time on a Friday for all their head-office staff, to indicate that working time should be limited. A management consultancy stated that from normal finishing time on a Friday to starting time on Monday morning employees should avoid work activities wherever possible. Similarly, Barclays Technology Services have 'go home on time days' (Kodz et al., 1998). Asda has required each store to sign up to 'ten commitments' on how to manage the work arrangements of their managers. These include the maximum number of hours per week, rota patterns and scheduled periods of time off. These commitments seek to balance the managers' needs with customer and subordinates' requirements for service and support (ibid.).

MEETING LIFESTYLE PREFERENCES

Flexibility at work can also assist in meeting people's non-work aspirations. Nine-to-five Monday to Friday jobs suit many who need to have a stable pattern of working hours and a regular source of income, but there are others who, either because of their situation or temperament, would rather have greater flexibility. This can be used to obtain a wider variety of work experiences or to move easily in and out of employment. Unlike the meeting of domestic responsibilities, described above, this is very much a matter of personal choice.

CASE IN POINT

'I am young free and single and using my skills to travel around the world. If I was married with kids and a mortgage, I suspect I would feel rather different.' (Dex et al., 1998)

Numerical flexibility in this context means taking on temporary work as a means of earning money to facilitate other activities. Students doing holiday, evening or weekend work might fall into this category. Overseas visitors to the UK, especially it seems from the Antipodes, take on short-term jobs to finance

CASE IN POINT

Employees at a production works were asked whether they would like to simplify the variety of shift patterns based on an 8-hour rotation to a standard 12-hour format of day, day, night, night, off, off, off, off.

There was quite a debate among the workforce, but the majority voted in favour of the change, despite many misgivings about working a 12-hour stretch.

However, it quickly became apparent that the workers liked their new regime. They became accustomed to 12 hours of work, and suffered the switch from day to night shift. What they really welcomed was the 4-day block of time off, which varied from week to week. Shopping and other domestic tasks were easier to complete during the week. The golf courses and swimming pools were relatively empty.

From being sceptical, these employees sang the praises of their new work arrangements.

their travels. More mainstream perhaps are those who in terms of personal characteristics are just like the workforce at large but prefer the possibility of job hopping. It gives them the opportunity of work variety (evidenced by the numbers who work for secretarial agencies) and the chance of career breaks to be used for long holidays or just doing other things. In the UK there are some half a million people in temporary employment who do not want a permanent job (Office for National Statistics, 1999a) – a substantial body of the workforce.

Temporal flexibility can be used in similar ways. Part-time paid employment may be combined with other activities, such as charitable work, where maximizing income is not the prime purpose of work. This can be seen in the case of those at the end of their career who might be winding down from employment, but like the stimulus of some form of activity with the bonus of a supplementary wage. The balance between income generation and time to do your own thing varies with age and circumstances.

Preferences over working time, or indeed place, can have added advantages for employees. Offshore oil workers may favour the extended shift system. That, together with high wages, allows people to live some distance from their onshore base. After all there is no commuting time to consider: once the workers are on the rig or platform they remain there until the helicopter comes to bring them back 14 days later.

More conventional shift working can be attractive for some people by, for example, giving extra time off in frequent blocks, as illustrated in the shift patterns example above.

Blocks of time off are sometimes attractive to shift workers. Others prefer particular non-standard hours, for example, early start/finish or permanent nights. An example of the benefits of the latter is given in the case in point below.

CASE IN POINT

The advantages of shift work were explained by a permanent night worker at Tesco: 'I took the job because the mine where I worked closed, but the hours suit my lifestyle incredibly well. I'd always been keen on playing rugby and night work gives me far more time than a day shift would. Four years ago my girlfriend's son was knocked down by a drunk driver and left partially disabled, and I can take him swimming and to physiotherapy. I've got used to sleeping in the day... The only time I find it difficult is on holiday. My body can't immediately re-adjust and I never get to sleep before 4 a.m. Overall, though, I've no regrets. I earn extra money working nights and the hours keep me out of the pub. I've lost five stone which can't be that bad for me.' (Crace, 1999)

There are those who make particular efforts to balance their work requirements with a particular lifestyle. The most obvious examples are the IT professionals who live in remote or certainly rural environments linked to workplaces in, from their point of view, less desirable areas. IBM featured one such employee in a marketing advert. Another more dramatic example is given in the case in point.

CASE IN POINT

A man working for a London bank decided that life commuting from his suburban home was no longer for him. He renegotiated his contract with his employers so that he reduced his hours to a three-day week. He and his family then moved to their holiday home in the French Alps. He now commutes overnight by high-speed train to work in London Tuesday to Thursday, giving himself a long weekend every week to walk, ski and bicycle.

TO MAXIMIZE EARNINGS

The most clear-cut way in which flexible work arrangements can be used to maximize earnings is through employment on a fixed-period contract. Employees can achieve this by moving from contract to contract, exploiting their increased knowledge and experience to increase their wages. Some may find that their pay increases when moving from a poorly paid sector on a regular contract to agency work in another sector. This is particularly true for those with clearly transferable skills. Employees can also exploit beneficial labour market conditions, where skill shortages allow some to bid up the price of their labour. By these means the workers' pay can rise faster than if they were in conventional employment, progressing through a standard salary structure.

Examples of this situation have been periodically seen in the IT industry both in late 1980s (exploiting the growth in financial services) and in the late 1990s (benefiting from the preparations for the millennium bug and the birth of the euro). Construction workers are often on temporary contracts, but their wages are even more cyclical.

More indirectly, adding skills through functional flexibility can improve employees' salaries. Many manufacturing organizations have decided to pay higher rates to technicians, as opposed to craftsmen, and part of the definition of a technician's role includes being able to demonstrate a wider variety of expertise. One organization used the following hierarchy to distinguish and pay for different skill levels:

Grade 1 – manual skills only
Grade 2 – skills with respect to working with machinery
Grade 3 – multi-skill – able to perform all jobs and operate in all areas, including the capacity to perform minor maintenance.

In the operating-theatre team of Nottingham City Hospital pay progression is linked to skill acquisition (Johnson, 1999b); this gives employees the incentive to add competencies and receive recognition for using them. Sometimes skill acquisition is rewarded by a one-off bonus rather than through base pay adjustment.

Maximizing earnings can, moreover, be seen in the premium rates of pay given for overtime working. Some employers have successfully removed the concepts of time and a half or double time, but others find that overtime paid at premium rates helps to meet their business needs or is the only way in which the work can be completed. Some employees come to rely on this additional income either to get a decent wage or to provide the money for the extras in their lives.

Profit sharing or gainsharing schemes, which we have described as a form of financial flexibility, also deliver extra money to employees when the company meets its profit or performance targets.

IMPROVING CAREER OPPORTUNITIES

It may not be entirely self-evident that adopting flexible work arrangements can enhance career prospects. There are, though, circumstances in which this can occur. Functional flexibility by adding skills can assist career development. As was indicated earlier, this could enable a craftsman to progress to being a technician. Beyond this level, it may be necessary to have a broad range of skills and knowledge to take on a supervisory role. This is certainly seen in the service sector, where broad product and process knowledge is necessary to progress. Banks lend out staff from branch to branch to cover absences, as a form of numerical flexibility in place of hiring in temporary staff. While staff may complain, as they apparently have done, of being pushed around (O'Reilly, 1992), in fact management has seen this as a means of giving employees wider experience that is good for their career development.

Another perhaps unlikely setting for career benefits can be found through outsourcing. This can enhance career prospects because the employee may be transferred to a firm with much better promotional possibilities. This may derive from being employed in a core rather than service function, where their skills are prime, not peripheral, and where their activities are 'on the revenue side rather than the cost side of the equation' (Labbs, 1993). This situation might occur to a chef working in a catering department where there are more chances of having a satisfying career with a specialist firm like Gardner Merchant than working in the kitchen of a company making ball-bearings. Similarly, there may be wider opportunities for IT specialists in, say, EDS than in an insurance company.

Flexible work arrangements may permit female employees especially to combine work and home life, not just through mitigating the problems associated with juggling the two, but also through allowing them to progress through the ranks of their employing organization. Not all companies facilitate the career development of those on shorter or flexible hours, but in others women can reach senior positions while still working non-standard hours.

In some cases, workers may see home-working as a stepping stone towards self-employment. If they are becoming fed up with office politics or the threat of redundancy, working from home may provide a useful means of beginning the separation from being employed by an organization to being self-reliant. It allows, on the one hand, ties to be kept with an employer, giving the benefits of a steady income and contact with colleagues, while, on the other hand, a taster of what being out on one's own feels like. There may be the additional advantage of networking with self-employed or other remote workers who live in the home locality.

SECURING EMPLOYMENT

In the UK the last Conservative government, as we have already seen, took the view that a flexible labour market provided opportunities for employment for those otherwise excluded from work. How successful this strategy was and continues to be is a matter of debate. Atkinson and colleagues (1996) found limited evidence that temporary work is a gateway to permanent employment for individuals coming from disadvantaged groups. However, the notion that temporary work is a route into permanent employment from unemployment is an attractive one to governments. In France, the Netherlands and Belgium there are active labour market policies based on these principles.

And it must be true that in some instances people take on work on temporary contracts because they cannot get regular employment, but see it as a means of getting into a permanent job. A survey of interim managers found that 40 per cent had entered the field because of redundancy (reported in Goss and Bridson, 1998). Not all of these were necessarily trying to find their way back into permanent employment, but one would imagine that some would see this kind of work as a means to that end. One reason for this view, validated by the Atkinson work (Atkinson et al., 1996), is that trying to get a job from being unemployed is much more difficult than being able to demonstrate the capability of working through being presently employed. European statistics bear out the logic of this approach. Around half of the temporary workers seeking permanent employment secured it via an agency (Bakkenist Management Consultants, 1998). The employers' survey by Atkinson et al. (1996) found that half the organizations in the sample had engaged a temporary worker on a permanent contract within the previous three years. So, if the employer has a history of expansion or high levels of wastage then an individual taking on temporary work may find it a good route to a permanent contract.

Indeed, some agencies see their role as facilitating the transfer of people to permanent contracts with their clients, if that is what is sought. Equally, there are employers that prefer to recruit in this way because they believe that the selection process is improved by their being able to judge the actual performance of workers, who already come with a reference from the agency. Familiarity naturally also comes for those directly employed on a temporary basis. As with those recruited through agencies, aptitude is demonstrated and induction time is reduced. In this situation, if your face fits, then you must stand a fair chance of getting taken on.

There are agencies that try to discourage transfers and charge fees for so doing. The government is minded to outlaw this practice and, at the time of writing, appropriate legislation is under consideration.

There is also trades union support for generating employment via some forms of flexible work arrangements. Annual hours contracts may be favoured by unions because they can replace insecure temporary jobs with permanent ones. This may be because the seasonality of the work can be managed via variation in working hours, rather than in numbers employed. In a food production company that operates an annual hours system, employees have cut their hours and pay to keep people in jobs who would otherwise have been made redundant: in this firm, team loyalty can be very strong.

Job sharing too can increase employment. The Amalgamated Engineering and Electrical Union (AEEU) secured a deal with Telecom Science Ltd in Airdrie which allowed job sharing as an alternative to redundancy (Trades Union Congress, 1998b). Although those who went from full-time to part-time work had their pay reduced, this was compensated for by payment of half the redundancy money that they might have received. Job sharing continued even when business picked up. Extra jobs that came from increased demand were negotiated as job shares to generate more employment.

TO TEST THE EMPLOYER

Some employers use fixed-term contracts as trial periods, that is as probationary employment, to test out the suitability of employees for longer-term engagement. This may also involve some element of training. From the employees' point of view the training offered may be a necessary way of getting into a trade or profession. Likewise, the trial period may work both ways since some employees may see it as useful way of testing employment, both the specific employer and/or the particular occupation.

DIFFERENT FORMS, DIFFERENT BENEFITS

These benefits may be exclusively associated with one particular form of flexibility (skill acquisition and functional flexibility), or may be realized through various routes (for example, testing an employer can be done via a fixed-term contract or working for an agency). Some types of flexible work arrangement may have multiple benefits. This is especially true of temporal flexibility. As a leaflet for Inland Revenue staff explains (PTC Inland Revenue, 1996), through setting their own working hours employees can 'make it easier to:

- take children to and from school, attend school assemblies, concerts and meet teachers
- be around for calls such as gas and electric, BT, washing machine repairs

Table 5.1 Ways the employee can benefit from flexibility

Employees can benefit by	Possible solution
acquiring skills	task flexibility cross-functional working agency temporary work
meeting domestic responsibilities	variable hours patterns
reducing employment costs or stress	tele- or homeworking
meeting lifestyle preferences	agency temporary work variable hours patterns
maximizing earnings	fixed-term contract gain- or profit sharing
improving career opportunities	outsourcing skills flexibility
securing permanent employment	fixed-term contract agency temporary work
testing suitability of employer	fixed-term contract agency temporary work

- split their days to care for dependants
- arrange regular leisure activities during the day.'

The different options to solve particular needs are summarized in Table 5.1. What the table shows is that flexibility can offer a number of benefits to employees, perhaps more than one might suppose from all the rhetoric surrounding the concept. However, if these benefits are to be realized they have to be secured in relationships that acknowledge employee aspirations and concerns. It is to the nature of employment relationships that we now turn.

CHAPTER SIX

Types of Employer/Employee Relationship

As should be evident from the preceding two chapters, employers and employees have a variety of reasons to be interested in flexibility. Sometimes these overlap, sometimes they are in conflict and sometimes there is genuine mutuality of interest. As Figure 6.1 suggests, at the extremities are relationships that suit one party rather than the other.

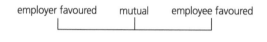

Figure 6.1 The flexibility spectrum

What we will contend is that mutual relations should be aimed for, precisely because they serve the needs of both parties. Before we look at circumstances of mutuality, we will examine the other types of relationship that occur as a result of differences in interest.

EMPLOYER-FAVOURED FLEXIBILITY

Some forms of flexibility are at best one-sided in their benefits to employers and, as we shall see, at worst exploitative. One-sided benefits to employers occur where there is no account taken of the needs of employees. We will call this situation Cyclopic flexibility after the mythical one-eyed giant. There are a variety of circumstances when this can happen, and it applies to all types of flexibility. The following examples serve to illustrate this point:

● organizations may hire employees on a series of short-term contracts that maximize their numerical flexibility, but, by inserting breaks between contracts, they deny their workers the chance to build up service-

related employment benefits (and, previously, protection against unfair dismissal)
● companies may use outworkers because they can pay them lower wages than those employed in the factory, and also minimize their health and safety responsibilities
● organizations may choose to institute home-working to save overhead costs but ignore the psychological consequences on some who feel socially isolated as a result
● employers may transfer workers to new working patterns that improve productivity but play havoc with employees' domestic arrangements
● employers may use split shifts to suit the pattern of work, despite objections from employees that these arrangements disrupt the balance between work and social life
● organizations may require employees to become self-employed, thereby reducing their own on-costs from national insurance, but simultaneously limiting employee entitlements to benefits
● organizations may employ people on particular types of contract specifically because of the ease with which they can dismiss them at the least financial cost
● organizations may outsource an activity so as to concentrate on core activities, with little concern for the impact this has on those that they used to employ
● organizations may change work tasks to reduce the effect of functional boundaries, but provide inadequate training such that employees feel overstretched in their work.

There have been plenty of examples of Cyclopic behaviour to demonstrate these points:

● a clothing manufacturer gave only small parcels of production to a large number of outworkers because in that way employment on-costs (for example, national insurance) could be kept to a minimum (Casey et al., 1997)

- a hardware store had a flexibility clause in part-time contracts that allowed any variation in hours to suit the employer's requirements (Neathey and Hurstfield, 1995)
- before the minimum wage was introduced, outworkers were being paid 25p per hour for assembling advertising folders or 50p per hour for painting ornamental cottages (Felstead and Jewson, 1999)
- a retailer said that the organization only recruited those who could work beyond contracted hours: if they 'persistently' failed to work overtime they would probably be warned (Neathey and Hurstfield, 1995)
- an insurance company moved to a greenfield site, introduced a twilight shift and abolished overtime, thereby excluding those who wanted to work normal hours. Instead, it switched recruitment to those who preferred non-standard hours (Rajan et al., 1997)
- a supermarket excluded those working under 16 hours per week and all temporary staff from sick-pay provisions (Neathey and Hurstfield, 1995)
- the practical exclusion of part-time employees from promotion in a number of retail companies because of perceived damage to continuity and consistency that would occur through working restricted hours (ibid.)
- a market researcher who had worked for a company for four and a half years on a zero hours contract was deemed by her employer to be self-employed and not entitled to any recompense when her regular hours were ended (Low Pay Unit, 1998)
- a university lecturer was employed on a casual basis and paid a third less per hour than her colleagues in substantive posts (MacLeod, 1999).

Cyclopic flexibility may derive from an employer ideology that takes little account of employee sensibilities. It could be that employers believe that employees must accept the implications of market pressures, that this sort of flexibility is ultimately in the best interests of the organization as a whole, even if it appears only to favour the employer. These arguments are based on market-driven or unitary philosophies that echo some of the thinking described in the transformation of employment school of thought outlined in Chapter 1.

It does not take much for one-sided benefits to become exploitative. As the director of an employment agency put it: 'there is a close relationship between E and F in the alphabet. E is for exploitation, F is for flexibility' (quoted in Legge, 1998). We will call this situation forced flexibility. In the UK such cases come before industrial tribunals (see case in point 1).

They are also reported in the press (case in point 2).

They are dealt with by bodies like the Citizens' Advice Bureaux (case in point 3).

CASE IN POINT 1

Two hospital nurses won an employment tribunal case in 1998 over their employers' unilateral change to their shift pattern. They previously worked an 8 a.m. to 8 p.m. shift arrangement. This suited them because they could also care for their children before and after school. The hospital trust which employed them changed their shift pattern to a rotating format. This saved the trust £315 000 per annum. But for these individuals the shift arrangement was incompatible with their home duties. As they would not accept the change, they were made redundant. The Bristol tribunal found that the nurses had suffered 'marital discrimination' and awarded them damages. The two nurses are no longer employed in the NHS – one works in medical insurance and the other at a supermarket. (Gibbs, 1999).

CASE IN POINT 2

A woman who had worked as a care assistant for a housing association was injured at work, and was denied statutory sick pay by her employers. This was because she was employed on rolling one-day contracts. She took the case to court and, despite opposition from the Department of Social Security, won her claim (Milne, 1996).

CASE IN POINT 3

A Citizens' Advice Bureau was contacted by an employee of a domestic service contractor at a local hospital. This person was employed on an 'as and when' contract. This meant that the contractor would telephone to invite the employee to work. This might mean immediate work; morning, evening or weekend hours; single or double shifts. No holiday or sick pay was available. Wages were lower than those in similar jobs at the hospital. Refusal to work the hours specified might lead to dismissal.

The employee did have a formal contract that made the pattern of variable hours working plain, but this was in contradiction to the verbal job specification at interview where specific hours were agreed. (National Association of Citizens' Advice Bureaux, 1997).

They may even be taken up by government departments (case in point 4).

CASE IN POINT 4

Ian McCartney, a minister at the DTI, reported in 1999 at a TGWU/Manpower conference on agency workers that a large agency wanted to terminate its employees' contracts over Christmas, only to re-engage the workers after the holiday period. This they said was to assist the employees to claim unemployment benefit.

These are the sort of cases that give flexibility a bad name, reinforce antipathy and provide ammunition for opponents. They give good copy to antagonistic journalists and fire the rhetoric of trades union speeches. They also keep the courts hard at work. Though undoubtedly people in the UK are becoming more litigious, this cannot explain away the dramatic growth in references to employment tribunals. Their workload tripled between 1988/9 and 1994/5 and the number of successful unfair dismissals doubled. Since then there has been a more modest 10 per cent increase in the number of cases disposed of.

Forced flexibility is characterized by organizations' failing to give employees written contracts of employment, the payment of low wages, unilateral variations of contract by the employer, denial of legal rights, dismissal in the face of challenge to such violations or impositions, and avoidance of employment-related costs. Some of these violations have a significant impact, others are more of an irritation. As one woman put it: 'a lot of people working in shops part-time are at the beck and call of their master, who changes hours at the drop of a hat.' Or as another explained: 'They can ask you to stay longer than you expected which is much more important when you are working part-time. You are actually doing the hours because you need to be somewhere else' (Industrial Relations Services, 1994).

Despite recent attempts to give legal protection to all types of workers, exploitation can still result from employer ignorance of legislation, or wilful disregard of it. Some organizations are merely careless with respect to their responsibilities to employees; others appear deliberately and knowingly to flout the law. Managers may be under so much pressure to deliver business results that they neglect to think of the consequences of their actions on the people they employ. Or they simply do not believe any such responsibilities exist – the business imperative overrides all.

Yet if employers only stopped to think they would realize how serious the implications of their actions are for their workers:

● the problems presented by variable hours or

zero hours contracts in arranging child- or eldercare

- the difficulties of arranging mortgages or any other form of credit where regular income is not guaranteed
- the denial of contractual employment rights, for example to holidays, pension entitlement, sick leave and so on, that occurs if continuous employment is prevented and service with the employer is not maintained
- the negation of legal rights, for example to redundancy pay, to protection against unfair dismissal, to statutory sick or maternity pay and so on, if the employment status is not properly determined
- the inability to claim state benefits (in the UK, for example, family credit or statutory maternity or sick pay) if hours or wages are below statutory minima, which may arise if working hours fluctuate significantly
- the exclusion from certain social security benefits (for example, pension, incapacity or unemployment) if national insurance payments have not been sufficient, again where wages are low.

The damage can be practical (lack or loss of income) or emotional. As a woman sacked for refusing to work 16-hour shifts put it: 'When I woke up next morning I didn't know how long I would be able to pay the mortgage for, or be able to feed the baby. There was the realisation that these people who were supposed to be caring for me for the last 10 years didn't care a jot about me' (reported in Gregoriadis, 1999). Another example comes from the education sector, where a university lecturer employed on a temporary basis came back from holiday to find her computer missing. When she reported what she thought was a theft, she was told her job had ceased. She described the experience as 'traumatic' – probably something of an understatement! (MacLeod, 1999).

Of the types of flexibility we have discussed, those that most risk exploitation are zero and variable hours contracts, because the benefits are largely, if not completely, on the employer's side, and the risks and uncertainties lie with the employee. Problems can occur too with 'serial' temporary contracts, such as the journalist who was employed on five successive one-year contracts – this manoeuvre denied the employee the chance to build up employment rights. The Employment Relations Act provides new statutory protection against unfair dismissal in this situation, but contractual, service-related benefits and statutory redundancy entitlements may still be denied. From the employers' point of view, repeated short-term contracts allows for easy downsizing, but from the employees' perspective getting rid of people is all too easy. As a university lecturer employed on short-term contracts bitterly observed: 'We are the cannon fodder. If there is any slack we go and full-timers stay. We are flexible to the point of bending in two – all they have to do to get rid of us is do nothing' (MacLeod, 1999). A similar abuse arises from those situations where workers are forced to be self-employed even when by legal definition they should be regarded as employees. Some employment agencies also connive with their clients to obstruct continuity of employment to prevent employees building up service-related entitlements.

Some of the worst mistreatment of employees seems to arise from outsourcing, when the law on transfer of undertakings is ignored. Cowboy contractors may not only violate the law, but in their desperate desire to maximize profits they offer pitiful terms and conditions to people in no position to refuse.

Exploitation tends to affect the most vulnerable in the labour force. They are often the least skilled and worst paid. They are the sort of people described in Chapter 2 as forming part of the underclass, those at the margins of employment. Such people are therefore particularly at risk when the labour market is slack and there is a plentiful supply of people available. Clear-cut violation and abuse of the law tend not to be found so much among the large and better employers. However, organizational change can affect all in the workforce, and transferring work to agencies or contractors can challenge the well-being of those involved, whatever their status. The impact of outsourcing can be serious on employees, even if transfer of undertakings has been applied correctly. Think of the bank employees transferred to a contractor with their work, who were subsequently made redundant as the contractor sought to cut costs. There were those with 20 plus years' of service with the bank, who, instead of receiving a generous, ex gratia pay-off based on their term of employment, ended up with limited statutory redundancy pay.

EMPLOYEE-FAVOURED FLEXIBILITY

One-sided benefits, however, can be found in favour of employees. This may not be as common as the reverse situation, largely because it is rarer for the employee to have the power in the relationship. It can, however, occur where labour market tightness, especially for specific occupations, means that individuals are in a strong bargaining position. Examples of this are seen in fixed-term contracts where the employee is able to negotiate extremely good terms, better than those that apply to permanent employees. Organizations accept and justify this situation on the grounds that these staff have valued skills, rare in the labour market. Nevertheless, there are times when the employer feels 'over a barrel' with little choice but to accept the terms demanded. Just look at what manipulating contracts is doing for the value of European footballers at present, Roy Keane at a reported £50 000 per week being the most prominent example! Employers cannot appeal to fixed-term contractors' long-term loyalty as they can with those on permanent contracts, but, precisely because they are on fixed-term contracts, they can, however, ring-fence them from the rest of the workforce.

A strong bargaining situation for employees also arises where organizations are vulnerable to industrial action, perhaps because they make a time-dependent product. The print industry suffered in this way, where every day the employees could, if they wished, irrecoverably halt production. Even if this no longer occurs, there are still examples where employees can exploit their position. London electricians finishing off the Jubilee Line against the millennium deadline did very well out of the situation. A personnel director of a hospital trust reported that when only two out of three senior medical staff were supplied by an agency, the two who appeared claimed double-time pay for the extra work pressure they alleged would result from their being understaffed.

Labour supply shortages may lead the organization to offer or maintain flexible work arrangements that provide no benefit to it, and indeed even some pain. Thus to attract or retain staff, part-time contracts may be offered. This may not prove to be much of a disadvantage in itself to the employer. However, trying to suit all employee preferences can produce a multiplicity of contracts on different time bases, which can add up to ever-increasing administrative complexity and cost. Job sharing can work well but, done badly, can lead to inefficiencies if handovers are missed or incomplete. It may break down entirely if one of the parties resigns and there is no job-share replacement. This leaves the organization with only half a job covered, or, if a full-time person is drafted in, with a surplus part-timer.

CASE IN POINT 5

A new managing director was appointed to a research laboratory. After a short while in charge, he became irritated by the fact that he could never find people at work when he expected them to be there. He discovered that this was because of the effects of a flexitime arrangement with minimal core hours that were hardly enforced. As he dug deeper, he found that going off-site at lunchtime was common for some groups, especially for trips to the pub on Fridays. He found out that they did not clock out for this period, as it had been agreed to operate the flexi clock at only start and finish times.

Not only was he worried by this problem, but he also became aware of the fact that both external and internal customers were complaining of the same difficulties that he had experienced.

Flexitime may be introduced at employee behest, but at the potential cost of having fewer workers on standard hours with the result that customers, be they internal or external, are less well served. As one company manager put it: 'too many staff wanted to leave early in the day and it was found to be affecting the efficiency of the business' (Industrial Relations Services, 1996a) (see case in point 5).

Another case of employee-favoured flexibility may result from overtime. This should, in theory, be used by employers to manage variations in the workload, but it can instead become an expensive inefficiency if it degenerates into something manipulated by employees. This is done to increase earnings or maintain them at a much higher level than base pay.

Employee-favoured flexibility can breed an attitude of mind that suggests that the employer's job is to adjust working patterns to suit the employee, and the purpose of the employment can go hang. An example of this occurred among a group of health professionals where employees were given a great deal of freedom to arrange their work activities. Some in executing their duties gave a higher value to organizing their domestic arrangements, by starting late and finishing early, than to meeting the needs of their clients. They seemed to have difficulty in comprehending that they were employed to give their first attention to their patients and not to themselves.

INCIDENTAL FLEXIBILITY

We have looked at situations that favour one party to the employment relationship rather than the other. There are also situations where there may be benefits to both, but we would not call them mutual arrangements because they are not positively chosen as such, having come about more by accident than deliberate decision. This incidental flexibility can occur when organizations are required to accept legislative requirements that favour employees. The limiting of working hours with the introduction of the Working Time Regulations or new statutory rights for part-time workers are examples of this. We will see later that the law can be implemented to achieve mutual benefits – but, as we have just seen, in some organizations the law is flouted or circumvented in a truly Cyclopic way. Alternatively, employers can choose a route of minimum compliance, but incidentally derive some benefits themselves. The Working Time Regulations may permit shorter hours for employees, while at the same time cutting overtime costs for the organization. The requirement to give part-time workers the same statutory rights as full-time staff may drive employers into revising their terms and conditions, but thereby improve recruitment by making the deal on offer more attractive to new recruits.

Benefits to both parties may also arise in circumstances where the organization pushes for a particular solution that incidentally gives some help to employees. Reducing accommodation space to save money might lead an employer to permit a degree of homeworking previously resisted for fear of losing control over work outputs. Some employees may find this an attractive option, even if the employer's motive was not to help staff reduce their commuting costs.

Outsourcing may be initiated by an organization wishing to cut out a non-core activity. Employees may be fearful at first of the implications, yet become pleasantly surprised in what they discover in their new home – be it more resources, greater recognition of their work or more attractive terms and conditions.

Functional flexibility may be introduced by management merely for reasons of efficiency. Nevertheless, there may be a spin-off advantage to employees that they improve their internal and external marketability because they are able to offer a wider range of skills.

Fixed-term contracts may be used for graduate entrants because the organization wants to test how the employee shapes up over an initial period. Coincidentally, this may suit the new employee who prefers what is in effect a three-year assignment before making a longer-term commitment.

Incidental flexibility is therefore characized by situations in which both parties benefit but by chance or through external compulsion, not by design.

MUTUAL FLEXIBILITY

The difference between incidental and mutual flexibility is that in the latter there is a conscious decision at least on the part of the employer to meet the employees' needs as well as their own. This chapter should have demonstrated that there is a choice for employers in the sort of relationship they can have with their employees, and in the way in which they select and implement any flexible work arrangement (see Figure 6.2). The relationship can be of the exploitative kind found in forced flexibility; it can be similarly narrowly one-sided in conception as Cyclopic flexibility; it can happen more by luck than judgement – the incidental sort of flexibility. Or, if it is not biased in the employee's favour, it can be mutual.

Figure 6.2   Spectrum of flexible relationships

What are the characteristics of mutual flexibility?

● it recognizes that employers and employees have their own needs to serve
● it appreciates that these needs are different
● it respects the importance of satisfying each other's requirements
● it benefits both parties
● it is freely entered into by both sides
● it acknowledges that circumstances may change and with it the needs of the parties.

Thus mutual flexibility is about both parties creating a relationship on the principle that they have different interests, but that these can be reconciled through acknowledging the differences and working to find common ground between them. It asserts neither the

primacy of the employer nor that of the employee.

Mutual flexibility has another fundamental characteristic that distinguishes itself from other forms of flexibility: it addresses more than the economic needs of the person – it concerns itself with psychological well-being. It has been widely argued that the attempt to separate the economic from the social person is flawed. Employees relate to organizations as if the latter were people: a kind of marriage is contracted. In many organizations in recent years the marital status has been threatened by the nature and extent of organizational change. The implicit contract between the employer and employee has in many cases between damaged, sometimes fatally (Herriot and Pemberton, 1996). Instead of this contract having a balanced basis – for example, the organization offers employment security in exchange for employee commitment and responsiveness to business needs – it has become one-sided, so the reciprocity of the contract has been lost. The organization still requires adaptability on the part of the individual but offers only insecurity in return. The violation of the psychological contract may indeed be more at the relational than instrumental level. Those who are retained by their companies may be paid well in cash terms, but may not be satisfied at the emotional level. Keeping to the marriage analogy, many employees have been divorced by their employers; of those that remain tied to their partner, many feel they are in an unhappy relationship. They too would like to divorce but for the sake of the children or to pay the mortgage they stick with it.

We have in general seen a move from paternalistic management, expecting and receiving loyalty in exchange for stability of employment. This is exemplified by a statement in W.F. Whyte's *Man and Organization*, written in 1959: 'Be loyal to the company and the company will be loyal to you. After all if you do a good job for the organisation, it is only good sense for the organisation to be good to you, because that will be best for everybody.' Figure 6.3 illustrates how the psychological contract

	pre-1980	1980s	1990s
Employers' offer to employees	• good pay • good conditions • excellent career • job for life	• good pay • no lifetime employment guarantee • severance and outplacement • pain of change minimized by company	• performance-driven pay • personal development supported • constant business change • frequent role transition necessary
Employees' response	• work hard • do your best • keep your nose clean • offer loyalty and sacrifice	• work harder • work smarter • take more initiative • be cost-conscious	• be flexible • be self-accountable • learn • perform

Figure 6.3 The changing psychological contract within one organization

has altered in one large organization. Looking at the example, how fair the exchange is depends upon how the underpinning principles are worked out in practice. Does 'perform' mean working long hours under pressure with little hope of advancement and with the ever-present risk of redundancy? If so, this is unlikely to be a balanced contract. Alternatively, if support for personal development really means encouragement of learning in order to make the employee more marketable (should business change mean job reduction), then we are closer to mutual arrangements.

There is a natural tendency for contracts to become more relational over time. Without the impact of external events, this is what one would expect. Longer-serving staff should see a transition from contract precision about effort and reward to greater scope for individual discretion. Growing trust should mean that employees can be left to determine their working patterns with less managerial intervention.

In fact, the volatility of business life is pushing contracts in the opposite direction. Figure 6.3 is thus the norm rather than an aberration. Concepts like 'jobs for life' which may have underpinned these relational contracts have been replaced by the more

ambiguous 'employability'. Others have shifted their meaning: 'career' is no longer primarily about onward and upward promotion, but now is more about development of skills within and between jobs.

So, mutual flexibility is set within a context of employment relationships that recognizes the plurality of interests. It aims to find ways of reconciling these differences that take account of the varying requirements of the parties. There is acknowledgement that the satisfaction of employees goes beyond merely the payment of wages – it includes social as well as economic needs. Hence the connection between mutuality and the psychological contract. Getting the employment relationship right provides benefits to employees both in terms of attitudes (for example, commitment, satisfaction and so on) and behaviour (manifested in such things as attendance, effort and retention); getting it wrong naturally has the opposite consequences. This helps explain why organizations should bother with the concept of mutual flexibility when they have enough problems surviving from day to day, and leads us to consider in more detail why organizations should choose the mutual route to introducing flexible work arrangements.

CHAPTER SEVEN

Why Choose Mutual Flexibility?

We may sympathise with the plight of individuals in unhappy relationships, but why would organizations of their own free will positively choose a mutual approach to flexibility? There are various reasons that we will examine in this chapter. They are roughly grouped under four headings:

- recognizing the experience of success
- responding to external pressures
- listening to the research evidence of its benefits
- realizing the risks of ignoring mutuality.

So organizations may have had some experience of the benefits of mutuality; they may be doing no more than acknowledging pressures from the labour market or from legislation; they may have heard about the advantages, especially through the volume of research that has been published to this effect, or seen the advantages that have accrued to others; or they may have recognized that to ignore mutuality is a high-risk approach in managing change over the longer term.

In considering these issues under separate headings, it should be borne in mind that these categories are not discrete, but overlap. Moreover, as was pointed out in Chapter 4, influences on management thinking and their effects are not as clear-cut as reading this account might suggest.

EXPERIENCE OF SUCCESS

It may be that the organization is attracted to mutual flexibility because of past experience of its success. This may have arisen through a number of routes:

- a conscious choice to develop a partnership approach
- the positive response by employees to a crisis or to the trust placed in them

- manifestations of the practical benefits of having a more committed workforce.

PHILOSOPHY OF PARTNERSHIP

The advance to flexibility may be subsumed as part of a wider approach to partnership in employee relations. The Involvement and Participation Association (IPA), a pressure group which advocates employee participation, defines a partnership as one characterized by:

- a commitment to business success
- recognition that flexibility and security questions need to be addressed
- the building of relationships at work that maximize employee influence.

In place of the previously antagonistic and confrontational interaction, the aim is to sort out problems in a consensual manner. This is within the context of employees understanding the business imperatives and being responsive to their implications. But the benefits of this approach need to be mutual, not one-sided – hence flexibility with security. The employee voice needs to be heard via communication and consultation channels. This is achieved both through formal mechanisms, but also by direct participation in work decisions. Building trust has been found as a necessary prerequisite. As the Hyder Water company explained, trades unions must be seen as 'being inside the communal tent and sharing the responsibilities which lead to success' (Department for Trade and Industry, 1998).

Many other companies in the UK have gone down the partnership path. Partnership deals involving Littlewoods, Tesco, Scottish Power, Barclays, Unisys, Legal and General, Go, Rover, Blue Circle Cement, Stagecoach, Bulmers and others have been reported in the press. There are differences in content between these cases. Often the partnership deal serves to bring a number of important items together under one roof. At Blue Circle Cement, for example, a joint management and union task group identified the key issues for employees and management. These included questions of pay, job security, harmonization and flexibility. The agreement struck between the parties allows some of these items to be traded off against each other. Thus job security for employees is linked to achieving business plan objectives (including cost reductions through workforce cuts, achieved through voluntary means) and employee flexibility, especially in taking on new tasks.

There are some obvious benefits to employers. An IPA survey (Guest and Peccei, 1998) found that 65 per cent of companies claimed that partnership was good for business, as demonstrated by improved productivity, quality and customer service. As Andrew Coker, a Tesco manager, graphically put it: 'More costs, yes, but it also means more beans on shelves' (Involvement and Participation Association, 1998a). Other practical benefits reported include more stable employee relations and less conflict and confrontation with representative groups.

Trades unionists are generally supportive of the partnership notion, even if sometimes doing deals has been a defensive reaction to avoid the worse fate of de-recognition. John Monks has been an ardent campaigner in favour of partnership, and he used similar language to that of Hyder when, at the October 1998 Institute of Personnel and Development conference, he emphasized that it must add value to the organization and that it required a 'joint commitment to the success of the organization' which is more than a 'ritual' or 'sham' of union involvement. The mutuality of this approach was described by a lay employee representative: 'We're not here to wreck the company. We care about the same things as the company. We just want employee representatives to be part of the circle of opinion makers in the taking of decisions.'

From the trades union point of view, the following would be listed as characteristic of a partnership deal:

- involves protection and minimum standards for workers
- promotes company response to changing business and technological demands
- recognizes the need for good-quality products and services
- encourages skill development
- advocates developing individuals' employability
- generates organizational success through high-level employee performance
- argues for rights and responsibilities for all parties in the workplace
- supports family-friendly working practices and childcare provision.

Ed Sweeney, general secretary of UNIFIL, the banking trades union, explained the union position at the 1999 TUC Conference: 'If there is open and honest dialogue between the parties, differences can be worked through more easily than by going down the historical route of conflict.' This requires, according to the unions, respect for the employee viewpoint and involvement in decision making. If this occurs, there is more likely to be joint commitment to the success of the organization, which will bring benefits to both parties.

POSITIVE EMPLOYEE RESPONSE

Within or outside the context of a partnership deal, employees may have responded positively to a crisis, demonstrating their commitment to

CASE IN POINT

A manufacturing operation negotiated a no-redundancies agreement with trades unions in exchange for improved workforce flexibility. Unfortunately, soon afterwards the bottom dropped out of their market. It was unclear at the time whether this was a temporary hiccup or a longer-lasting problem. Faced with this dilemma, management stuck by their no-redundancy deal even when income was hammered. The result was that employees responded with higher levels of flexible working than ever before.

the future of the organization and encouraging their employer towards mutuality in employee relations. The case in point on p. 81 illustrates how employees may react if the organization has faith in them.

Another situation where employees may repay the trust placed in them is the way in which they treat an honour flexitime system. In other words, rather than there being a closely scrutinized method for monitoring timekeeping, employees have been left to manage their own hours and have done so honestly.

PRACTICAL BENEFITS

Organizations may have consciously or seren-dipitously found advantages in a mutual approach to employee relations. There may have been planned initiatives or surprising side effects to apparently unconnected develop-ments. Whatever the cause, the practical benefits of mutuality may have been realized. It may have:

- assisted organizational change, by facilitat-ing agreement
- provided a balance between the freedom of managers to manage and the employees' need to set limits on what is expected of them
- fitted with the move to empower people
- encouraged employee motivation
- led to better productivity and quality

- lowered absenteeism, wastage and other employment costs
- improved labour relations.

It may be clear that employee support is a prerequisite for the acceptance of the introduc-tion of flexible work arrangements. This may not just be in the narrow sense that negotia-tions have to be conducted with trades unions, though this may be true, but because it is necessary to win the hearts and minds of employees if change is to be successful. It may be clear that mutually agreed flexibility improves employee motivation and commit-ment to the success of the introduction of new contracts, hours or ways of working. Organiza-tions can then see the value in the way that change can be positively managed (see Figure 7.1).

Greater task discretion meets a psychological need most people have for some control over their work. Organizations may have realized that, especially in a tight labour market, volun-tary support is preferable to that obtained through coercion. Pressed men are never as committed as volunteers. And in any case, trying to specify all that the organization requires through detailed contract specification or union agreement is extremely difficult. Employers have found that they are better served trying to get employees to see the importance of the organizational goals, and why these are being sought, than merely

Figure 7.1 A virtuous change circle

instructing them blindly to follow rules. The push towards IiP and integrated forms of performance management are evidence of this. If there are clear benefits that will arise simultaneously for employees, be it in terms of greater job security or higher wages, then we have mutual flexibility providing a win/win situation.

CASE IN POINT

Henry Stuart, founder of Happy Computers, describes his philosophy: 'When I established my own company I wanted to harness all that enthusiasm and creativity people have in their private lives. It gives the company a competitive edge. But it is a lot more than just hugs. It is about trusting people and giving them control over their jobs – empowering them and allowing them fulfilment even if the job is mundane.

'We don't go for short-term contracts and we don't go for working ridiculously long hours; nonetheless in some ways it is harder to be a whole person at work because it means you have to engage yourself with your environment instead of just cruising through on auto pilot.' (quoted in Benardy, 1999)

Some organizations have been tempted to follow a coercive route. They have constructed contracts which allow them to determine the workers' duties in any way they wish. The difficulty with this approach is that it flies in the face of the simple psychological proposition that employees like to know what is expected of them and what their reward will be for their efforts. If this is not provided or is unclear, the parties may well have different expectations of what is to be delivered and at what price. This is a recipe for conflict, which may be held in check when the demand for labour is weak, but which is likely to surface if workers are ever in the position to have a real choice of employer.

There is the further difficulty that the more organizations decentralize or devolve power, the more they introduce complex organizational forms, the more they create self-managed teams, the harder it will be for management to control individual behaviour. How work will be completed will be settled by the teams themselves. This may apply to working hours or the allocation of tasks. The sort of close supervision of the sort advocated by those adhering to the philosophy of F.W. Taylor will not be applicable in this situation. Taylor believed managers should manage and operatives should follow instructions. The increased knowledge input into work and greater sophistication of the employees' contribution means that employees have to be more self-reliant, not directed from above.

Even where close supervision is still the predominant management style and is applicable to the working conditions, neglecting mutuality may still have adverse consequences. Call centres are a prime example. They have generally been set up in order to provide a fast, efficient and consistent service to customers. This has led to management seeking to specify working patterns in minute detail, monitoring performance very closely and controlling employee behaviour very carefully. However, there is evidence that some employers have gone too far. This is shown in poor retention and absence figures. It has been claimed that average turnover is as high as 30 per cent per annum (Davis, 1999), but can be as low as 3 per cent. Those at the latter end of this scale have avoided a battery-hen model of operation, where output is maximized but the needs of those employed are neglected. Firms like Freemans, near Sheffield, have attended to these needs by providing a good working environment and easy access to work (North, 1996). The Woolwich service centre in Essex has worked on training and development, and on reward as a means of attracting and retaining staff (Davis, 1999). Turnover is not just a matter of labour market conditions allowing employees to job hop as they fancy – it is also a rejection of an over-managed working environment. People today are less tolerant of being dictated to and directed, and will rebel if they have the chance. The irony is that successful customer service relies upon having staff that are friendly and helpful. Surely organizations would find that well-motivated and committed employees will offer this kind of response?

Going the extra mile, which so many organizations want, be it in a self-managed team or even call centre, is not likely to occur if employees are expected to adhere rigidly to a pattern of work laid down for them. If employees have freely entered into an agreement with their employer, if they understand the organizational aims and support them, and if they feel that they themselves are valued and rewarded for the efforts, then staff are more likely to please the customer and meet his or her needs. This is not just a matter of some individuals being harder workers, but of creating a culture in which positive behaviour is endorsed. Peer pressure can be exerted to discourage skiving and skimping at work. Lower turnover and absenteeism may result, especially when teams are given responsibility for arranging their work pattern. Organizations can engender an atmosphere in which hard work is applauded and delivering what is required is seen as the norm.

If people are involved in shaping their work and their needs are taken care of in a mutual way, employee relations are bound to improve. This has the added benefit of relieving management time from dealing with work disputes to attending to other tasks, such as improving the quality of production or service.

These benefits are summarized in the NHS case in point.

CASE IN POINT

An NHS taskforce on staff involvement assessed the impact of greater employee participation and reported:

'We have no doubt – because we have seen it with our own eyes – that employers in the NHS who involve staff in decisions, planning and policy making:
- improve patient care through better service delivery
- manage change more effectively
- have a healthier, better motivated workforce and reduce staff turnover.' (Involvement and Participation Association, 1999c)

EXTERNAL PRESSURES

In the UK some of the pressure for mutuality is not born of experience of success alone, but comes from external sources. These include the need to respond to the ambitions of the European Commission, to the views of the present government, to deal with the effects of the legal system and the labour market. Naturally, this is a fast-moving picture in which the debate shifts with the prevailing climate and the transfer of power between political players. The labour market, too, is frequently in a state of flux, benefiting the employer and employee by turns.

EU INTERVENTIONS

The European Union has had a major impact on employee relations. The Commission has consistently promoted the view that economic change should be achieved at the macro-(national) level via 'social dialogue between governments and social partners'. This should aim to foster permanent work contracts by avoiding 'excessive regulation' and to extend 'social protection' to non-standard forms of work' (Commission of the European Communities, 1999). At organizational level, the Commission similarly argues the benefits of partnership between management and trades unions in achieving work modernization. It believes that success is built upon co-operation and the development of a common interest. Works councils are seen as a means of promoting greater workforce adaptability. In early 1999 European Commissioner Padraig Flynn commended the setting up of national works councils by saying that they would 'help create a more positive and flexible approach to re-organisation and change' (Involvement and Participation Association, 1999a).

With respect to flexibility, the Commission sees the importance of achieving a balance with employee security. In this context employees are more likely to add skills and be more adaptable, thus helping organizations themselves be more responsive to changing demand. Additionally, 'this security for workers can also provide employers with increased security in the form of a more stable, versatile and contented workforce' (Commission of the European Communities, 1997).

The European Commission's position can be summed up as follows:

> For management, the challenge is to achieve a fundamental renewal of their organisation in such a way that they create a climate of trust and partnership, based on the concepts of flexibility and security. For trades unions, the challenge is to ensure that they exercise a constructive and active role in the innovation and modernisation process within the firm so as to achieve a sustainable balance between their social and economic objectives. (Commission of the European Communities, 1997)

The practical manifestation of this position varies depending upon the political climate and the forcefulness of the commissioner responsible. The Greek commissioner, Anna Diamantopoulou, who replaced Flynn in 1999, may have a different view of employee relations and may steer the EU along a changed course. There is also the new and more important role of the Parliament to consider.

For now, the EU Social Action Plan for 1998 to 2000 is drawing to a close. Its themes have included:

- creating jobs and preventing unemployment
- modernizing work organization and promoting adaptability (the preferred term now for flexibility)
- anticipating industrial change.

Under these banners, the Commission has been keen to promote family-friendly employment strategies, encourage greater employee financial participation and define minimum standards in information provision and consultation. Attempts have also been made by the Commission to extend works councils to the national level and to companies employing 500 staff. At the time of writing this last measure has been blocked.

There has also been bargaining between the social partners ETUC (the European Trades Union Confederation) and EUNICE (the Union of Industrial and Employers Confederations of Europe) on what, in practical terms, the Action Plan might mean for flexibility. The result has been:

- an agreement between ETUC and EUNICE on the regulation of fixed-term contractors which limits their use, provides employees with minimum employment rights and seeks to control the granting of successive contracts
- the beginnings of a discussion between the same two parties on agency employment
- a move to regulate teleworking promoted by ETUC which is being resisted by EUNICE.

Future developments may build upon the notion of minimum employment standards being set across the Union. There may be a desire to offer the European workforce a sense of the benefits of being part of the EU through improvements in employment conditions in some way. Further legislation might also spring from the review of previously enacted legislation, like the Working Time Directive.

What we have yet to see is how the arrival of the euro will impact on employment. The drive for still greater labour market harmonization across the Union may come from the Commission's wish to ensure a level playing field in employment costs and employment rights. Uneven job protection measures within the EU prevent a proper flow of labour, and they may come to be seen as an important impediment to the operation of the free market. This does not necessarily mean the imposition of a highest common denominator in regulations. Instead, European convergence may reflect the desire to have minimum standards in operation.

THE UK POLITICAL SCENE

The Blair government has also shaped the context of employee relations in a number of ways, having:

- more readily accepted EU legislation than

its predecessors – but it has put limits on how far corporatism should develop

- emphasized the requirement of organizations to respond to market pressures – but it sees value in supporting partnership deals
- supported the notion of a flexible labour market – but its practical emphasis is in giving support to family-friendly employment policies and other supply-side measures to get people into work
- retained much of the Conservatives' industrial relations law – but it has eased the means by which trades unions can be recognized at company level.

This does not add up to an agenda of encouraging mutual flexibility, but there are elements within it that give a strong push in that direction.

In its attitude to the EU, Labour has largely been happy thus far to implement legislation that fosters co-operative employee relations. It has signed the social chapter of the Maastricht Treaty, which has brought works councils to trans- and multinational companies (applying to those with more than 1 000 employees within the member states of the European Union, at least 150 of whom are employed in two different member states). It has extended consultation rights on redundancies and company transfers. It uses the same 'flexibility with security' expression as the European Commission in emphasizing that it believes in a partnership approach. Furthermore, the government has established a partnership fund to support initiatives in the training of managers and employee representatives.

The government has also supported financial participation with the aim of getting a greater degree of identification of employees with their firm. Profit-sharing schemes have been encouraged, and generous tax breaks were offered in the 1999 budget with the aim of doubling the number of share schemes in operation. Tax-favoured schemes will have to ensure that they apply workforce-wide, rather than being limited to those in the boardroom.

With respect to supply-side measures, there have been a wide range of initiatives to encourage the economically inactive to find a job. In the context of flexibility, the government has been keen to promote family-friendly working. This formed a key part of the Employment Relations Act (ERA). Secretary of State at the DTI Stephen Byers, when launching the bill in January 1999, said:

> The Bill will promote the best of modern employment relationships in all our companies, encouraging a culture of fairness and trust in the workplace which is so important to the competitiveness of our economy. It will help millions of parents who give their all, day in day out at home and at work. For the first time people will be able to care for a sick child or an ailing relative without running the risk of losing their job. (Department for Trade and Industry, 1999)

The government has supported pre-school nurseries and out-of-school childcare centres, and introduced the childcare tax credit for low-income working families. Ministers have aimed to expand the number of those working in the childcare sector and to ensure that staff are better trained. The ERA has given employees the right to take unpaid time off work for family emergencies, and the right to up to 13 weeks' unpaid parental leave. All this is intended to help parents, especially single parents, be able to get into work and stay there.

Ministers have attacked the long-hours culture of some firms with its consequent impact on family life. They have more readily accepted the Working Time Directive because of its aim to achieve a better balance between time spent at work and at home. Tony Blair himself has promoted initiatives to get a better work/life balance. In March 2000 he launched an alliance of employers committed to family-friendly employment practices.

The desire to give employees greater protection at work has also been seen in enshrining in law the non-discrimination of part-time workers and prohibiting unfair-dismissal waivers in fixed-term contracts. At least some of the employment rights of permanent employees are being extended to other workers. The route to trades union recognition has also been eased, on the basis that employees should be freer to have the support of the representatives of their choice

The government is keen to ensure that employers recognize their responsibilities. Part of the point of having a national minimum wage is to prevent situations where employers get away with low wages knowing that the state will pick up the tab. The government has also chosen to re-legislate to control the behaviour of employment agencies to stamp out excesses.

While the trades unions have largely supported this agenda, the Conservative Party, the CBI and the Institute of Directors have, to varying degrees, objected. They have complained of the added burden of costs arising out of regulations such as the minimum wage, Working Time Directive and ERA. They see this sort of regulation as weakening the UK's competitive position and shifting the balance unreasonably in the employees' favour, a view strengthened by what they regard as a one-sided deal favouring the unions on recognition rights. They object to compulsion rather than voluntary adoption of measures such as works councils. They dislike what they consider to be the 'corporatist' approach of Labour, 'flirting with continental style' partnership ideas. Sir Clive Thompson, then president of the CBI, saw partnership with trades unions as a 'Trojan horse' through which they would gain greater influence (Coupar, 1999).

In fact the government has seemed to be sensitive to these criticisms. It has sometimes done the minimum necessary to comply with European directives or court decisions, such as on employee consultation rights regarding redundancy and company transfers. It upset the trades union side by taking on board some of the employer objections to the union recognition process. In the implementation of the Working Time Directive, the government has wavered between softening its impact, by excluding all managerial jobs from the effect of the regulations, and appeasing the unions by including all but the most senior executives. It finally settled on a compromise. It has resisted pressure to treat paternity time off as paid leave of absence and has restricted its application to the parents of children born on or after 15 December 1999; it has chosen to phase in the ERA; it has seemingly cooled to further interventions on employment law from the European Commission. Stephen Byers said his aim was to 'ensure that there is no new raft of proposals from the EU' and, specifically, that there was no compulsion to national-level works councils (Walsh, 1999b).

This illustrates the tension within the government between promoting employment rights and at the same time recognizing global economic trends that necessitate companies' being able to respond and adapt quickly. This lies behind what was said before (Chapter 1) about the government's attitude to flexible labour markets – wishing to give employers the freedom to manage, yet perceiving that co-operation with employees brings its own rewards. Tony Blair would probably explain this conundrum by talking about both organizations and workers having rights as well as responsibilities in the conduct of employment relations.

THE LEGAL PROCESSES

Employer behaviour on flexibility has to an extent also been affected by the rulings of the courts – both UK courts and the European Court of Justice (ECJ). The latter has had a significant impact by clarifying or seemingly extending the law, for example on staff consultation rights, on discrimination against part-time workers and on the interpretation of the Acquired Rights Directive. However, it has to be said that the Court can sometimes confuse and restrict legal application, as indeed it has also done in relation to the Acquired Rights Directive. The ECJ's decisions have also led to the introduction of primary legislation, for example on pension rights for women. The UK legal system has had to interpret employment law initiated in Britain as well as European legislation.

Successful cases have been brought by employees asserting their rights to equal opportunities at work, but also to the reasonable introduction of new work arrangements and to changes in the deployment of staff. For example:

- a female tube-train driver won a case of sexual discrimination because London Underground introduced a new roster system which she claimed to be incompatible with her parental responsibilities (Dyer, 1998)
- there was the 1994 ruling that excluding part-time workers from occupational pension funds amounted to sex discrimination because more women than men work part-time.
- indirect discrimination has been proved where employers have refused women requests to work part-time after maternity leave.
- in 1999 a woman won £67 000 damages for stress when she was moved to a new activity but not provided with the necessary training or support (Whitehead, 1999c)
- a single mother, sacked because she refused to work 16-hour shifts, was awarded three years' salary in compensation at an employment tribunal in 1999. It found South African Airways had breached sex discrimination legislation, and was concerned about the safety implications of long working-hours in an airport environment (Gregoriadis, 1999).

These decisions illustrate that employers at the very least need to be mindful of legal precedent. But they also show that if the world is only viewed from the employers' perspective, then the impact on employees will be neglected. If the impact is severe, organizations may find themselves in court having to justify 16-hour shifts or redeployment without training. It seems that in the UK the legal system is increasingly likely to punish those that ignore the implications of their actions and cannot justify them on grounds of economic necessity.

THE LABOUR MARKET

One of the most obvious external pressures on employers comes from the labour market. If the labour market is tight or scarce resources are being sought, organizations may have to offer terms and conditions that are attractive to potential recruits and that develop a positive image in the recruitment market. These terms and conditions may include flexible work arrangements that suit specific groups of people that might only be tempted into work this way. Women, the disabled, and single parents may be groups, previously neglected, who might be interested in non-standard working contracts.

Labour market conditions may also dictate that if the appropriate flexible work arrangements are not on offer, retention of existing staff may be difficult. This may be because employees choose to resign to find more desirable conditions elsewhere or to withdraw from work altogether. This can be particularly true for women who find certain patterns of working hours difficult to cope with.

CASE IN POINT

Lands' End management explains: 'We make a lot of compromises with our employees because they're trained and we want their skills. We want to keep them, so contractual hours vary according to individual need.' (Industrial Society, 1998)

RESEARCH EVIDENCE

If managers reading this are in any further doubt of why mutual flexibility is a route that should be chosen in place of, say, forced flexibility, then they should consider the recent research published that demonstrates that a positively employee-centred approach is likely to deliver business benefits.

Some of the research evidence suggests that clusters of high-commitment work practices are associated with employee productivity and business success. These practices include, in our context, providing employment security, encouraging employee ownership, sharing information with staff, adopting employee-participation practices and changing job design in an involving manner (Pfeffer, 1994; Ostroff, 1995; and Huselid, 1995). Other research (Arthur, 1994) has demonstrated the productivity, quality and employee-retention benefits of creating psychological links between organizational and employee goals. Caffman and Harter (1998) describe the impact of employee engagement on business results. They emphasize the importance of employee contribution allied to development. Lawler and colleagues (1995) found that those organizations using an employee involvement approach to total quality management had a better financial performance compared with competitors that did not. Tsui et al. (1997) found that employee performance was most effective where a 'mutual investment' approach applied. This occurred when the employer invested in the employee through such things as training and development, and the employee reciprocated by demonstrating commitment to organizational goals by being flexible in the way in which he or she worked. Black and Lynch (1997) concluded from their research that 'simply introducing high performance workplace practices is not enough to increase productivity. The increased employee voice that is associated with these practices seems a necessary pre-condition to making the practices effective.'

There is also the case study at Sears (Rucci et al., 1998) that found that employees' attitudes to their work and company fed through to an effect on the customer, which resulted in improved revenue growth. Finally, there is specific support for family-friendly forms of employment reported in the US by *Fortune* magazine: those companies using family-friendly flexibility policies out-performed the average (Stevens, 1999).

This US evidence has been vindicated in the UK. Patterson et al. (1997) found that positive HR practices explained nearly one fifth of the variation between companies in terms of productivity and profitability. Job satisfaction and employee commitment were also demonstrated to influence profitability; HR practices relating to the acquisition of skills and job design were particularly important. Gallie et al. (1998) found that where there were greater opportunities for employees to be directly involved in decisions concerning their work, they were more receptive to change and better employee relations resulted. Barber et al. (1999) have replicated the Sears model in a UK retail company, finding a strong correspondence between employee commitment and sales, mediated through customer satisfaction and lower staff absence. What was particularly interesting in this case study was the positive effect of front-line supervision on employee attitudes. This involved managers supporting staff, valuing them as people, giving and receiving information and feedback, and allowing them to grow and develop. This positive attitude of managers generated a culture that fostered these sorts of management behaviours in what it valued, supported and promoted.

This research evidence supports the argument that increasingly organizations compete more on the basis of their human capital than on their physical assets. This is because it is easier to replicate a product or service: what is much harder to do is to copy intangible assets. Hence the interest in developing or protecting the brand image. Likewise, employees' own knowledge and the organizational culture within which staff operate are almost impossible to imitate fully. And if Western economies are going to be sustained by their intellectual added value, then once more the employees' contribution will be vital.

THE RISKS OF IGNORING MUTUALITY

Another way to look at why organizations might choose to adopt mutual flexibility is to consider the consequences of ignoring this approach and instead opting for the coercive route. The danger of Cyclopic or forced flexibility, where the organization ignores employee interests or tramples over their rights, is that it makes the change process all the harder to implement. Employees may respond by:

- leaving the organization
- taking industrial action
- initiating legal action
- demonstrating their lack of commitment through poor productivity
- refusing to do any work outside their own specified area of duties
- requiring payment for any additional tasks.

So, instead of the virtuous circle shown in Figure 7.1, you may end with a vicious circle of the sort shown in Figure 7.2.

These problems may not be apparent in the short term, or may appear to have only a limited effect, but they may have a greater impact over the longer term. People may leave once the labour market improves. Sickness levels may rise if people feel overly pressurized in their work and, as they feel less committed, are not prepared to struggle in when it might be easier to stay in bed. They may refuse to carry out new duties or take industrial action if the balance of power shifts away from the employee. People have long memories over a perceived violation of the psychological contract. Evidence of the post-traumatic stress on survivors of redundancy is indicative of this point. The employee who sees a colleague made redundant may fear that he or she is

next in line. Employees put psychological distance between themselves and their work. They become emotionally detached, and are likely to see their relationship with their employer more in terms of a transaction (I am only here for the money) and less on a relational basis. Their emotional sustenance may come increasingly from outside work. Organizations that seek flexibility from employees but go about it in the wrong way may, ironically, produce an attitudinal inflexibility that will imperil the objective they set for themselves.

Less dramatically staff may feel disillusioned by management behaviour, and be less prepared to 'go the extra mile' or to think up solutions to problems themselves. Instead there is compliance or indifference. There is indeed some evidence to suggest that the consequences of the last recession left managers more detached from their employers than previously and keen to leave if they could (Wilson et al., 1994). This is borne out by an Institute of Management survey which found that two-thirds of the 1300 managers who replied felt that morale and job security had fallen over the previous year, with half believing that motivation and loyalty had also suffered (Institute of Management, 1997). What was more striking still was that responses differed depending upon managerial level.

Figure 7.2 A vicious change circle

Nearly 80 per cent of junior management felt that morale had suffered over the last 12 months, whereas only 21 per cent of chief executives/managing directors had the same opinion, suggesting that experiences depended upon whether one initiated change or was on the receiving end of it.

It should of course be acknowledged that some circumstances are so serious that employees accept the approach chosen by management. They are more likely to do this if they trust management's motives and competence. Whether they do so or not depends upon management's previous behaviour. If in the past management has described the organization's problems as real and significant, and this has turned out to be the case, employees are naturally more likely to believe them the next time. The opposite is also true: employees are wary of managers' crying wolf. And equally, if, in the eyes of staff, management has successfully and sensitively dealt with any difficulties, then employees will have faith in them again.

So a failure on the part of management to communicate the extent and nature of a problem is likely to generate employee suspicion. If there is a genuine crisis, employees may respond positively; if they do not, they may demonstrate their alienation. It is much harder to get employees to engage if they do not see that a crisis exists. As Kurt Lewin's theories on change management suggest, people want to change only if they perceive their current position to be untenable or a source of major dissatisfaction. They need to see and believe in an alternative future vision of events. Should management not be able to demonstrate the unacceptability of the present and the desirability of the future, then change will have to be driven through and employees coerced.

Coercion may work up to a point and for a while. Some employees are too vulnerable to challenge their employer's behaviour. Labour market conditions may mean that employees have no alternative. But the organization risks storing up the problems reported earlier. These may reveal themselves in a rational response – leaving the job because of the unacceptability of what is on offer – or an emotional reaction to a perceived abuse. Once this happens events may take their own course with negative consequences for both employees and employees (see the case in point). What is certain is that more management time and energy will have to be invested in managing this sort of situation. Transactional costs are then higher because of the limited trust felt by the parties.

So, the organization's ability to move to a new way of working will be harder if:

(a) the company is seen to be still performing well, that is generating high levels of profit
(b) the negative effects of change are only

CASE IN POINT

A manufacturer responded to difficult financial conditions by agreeing greater pay flexibility with the trades unions, instead of making redundancies. Times changed; business improved. A new managing director arrived wanting greater workforce flexibility. The unions sought improved pay, but were prepared to accept greater flexibility in a 'partnership' deal. No deal was agreed and the employees' response to the company pay offer was to go on strike. The company demanded a return to work with a guarantee of no further industrial action. When this was refused, the company fired the strikers, de-recognized the union and hired new staff.

The unions believe that employees lost trust in management's capacity to deal with them fairly. Management says the unions were intransigent and that with a 'refreshed' workforce it has better productivity and flexibility. The cost: temporary loss of production, bad publicity, a 20-month union dispute and the dole for many former employees.

visited upon certain (more junior) groups of employees, through a deterioration in terms and conditions, for example

(c) those at senior management level disproportionately benefit from the change, for example through substantial pay increases.

Perceptions of a one-sided employment deal on flexibility may be seen by employees to occur in circumstances where:

- there are fewer full-time jobs on permanent contracts
- older serving workers are 'retired' and replaced by cheaper new recruits
- base pay is restrained, but performance-based bonuses are offered
- there is greater insecurity of future employment
- management itself is untouched by the change or realizes its benefits through the growing value of their share options.

Organizations can spot signs of employee dissatisfaction and act upon them. Negative experience of how change has been managed does lead organizations to the conclusion that mutual flexibility is the right way to proceed. For example, an organization may find that without mutuality the process of change is too costly, with the interminable guerrilla warfare

CASE IN POINT

The EDAP scheme introduced by Ford is another illustration of how partnership at work can produce wider dividends. It was a self-conscious decision on behalf of management and the Transport and General Workers' Union to change the nature of their relationship, which had been characterized by conflict. Developing EDAP was used at one level as a means to achieve better working relations between the parties, and at another level as a way of realizing the talents of the workforce. The learning organization concept suggests that giving people the experience of learning in one sphere will translate into learning in another setting. So one can move from basket weaving to multi-skilling. An important characteristic of this approach is that it is centred on the individual, who chooses the approach to take.

over employee relations taking up too much management time with little to show for it. It is said that Ford's Employee Development Assistance Programme (EDAP) scheme was born out of frustration felt by senior managers and trades union officials at the traditional nature of antagonistic industrial relations; see the Ford case in point above.

The Tesco example (see case in point below)

CASE IN POINT

Lesley James, formerly Tesco's HR director, explained how these issues presented themselves at Tesco: 'In the mid 1980s the company was run according to a financial model. The culture was one of managing by fear and intimidation. Our staff were frightened of their managers and labour was used as a balancing item in our accounts. So if we were strapped for cash, we would fire people. They weren't paid well or well managed. Hardly

surprisingly, staff were surly and indifferent.'

Tesco decided on a new approach. This included an overhaul of terms and conditions and changing managerial behaviour. The benefits were twofold:

- a cut in wastage rates, down from an average 75 per cent per annum to 30 per cent
- better customer service.

'We wanted to foster lifelong relationships with customers, and

to do that we needed longer relationships with staff. We want them to be helpful and show initiative. In a big impersonal world, customers love it when they are recognized.

'If margins were squeezed in the future, Tesco will undoubtedly take a longer term view than in the past. In the old days we would have slashed jobs, now they would try hard to save jobs.' (Benardy, 1999).

shows how management realized that their style of operation was affecting both customer service and employee retention. It also bears out the fact that employees often leave organizations not so much because of the money, but because they do not like the treatment they receive at work, especially from their manager (Bevan et al., 1997). It also validates the research reported in this chapter that the relationship between the immediate supervisor and employee is critical in the way that staff perform and in their attitudes to work.

In these circumstances the organization will discover the merits of mutual flexibility through gaining new flexibilities or increased productivity, and losing the costs of policing and regulating behaviour. In many cases organizations have moved across the spectrum of employment relationships from Cyclopic or incidental flexibility towards mutuality. They have done so for positive or negative reasons; either way, they have shown the importance of learning from experience. Others may need to go down the same path, having seen or read about the success of others, or being pushed down this route by the pressures of legislation.

CHAPTER EIGHT

The Model

So how do you achieve mutuality, having decided it is the approach to use? I have taken a model from career contracting (Herriot and Pemberton, 1996; Herriot et al., 1998) to help organizations approach this subject. It is shown in Figure 8.1.

The basic features of this model are that mutuality:

- involves discovering what both employees and the employer need out of flexibility
- requires both parties to be aware of each other's 'wants'
- operates at the individual rather than collective level
- requires negotiation in determining a consensual outcome

- does not assume that performance of the contract will occur as agreed – it needs monitoring
- accepts that needs may change over time, so further negotiation may be required
- is framed by what is happening in the world outside the organization.

The model is thus characterized by the fact that it is a two-way process since it involves both parties. It recognizes the legitimacy of both 'sides'. Thus it dismisses the HRM assumption of a unitarist vision shared by one and all. It recognizes the diversity of interest. It allows employees to shape their own world of work rather than have it wholly determined by their employer. It thereby rejects domination

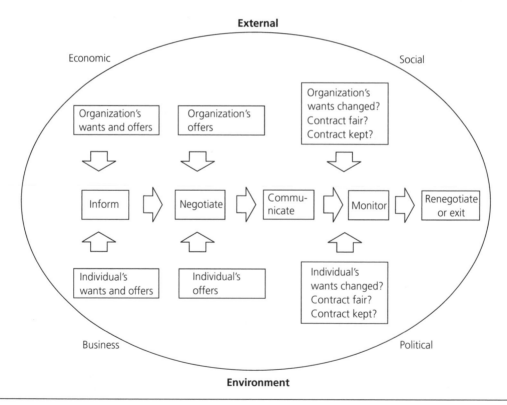

Figure 8.1 A model of achieving mutual flexibility (adapted from Herriot et al., 1998)

by either party, whichever way round it might occur.

The process is open and explicit – it tries to avoid hidden agendas. This is critical at a time when trust is at a low ebb and where the 'deal' under which the parties are operating may have shifted, unrecognized, over time. Indeed, a multiplicity of different contracts may have arisen, but only one model is seen as the 'norm'. It is important to respond to these developments because a lack of clarity in what is expected of the parties risks misunderstanding and conflict. The deal is iterative: it does not stand still – an important aspect, with so much change happening inside and outside the organization, both for the employer and employee.

The model offers primarily an individual approach. This is in itself an important change in perspective. In the years dominated by industrial relations, we came to think only in terms of blocks of people, blocks of interest. It was seen in the card votes at TUC conferences. It was seen in the national deals done to cover whole industries or companies. While this approach has much merit in simplifying what could be complex processes, in ensuring that the democratic majority view is not hijacked by minority interests and in providing egalitarian solutions to problems, its weakness is that it did not address the personal needs of those represented. This might have been easier in the days of greater labour market homogeneity – the time of the white, male, full-time worker. But now we have a more diverse workforce. Individualism is more prevalent, people want to satisfy their own aspirations, they have less need of the group or community. In this world, it is ever more important to understand and respond to individual employee needs, and not just assume that they can be swept in together with those of all the others. As the research indicated in the last chapter, employees who have control over their working lives will produce better results for their employers: the very fact of being part of the bargaining process will go a long way towards achieving that.

We will go through each stage of this contracting process.

STEP 1: UNDERSTAND THE ENVIRONMENT

The point has frequently been made in this book that the external environment, be it social, political or economic, has a profound effect on how relationships operate within an organization. In the context of flexibility we have noted that employees are affected by the changing family structures, the growing numbers of women at work, the need to care for the elderly, the pressure to maintain an income in these uncertain times.

For organizations there are economic pressures, technological innovations or changes in regulatory frameworks (especially through employment legislation) to cope with. In responding to the competition there may be the need to cut costs, to restructure or to merge or acquire other businesses. These issues may impact directly on the desire to introduce flexible work arrangements, but there are indirect effects too. The state of the labour market will influence how easily organizations find it to recruit or retain staff. The outflow from schools, colleges and universities will bear upon the size, nature and quality of that labour market.

More subtly the importance of organizational culture should be recognized, the 'how things are done around here'. While organizational culture does change, and indeed as we have seen those who believe in the transformational effects of flexibility use it to that end, it is slow to shift. So how organizations confront their problems is mediated through their culture.

STEP 2: MUTUALLY INFORM

No process of reaching mutually agreeable flexibility is likely to occur in a state of ignorance. As John Monks said at the 1998 IPD conference, 'partnership demands a sharing of hard, unvarnished information' at an early stage. Therefore it is incumbent on both parties to find out about the needs of the other. This is all the more so since we are operating at the individual level. How can this be done?

Organizations need to inform their staff what the business objectives are, and what are the pressures that they operate under. Management has to make clear to employees what they want from them, and what the employees need to do to meet these objectives. To be meaningful the broad business strategy has to be translated into the particular requirements that affect employees. Managers can explain the demand for products and services. They can say what effect this might have on workforce numbers short term, and on projections for the longer term. They can talk about any changes necessary to work schedules or in the sort of work that needs to be carried out. They can draw out the implications for skill requirements and hence for training.

So in practical terms this may involve cascading the business strategy, holding briefing sessions and arranging meetings. It will probably necessitate several question and answer sessions so that employees can get a good feel for both the organizational imperatives and what the specific consequences are for them.

Employees must reciprocate and make known their views to management. They can do this by having individual discussions with their line managers. Management itself can help this process by ascertaining staff preferences through attitude surveys. Consultation with employee representatives may also provide background information on employee opinion. Through these sorts of means, management can discover employee views about such things as working hours, work location, training needs and what causes them to stay with the organization – or might incline them to leave.

STEP 3: NEGOTIATE

The third step involves negotiation. This should have both process and content aims. It should address the questions of how individuals can become more involved in a true exchange of views and what subjects the discussions should cover to make them meaningful. These are not straightforward issues. Many consultative forums have fallen into disrepute because they have ended up as talking shops discussing tea and toilets. Even in those committees that have tried to be strategic, representatives may struggle to cope with the language and complexity of business jargon. Employee interest in consultative structures has often been very low, and persuading the average worker to participate has proved extremely difficult. At the other extreme, collective bargaining may cover matters wholly pertinent to employees – that is terms and conditions of employment – but again without much real participation beyond mass voting. The negotiation we propose should tackle issues relevant to employees, such as how their work is organized, and should offer a mechanism to get individuals directly involved. Past experience may not have prepared people for such an approach, so organizations will have to work hard to convince managers and employees of the value of these ideas and to give them confidence in a worthwhile outcome.

The negotiation is likely to require give and take on both sides. This process will be greatly assisted by both parties thinking through what they really require rather than what they think they do. So, for employers, this means recognizing that many of the advantages that come from flexible work arrangements will not be lost by making concessions to employees. Providing pro-rata terms and conditions to atypical workers may add some cost, but it does not threaten the basic benefit of workforce flexibility. Offering access to training likewise means money has to be spent, but a more effective workforce may result. Similarly, employees need to see that meeting all their flexible requirements may put too great a strain on the operation of the business. As with management, there has to be an understanding that complete flexibility costs money and that it is better and cheaper to aim for useable flexibility.

Negotiation is not something that is usually neatly concluded in one go. Ideas need to be tested, and piloting new flexible work arrangements will enable the organization to learn what is turning out to be successful and what not. At the individual level, personal trials of new work patterns may be helpful to see if practice is as effective as theory.

STEP 4: COMMUNICATE

Once it is clear what flexible work arrangements are to be, before proceeding any further the nature of the agreement needs to be widely communicated, especially if there is a collective element to it.

There is of course a panoply of ways of doing this, from the traditional team briefing to the use of the latest communications technology. In fact, a multi-level approach is likely to work best. Employees will want to hear directly from senior management of any proposed changes, to understand the rationale behind them. They will wish to talk face to face with their immediate supervisor to discuss the implications of change, the impact it will have upon them and what scope there is for their input.

Finally, employees will need the sort of detailed information contained in booklets on, say, options in working hours or patterns. The intranet provides a cheap modern way of doing this, and more sophisticated decision tools allow employees not only to understand the implications of the choices on offer, but also to make decisions based on modelling their options. This methodology is already used for cafeteria-style benefits schemes, where employees can choose their personal benefits selection from a menu. The concept can be extended further. It makes employee participation more of a reality.

STEP 5: MONITOR

The next step is to monitor the deal to make sure it is still working to mutual satisfaction.

The first point of monitoring the contract is to see that it has been properly observed, that both parties have kept their side of the bargain. Has management stuck to the agreed working hours; is the notice of call-out as decided; has the training been given as required; do the numbers of temporary agency people reflect

what was anticipated, and so on? For their part, are employees carrying out the tasks in the way they were asked to; are they learning new skills; are they working overtime when requested; are they accepting the temporary staff drafted in, and so on?

One reason why the deal may not be working out as planned is that things may have changed since agreement was reached. This is the other main reason for monitoring: to see whether the external or internal environment have altered. The business situation may have changed. The pressure on the company to cut costs may have grown because a new low-cost competitor has arrived. The organization may have restructured since the last deal and the new arrangements might need to be reflected in the way work is carried out. The firm may have merged with another similar business, and the two organizational cultures may have to come together. Legislation (such as the Working Time Regulations or minimum wage) might have been introduced which affects work patterns or contractual terms.

On the employee side, the context too may have shifted. Individual circumstances may have altered. Children may have started school; elderly parents may have arrived to stay long term. A partner may have been made redundant, requiring the employee to earn more by going from part-time to full-time. Besides changing domestic situations, the labour market may have got tighter, giving employees more chance of alternative work, or slacker, leaving them in the opposite position.

Some of these changes may be obvious to the parties and recognized as such. In a trusting environment it may be that the parties can still work round the difference between what they agreed and what is happening in practice. At the opposite extreme, the employees may feel that their deal has been violated without acknowledgement by management. At a collective level, this might occur after a takeover, when the employees feel their relationship with their employer has shifted markedly. A new management might not understand or accept the culture of the acquired company, for example an attitude of give-and-take over working hours. At the individual level, a parallel situation might occur when a new manager comes on board and reneges on a previously agreed arrangement. If the violation is inadvertent, then monitoring the performance of the deal will have value in drawing it to the attention of the parties, which allows for the possibility of remedy. If the violation is deliberate, then it may be fatal to the basis of the bargain.

Finally, monitoring allows the parties to check the fairness of the deal. Do they still feel comfortable with it? Are they certain that the wool was not pulled over their eyes and the reality fits with what they expected?

STEP 6: RE-EVALUATE

Following a meeting to check on the performance of the deal and to see whether it is fulfilling its requirements, the final stage is to decide whether to take remedial action through renegotiation or to terminate the deal. Clearly the choice will be affected by how far the deal is failing to meet mutual needs. If the whole process has failed because of fundamental non-observance, then either party can decide to exit and find other ways to sort out the problem. If the difficulties are not so serious, then the parties can work to find an appropriate solution. Which route to go will depend not just upon the extent of the violation, and whether it is deliberate or inadvertent, but also on the quality of the existing relationship. If suspicions already exist then non-compliance will reinforce these feelings. In a more trusting relationship there may be greater tolerance of non-observance. In addition, if it is recognized that the violator of the deal had little choice, then clearly this will affect the reaction.

Renegotiation of the deal might involve some compensation against previous loss. The most obvious is management offering to pay more money to offset a loss of freedom, or to offer an alternative arrangement. Thus management might want to abandon a flexitime system, but offer early closure on Friday as an alternative. Multi-skilling might be extended with the promise of extra pay for extra skills. If the value of what is on offer matches or exceeds what it is being removed, there should be no problems. The difficulty is that some things have a greater symbolic than actual value. Flexitime might be more valued by employees – because it gives them control over some aspects of their working hours – than the actual take up of the flexibility offered might indicate. An early Friday finish might be in practical terms more useful, but it cedes control to management.

It would be naive to ignore the reality that any deal struck will reflect the respective power of the participants. Management has the power to cut numbers or change systems, processes, structures, technology and so on, but it exercises its power in relation to the external context – especially laws and the labour market – and the reaction of employees. The latter can look elsewhere for employment, take legal action, withdraw co-operation or even strike, but again their real choices are determined by the same context. Nevertheless, without a fundamental breakdown in relationships, even the less powerful party can have an impact. Usually this is the employee. If he or she feels that the deal has been broken, then sullen acceptance rather than active challenge may still have costs to the employer. Demotivated employees stop well short of 'going the extra mile'; they do the minimum necessary to comply. Productivity, customer satisfaction, quality of output all suffer.

The aim of a mutual approach is not to deny these realities, but to acknowledge them and take them into account. The objective of the deal should be to gain consensus and respect the needs of the parties. Point-scoring in negotiations might be fun at the time; putting one over your 'opponent' might give you short-term advantage. In the end, these tricks are futile. Long-term success can be achieved when the employer and employee are both committed to the deal and want to see it through, if at all possible. This means it has to be balanced. It cannot require unconditional demands being placed on the workforce (complete flexibility) in return for heavily conditional promises in return (job security dependent upon productivity increases, cost reductions, profits rising, etc.). The bargain cannot be what Bill Morris, General Secretary of the Transport and General Workers Union, has described as the 'bacon and egg' partnership – total commitment from one participant and merely a contribution from the other.

CHAPTER NINE

Mutuality at Work

Before summarizing what organizations need to do to make the model work, it may be helpful to give some illustrations of mutuality at work. It is not easy sometimes to distinguish between organizations that have acted out of self-interest, with incidental benefits to employees, from those where mutuality is genuinely present. The distinguishing feature of a mutual approach is that there is purposive intention. An organization that acts in a mutual way should see benefits to employees as a good thing, an end in itself. Mutuality is prompted by a wider social philosophy that values the contribution of employees and recognizes their needs, as well as appreciating that there may be a bottom-line benefit.

In practice enlightened self-interest can look very much like mutuality. Perhaps this does not matter, so long as the result is mutually beneficial. However, if mutuality is to be sustained, it should ultimately be a self-conscious process.

The illustrations below loosely follow the steps of the model.

RESPONDING TO THE ENVIRONMENT

Understanding the environment within which organizations and their employees operate is something that is to be found in any good strategic thinking process. Sometimes called environmental scanning, sometimes PEST (political, economic, social and technological) analysis, it should feed into the debate about the business direction. The danger is that this analysis is not well connected with decision making – it is merely window dressing, while managers choose to do what they always intended. But there are examples where organizations have used PEST analysis to understand the likely issues facing them with respect to people, and respond to them.

In the case of flexible work arrangements, there are several types of organizational response to the external environment. Many relate to the fact that, as described in Chapter 2, the workforce of tomorrow is likely to be more diverse than in the past with more women workers and a greater proportion from ethnic minorities. More employees are likely to have to balance home and working life in dealing with domestic responsibilities, both of child and eldercare. Attitudes to work may change as a result.

There are, therefore, companies that have taken account of changing labour-market conditions to reframe their personnel policies or offer new benefits to employees. This has been seen especially in the area of family-friendly flexibility. Policy initiatives have been intended both to attract or retain female employees and to support wider developments in offering equal opportunities.

Support for those caring for younger children is a particularly common aspect of this approach. A Department for Education and Employment (DfEE) survey in 1996 (Forth et al., 1997) found that 77 per cent of organizations it surveyed offered some type of childcare help, taken in the broadest sense. Options on offer to employees as shown in this survey and others include:

- advice services to guide employees' choice of support
- nurseries in the workplace
- time off work (from career breaks, through voluntary reduced hours to paternity leave)
- homeworking
- flexible start or finish times
- vouchers to spend on childcare arrangements
- adoption leave
- job sharing
- paternity leave

- phased return from maternity leave
- financial help in the form of allowances.

Employers can see the benefits in assisting with childcare responsibilities through:

- better productivity (a local authority found that, not surprisingly, nearly all their female employees spent time at work worrying about care of their children, but, more disturbingly, half resolved any difficulties that arose while at work)
- lower absenteeism – female employees often take time off, officially or not, to deal with ill children
- better retention (the DfEE survey discovered that women were twice as likely to return to work after birth of a child if the employer provided childcare)
- quicker return from maternity leave
- using this assistance as a selling point in a recruitment campaign to attract those with children.

The Workplace Employee Relations Survey (1998) reported similar positive results from employers, with 80 per cent of respondents saying that these initiatives were introduced at minimal cost.

In another example of reacting to the changing social climate, HSBC recognized their childcare arrangements were not meeting the needs of their female employees. As a conse-

quence, they were losing a lot of good staff who did not return to work after maternity leave. Through introducing a childcare and family-friendly programme (involving career breaks, extended leave and company-supported nurseries), the proportion returning to work after maternity leave rose from 30 per cent in 1988 to 85 per cent by 1999. As Flo Armstrong, their equal opportunities officer, said: 'Employers are realising how much they stand to gain by supporting their employees. It is good for morale and for the bottom line' (Whitehead, 1999b).

Similarly, Lily Industries was prompted by shortages of labour to offer a range of options from which employees could choose. These included part-time working, job sharing and voluntary reduced hours. The hope was that these benefits would attract female staff especially (Daycare Trust, 1998).

The same issues present themselves with care of elderly or infirm relatives. Eldercare, however, has distinctive features compared with looking after the young. The most important of these is the suddenness with which the need for care can occur. Accidents, or more likely physical deterioration, can come quickly and unexpectedly. An apparently perfectly fit person can have a fall or a stroke, and go from being an independent home owner to needing constant care. Without the financial resources to deal with this situation, an employee can be

---

CASE IN POINT

Peugeot introduced a day-care centre for the care of the elderly relatives of its and other motor manufacturers' employees in the Midlands. It chose to offer help with eldercare rather than childcare because:

- it felt childcare was already well covered in the locality
- the closure of old people's homes left people with a need
- it felt that this need would

grow with the ageing of the population

- in an employee survey 150 of its staff admitted to be carers
- it had anecdotal evidence that some individuals were struggling to combine work with their responsibilities to the elderly.

The personnel director at Peugeot, Mike Judge, summed up the mutuality of the arrangement:

'People will say: "That's a nice company – they look after people". And that's a good reputation for an employer to have. I'm also convinced that it reduces sickness absence and means someone's mind can be on their work. It is an act of faith to some extent, because we can't measure the benefits, but that doesn't mean it isn't valuable' (Iziren, 1999).

faced with stressful and problematic issues, especially if the relative does not live nearby. Who is to care for the relative, and how? How long will this condition last? One new solution, of which there are as yet few examples, is for the organization to provide day-care centres for the elderly (see case in point on p. 101).

One consequence of the workforce becoming more diverse is that many employers have given greater attention to equal opportunities policies. Some organizations very explicitly make the link between the support given to carers and treating all workers equally. One life-assurance company introduced job sharing and term-time contracts under the equal opportunities banner (Neathey and Hurstfield, 1995). Littlewoods does the same and can point to a remarkable 98 per cent of women returning after maternity leave, and 30 per cent of senior management positions filled by women. Thus the company can argue that flexible work arrangements are promoting female career development, instead of parental responsibilities being a hindrance to progress (Johnson, 1999a). The Automobile Association used its approach to homeworking specifically as a means of encouraging the disabled into work (Industrial Relations Services, 1999).

Wakefield Council felt the need for a more practical demonstration of its claim to be an equal opportunities and family-friendly employer, where three-quarters of its staff are women. It provided employees with a menu of options to choose from:

- paid short-term leave (up to five days at a time and to a maximum of 15 days per annum) to deal with immediate caring difficulties
- unpaid long-term leave for more serious domestic crises
- term-time working
- temporary negotiated hours, where hours can be varied for up to a year.

Employees have the right to ask whether they can adopt any of these practices, but management has the right to refuse, with an explanation (Bigwood, 1996).

Some organizations anticipated the UK government's legislative programme, as described in Chapter 7. Littlewoods offered five days' leave to cover domestic emergencies and ten days' paternity leave, before the government legislated on the matter. Sometimes the aim is to deal with the effects of the law, but in a way that has more general benefit. Oxfordshire County Council, for example, launched a cutback on overtime to comply with the Working Time Regulations but also to link with family-friendly employment policies (*People Management*, 1999b).

There is no current legislative penalty against age discrimination, but a lot of exhortation to take account of the ageing of the workforce, as described in Chapter 2. Some organizations have deliberately altered their recruitment profile to hire older workers. This may have been done because of problems meeting their usual specification in a tight labour market or through a view that older staff are both more reliable and suitable for some forms of customer service – a position advanced by both B&Q and the Nationwide Building Society. For some individuals such work can be a godsend, particularly if the working hours are flexible, in easing them into retirement by winding down the level of employment.

Besides the family-friendly or equal opportunities agendas, there are political demands with respect to the protection of the environment. Though there is as yet no legislative requirement to reduce car use for environmental reasons – rather it is a Good Thing to do – some employers have given their support to the campaign. Vauxhall cars has had 'car free' days to encourage the use of public transport. More relevant for our purposes is the lead taken by the Highways Agency, which has adopted a 'Green Travel Plan' to address these issues. It seeks to reduce the environmental and transportation costs of commuting through greater use of home or local working.

INFORMATION FROM SURVEYS, WORKSHOPS AND TRIALS

There are many ways in which employers can gather information about their employees and the state of the employment relationship – what employees' hopes, worries and expectations are about work. Many large organizations use attitude surveys to garner employee views and feelings; fewer target them on specific policy issues such as flexible contracts or working patterns. The case in point is an example of where this happened.

CASE IN POINT

A financial services company was moving to a new form of service delivery that involved extended opening hours. Rather than impose a set of terms and conditions, it surveyed its current employees to establish the preferred patterns of working. It then determined the most appropriate contracts to be offered. The result was that absenteeism and turnover were lower on the new working hours than the old.

Tesco's partnership deal, reported below (p. 104), came out of an attitude survey which showed that employees felt that employee relations were dominated by pay issues to the exclusion of matters closer to staff's hearts, like training, careers and job security.

Focus groups or workshops can be used to gather employee views. Asda used these to discover managers' opinions on their preferred working hours, how they could fit business needs and how they could be regulated in a sensible fashion (Kodz et al., 1998). Hertfordshire County Council Social Services used workshops to decide how their flexible work arrangements would operate (Industrial Relations Services, 1999). This was both to determine who should become a mobile worker and who a homeworker, and to sort out their equipment needs.

Another way to gather information is to hold a trial in order to test a revised work pattern. The Automobile Association had a six-month pilot project to see how a home-based call-centre operation would work (ibid.). The pilot used both volunteers from existing employees and new recruits specifically recruited for the

homeworking concept. The pilot was seen to be successful both in terms of productivity gains and employee reaction.

Testing out ideas in this way may result from the efforts of a working group set up to tackle a problem. Hertfordshire County Council Social Services had to save large sums of money so set up a task group to propose how this could be done by reducing accommodation needs. Implementing the Working Time Regulations or the new consultation rules has similarly been achieved through the workings of a joint task group. Such consultative mechanisms as these have encouraged both 'sides' to see the value in co-operation over confrontation. One financial services company, for example, decided together with the relevant trades union to meet the spirit rather than the letter of the Working Time Regulations. They did this out of a philosophy of partnership to solve a common problem.

NEGOTIATING A DEAL

Negotiating a deal is in itself not unusual; doing so on a mutual basis is more so; and recognizing the needs of individuals at the same time is rarer still.

Some deals on flexibility are pretty traditional in manner: the parties bargain and the result depends upon their relative strength at the time of negotiation. Thus many deals on functional flexibility extended the areas in which employees would work, but put limits upon it. So, for example, maintenance employees might become flexible within the craft trades, but still not do any operational tasks. Similarly, there have been deals that allow temporary staff to be used only in specific and defined circumstances, for example for short-term cover or to obtain specialist skills but not to replace existing permanent staff.

The partnership deals referred to earlier are designed to improve processes in handling relationships between the parties, to avoid 'the meaningless ritual that characterizes adversarial bargaining' as described in the Tesco case (Allen, 1998). This finds expression in the creation of works councils, as at Tesco or Stagecoach. Sometimes these deals involve a trade-off between money and job security, as in the Blue Circle Cement case described in Chapter 7. Sometimes they go further and include flexibility of some kind, as in the Rover deal (p. 56). A local government agreement with trades unions in 1997 gave management the freedom to deploy people on the basis of capability, thereby removing demarcations, in exchange for improved terms and conditions (Claydon, 1998). Tesco's partnership arrangement, shown in the case in point, allows the company to pursue its business aims and respond flexibly to the market, while at the same time providing greater union involvement in business decisions.

Yet, however good the deals are, there is the doubt of whether they engage the active support of the workforce or merely their acquiescence. Tesco have tried to address this concern by trying to broaden the agenda of discussion beyond terms and conditions of employment, by setting up their works councils at all 586 UK stores and by insisting that all employees, including non-union members, select their representatives, who again may or may not be members of USDAW.

Some agreements negotiated between unions and management can facilitate individual discussions at local level. An example from the civil service is given in the case in point below.

The union itself had conferred with its members through a survey (PTC Inland Revenue, 1996), to identify which flexible work arrangements were of the most interest. Interestingly, just over half the male respondents, compared with 38 per cent of women, were attracted by the compressed working week; on the other hand, term-time working and the other forms of flexitime held more interest for women, with over 45 per cent of respondents positively inclined.

Two aspects of the PTC (now the Public and Commercial Services Union) agreement are of particular interest. Firstly, there is explicit

---

CASE IN POINT

In 1998 Tesco signed a partnership deal with USDAW (Union of Shop, Distributive, and Allied Workers). It is built on nine pillars, which include:

- high-quality individual representation of staff
- the union gaining understanding and promotion of the company's business goals
- co-operation between the parties
- the right for the union to challenge management, where it believes there to be problems
- the right for the company to retain its business flexibility.

CASE IN POINT

In 1990 the civil service concluded a national agreement with the CPSA (Civil and Public Services Association) on part-time working to apply in agencies and departments. Individual civil service agencies and departments then implement their own policy in the light of this general agreement. A Treasury policy circular, however, confirms that job sharers or part-timers may work any number of hours per week and be at any grade. The expectation is that detailed arrangements are concluded between job holder and manager. While the manager is not obliged to agree, a refusal can only be made if there are objective business reasons to do so.

At the Inland Revenue flexible work arrangements options have been taken further in an extended trial. In one IR region, employees can choose from a menu including:

- flexitime, with sub-options of
  - no core time
  - variable core time
  - compressed (for example four-day) working weeks
- part year or term-time working
- partial homeworking
- part-time work or job sharing
- working regular but non-standard hours.

recognition on the union's part that any flexible work arrangements have to work for management as well as for the staff. And secondly, it is acknowledged that interest in flexibility varies, and that some work patterns may interest only a few people. But the union states that these members 'should be given the choice of which pattern suits them' (PTC Inland Revenue, 1996).

Similarly, Littlewoods offers flexible work options, including part-time, job sharing, term-time, reduced hours and zero hours contracts. There is a job share and flexible working register to stimulate take up. Employees are encouraged to voice their needs and ideas for solving them. As far as management is concerned, Surinder Sharma, corporate equal opportunities manager, explained: 'family friendly policies are guidelines, because managers have to take into account individual circumstances. We like to encourage them to build on our policies and suggest new ways of doing things' (Johnson, 1999a). Managers are appraised on their family-friendly approach, not just on conventional business target measures.

When the Nottingham City Hospital theatre team were changing their approach to people management, all staff groups were invited at the outset to consider three types of work roster, and vote on which they preferred. Then individual discussions were held with each member of staff. Personnel explained the new arrangements on offer and how they affected staff. Employees were then free to choose whether to accept or not, or indeed to adopt them at a later date. Stephen Pugh, acting HR director, explained: 'We did it with staff, not to them' (Johnson, 1999b).

Without going as far as to make new flexible work arrangements optional, organizations can implement change in a way that recognizes individual circumstances. When Autoglass introduced annual hours contracts and abolished overtime, this posed difficulties for some of their employees. To ease the transition, some customer advisers were permitted to retain rights to overtime for a limited period. In addition, those who were keen to work extra hours in excess of their annual commitment were allowed to put their names on a list to be used in the event of extra staff having to be called in (Jones and Stredwick, 1998).

Individualized arrangements can be put in the hands of the employees themselves. At Barclays Technology Services (Kodz et al., 1998) working patterns are sufficiently flexible that a manager can work shorter days in the office, leaving early in order to look after the children, but return to work at home after the children have gone to bed. MD Foods annual hours arrangements can be personalized to suit individual preferences, but there is a team context. Some team members prefer permanent nights, others permanent days; both are acceptable so long as the facility is properly staffed at all times. This has improved co-operation between colleagues. They share home telephone numbers in order to allow shift swaps to be made. As one employee described how annual hours compared with the previous situation: 'it was quite fractured before, in that there were those who did and those who didn't do overtime' (Arkin, 1998).

INFORMAL FLEXIBILITY

Many examples of flexibility do not feature in management journals or indeed in employee handbooks. They are the everyday ways in which managers give employees scope to sort out their working hours. Time was when working hours were fixed and immutable – woe betide you if you did not conform. While lateness at work should still not be condoned, there is in certain jobs more 'latitude for adjustment'. This may involve coming in later and leaving earlier because that suits the transport system, domestic responsibilities or even individual biorhythms. Working from home to get peace and quiet to write a report (or even a book!) is more common these days. It is acceptable for an employee to say that he or she needs to be at home to let the plumber in, and being able to use a laptop there makes productive working possible. Clearly opportunities for this sort of flexibility vary by type of occupation, but they also vary with the corporate culture. In some organizations managers feel fully empowered to handle employees' work patterns with discretion; in other settings, managers are fearful of precedent or senior management displeasure. Indeed, there is a fine line between abuse and its opposite. An exercise in flexibility becomes an entitlement; a manager treats every example of discretion as a concession which can quickly be withdrawn.

COMMUNICATION AND MONITORING

Some organizations see communication with their employees as the bedrock upon which employee relations rest. Sir Stuart Hampson, chairman of the John Lewis Partnership, forcefully argued the case thus:

> Sharing information needs to be second nature and I can only regret that any business needs to be forced to talk to its staff. The existence of consultative arrangements should be seen as a source of competitive advantage rather than as a burden on industry. By avoiding the conflict of an Us and Them relationship, there is a sense of common purpose within the whole enterprise, feeling that everyone is working to advance our business and that the actions of management are fair. (Involvement and Participation Association, 1999c)

Of course there is a special relationship between employer and employee at John Lewis, given the partnership nature of the company, but there are many others who would argue the benefits of open communication. Nissan, for example, includes reference to informing employees as part of its company philosophy. Where communication becomes critical is during a change programme. If, say, flexible work arrangements are being introduced for the first time, there is a strong requirement to ensure that all concerned understand the aims, objectives and implica-

tions. This means positioning the change so that employees and unions know why any adjustment is being made and what is involved. Such was the radical nature of the change, MD Foods produced a video to explain their new annual hours system. This enabled employees to take the information home to explain to their families. The company supported this with shift meetings at every site, and every employee was individually taken through the working hours and wage implications of the change. Many other organizations have used briefings and booklets to explain organizational policy and employee choices, where these exist.

Monitoring can be done from surveys. Sainsbury's has tested employee opinion of the company's IT homeworking concept (Industrial Relations Services, 1999). Oxfordshire County Council validated the introduction of a menu of flexible work arrangements that employees can choose from via an attitude survey (ibid.).

Initiatives can be supported by following up their progress at normal management meetings or those specifically convened for the purpose. MD Foods tracks how well their annual hours system is operating in quarterly reviews between management and unions (Arkin, 1998). This has allowed refinements of the scheme to be made, including greater self-management by the operational teams. Solutions to problems that arise are communicated to all managers via a newsletter.

Communication of what is going on in the business can sustain partnership deals and keep trust going. At Borg Warner Automotive, management has taken the decision to have an open book regarding the company's past financial performance, as well as its future plans (Involvement and Participation Association, 1998b).

AN INTEGRATED APPROACH

A final illustration of mutual flexibility at work is given in the case in point. This example pulls together many of the strands we have seen in the chapter.

CASE IN POINT

Using a partnership approach in local government, Bristol City Council launched a pilot scheme to provide options in working hours, including varying the length of the working week. This was to give more choice for employees to fit their job to their domestic lives and at the same time improve services to their customers. A survey of employees found the scheme to be attractive to men as well as to women. Reasons given for the popularity of the scheme included having the time to meet caring responsibilities, to study or to engage in leisure pursuits.

In designing the scheme, management was aware that flexibility could mean long hours and little benefit to the employees. So, together with the participation of trades unions, there was a conscious aim to meet both parties' needs. Finally, there was a positive wish to place decision making in the hands of teams and individuals who had to take responsibility for their own time management (Walsh, 1999a).

As you can see, Bristol City Council:

- gathered data
- challenged shibboleths
- positively chose a mutual approach
- involved the trades unions
- pushed responsibilities downwards.

This case demonstrates the value of an integrated approach to flexibility with mutuality at the core of both its process and content.

As Table 9.1 shows, mutual benefits are to be found in all types of flexibility.

Table 9.1 The mutual benefits to be obtained from flexibility

Arrangement	Employer benefits	Employee benefits
multi-skilling	improved productivity	enhanced skills
agency labour	short-term cover	work variety and breaks
flexible working hours	better labour input	domestic needs suited
outsourcing	quality/cost improvement	better career development
gain- or profit sharing	paybill linked to results	provides financial incentive
teleworking	reduced overhead costs	less travel time/cost

Adapted from Reilly (1998)

CHAPTER TEN

The Prerequisites for Making Mutuality Work

The examples of experience in the previous chapter should indicate that the meeting of certain preconditions is likely to ensure that mutuality works. This chapter will explore these prerequisites to success in more detail.

DECISION MAKING WHERE IT COUNTS

The model described is predicated on organizations' discovering individual needs and responding to them in the light of their own business requirements. This approach should push decision making down to where it is easiest to discover individual needs and to respond to them. In most organizations this means giving the responsibility to first line supervision or management.

As I write this I hear the cries of my former HR colleagues: what about the problems of managerial inconsistency, favouritism, discrimination, soft- or hard-heartedness? These of course are real worries, but, if we are serious about getting flexible work arrangements that meet the needs of both parties, then we have to take these risks. We propose that risks are taken because of the potential prize. We have seen, especially in the Barber research (see p. 89), that line managers have a significant impact on how employees respond to work. As the research indicated, managers who support staff, value them as individuals, keep them informed and allow them to grow and develop, generate positive employee attitudes. This is just the sort relationship we wish to foster. It brings clear business benefits, while at the same time providing satisfying employment for staff. The area of flexible work arrangements must be one of the best situations in which these positive relationships should flourish. Managers keep employees informed of business developments, but listen to employees' own changing circumstances. Managers respect individual needs. Employees recognize the business imperatives.

So we need to see decentralized decision making. This means passing responsibility from the corporate centre of organizations to operating units and, within these, from top management down to front-line supervision. It also requires devolvement of personnel activities from the HR function to the line. Devolving responsibility to line managers is beneficial in itself because it locates decision making at the point where it is most appropriate, that is at the interface between management and the managed. It gives managers the chance to deal with the circumstances as they find them and adapt solutions to the situation they face.

And decisions can be pushed even further down the hierarchy. Empowerment has become a dirty word in many people's eyes because the reality too often meant more work, not greater responsibility. Where real transfer of power takes place there can be genuine benefits. British Airports Authority at Glasgow airport has devised 'empowerment zones' for its multi-skilled maintenance staff. Depending upon the task, they may have full or partial authority to act, or they may have to seek authorization from management. As the works service manager put it: 'The supervisor's traditional approach was "you will do this." The new culture means staff are more responsible, with more authority and freedom to carry out day to day duties. Supervisors have had to change their approach and now act more as facilitators' (Pollock, 2000).

CREATING A POLICY FRAMEWORK

Devolving responsibility and decentralizing power will only work well if there are policy frameworks within which localized decision making takes place. But here again, there is a need for a fresh approach. Personnel policies have too often been overly prescriptive. They have laid down the law. They have deliberately given managers little freedom of action, fearing that if they did, managers would make poor decisions – inconsistent, biased, discriminatory, and so on.

As many of the more progressive organizations have determined, this approach is disempowering of line managers precisely at a time when they are being encouraged to take greater responsibility for many aspects of their duties. In place of prescription, enabling personnel policies should be the order of the day. This means setting broad guidelines within which managers can operate. This might mean providing the sort of menu of options offered within the Inland Revenue trial or the scope for building on policy as practised by Littlewoods.

Guidelines will still have to be clear about the legal and contractual implications of the choices on offer. Managers cannot be left to choose whether a contract offers membership of a pension fund or not. They must be reminded of equal opportunities obligations. It must be made clear that any decisions must be made on objective grounds and be capable of being defended if challenged. But within the framework, managers should be left to manage. HR staff can provide the broad policies, but even these should be constructed with input from both managers themselves and from employees, and their representatives. Thereafter, HR staff should see their role as advising managers on the application of policy, especially the legal implications, and employees on their rights and the choices open to them.

RECOGNIZING INDIVIDUAL NEEDS

If the model we have described is going to work, some line managers will have to adjust their way of thinking. In particular, managers have to understand and respect the differing needs of staff. This means that they cannot simply lump everybody together as a single entity. It means that they cannot get away with saying that the union is responsible for protecting employee interests, and therefore one's personnel responsibilities are discharged by dealing with union representatives. This has too often been the cop-out in the past. What we are talking about is taking an interest in what are the concerns of individual employees, their personal needs. It is a case of viewing the whole person. It means encouraging people to discuss their problems, not hide them behind other excuses, such as sickness. This may be an uphill struggle, given that the BT Forum discovered that 61 per cent of employees surveyed felt unable to discuss home issues at work, or indeed vice versa (Foster, 1996).

So are we proposing a return to the welfare role that was once performed by personnel and is now to be devolved to the line? If so, how can it work in a world of organizational turbulence, where jobs change rapidly, companies appear and disappear at staggering rapidity, where downsizing exercise follows downsizing exercise? Moreover, the line managers who are being asked to perform this role may themselves be suffering from overwork and insecurity, as the Institute of Management survey reported (Institute of Management, 1997).

There are two answers to this complaint. Firstly, we would reiterate that if organizations are to be successful in the future they must be able to maximize the performance of their employees, since this will be the key to achieving competitive advantage. As the MD of British Chrome and Chemicals told a DTI study: 'There is no other source of our competitive advantage. Others can copy our investment, technology and scale – but NOT the quality of our people' (Department for Trade and Industry, 1997a). And, we have repeatedly pointed out, the way to generate high levels of employee contribution is through people management practices that involve, encourage and energize those at work.

The second point to be made is that we have had a tendency, especially in the 1980s, to consider only the economic aspect of life. We have emphasized market relationships; we have responded to materialistic aspirations; we have assumed that it is only money that talks. While there is no denying that there is an acquisitive side to our society, this is not the whole story. People also come to work for social reasons, to have contact with others, to chat, gossip and discuss the issues of the day. The social person also has hopes at work that are not purely money oriented. People want to take pride in their work. They want to gain pleasure in what they do and derive satisfaction from doing it well. They use their employment to boost their sense of self-esteem. In all these responses to work we can see that feelings matter. Employees seek emotional as well as financial well-being. They may understand the uncertainties inherent in their continued employment, but they hope and expect that note will be taken of their feelings, that they will be treated with dignity and respect. If they are not, if their managers do not behave appropriately, then employees will leave, given an alternative possibility. One employer I visited realized the importance of this point. Unable to improve terms and conditions in a fiercely competitive market, the company sought to adopt a management style that encouraged and supported employees. It benefited from lower wastage and even re-recruited staff who had found their treatment with other organizations less than appealing by comparison.

There is plenty of research (for example, Tyler and Bies, 1990, or Thompson, 1993) to demonstrate that it is procedural justice, rather than distributive justice, that counts in people's judgement of fairness. It is the process of how I am treated rather than what is the outcome that counts most in people's minds. Ask those who have experienced redundancy, and the discussion is less about the causes and more about the process by which it happened. Evidence of this fact is the growth of the outplacement industry, with its emphasis on handling job reductions in a sensitive and humane way.

There are relevant parallels with our model of mutual flexibility. If managers are to make this work they have to deal with individuals as individuals, with the whole person, feelings and all. They have to show respect for the individual, to avoid biases and to stick to the agreed rules.

INVESTMENT OF TIME AND ENERGY

There are clearly costs in managing employee relations in this way. It is a lot easier and quicker to treat employees as one collective mass or to relate to them only through their representatives, though even here to involve employees through indirect consultative channels can be expensive. The most obvious cost is one of time to be invested. Supervisors will need to talk to individual employees. They will need to explain work requirements. They will have to listen to employees' reactions. They will have to take action in response to what emerges as the best balance between corporate and individual requirements.

However, these costs should not be exaggerated. Good supervision knows its staff. Managers talk to their employees about their responsibilities, their tasks and any constraints on their ability to meet these targets, be it a shortage of resources, lack of training, or inadequate time. In most large organizations there is the annual performance discussion, which increasingly covers all levels of employee. This provides a formal opportunity to talk over work-related matters, and, if it has a development aspect, to discuss future aspirations. So, both formally and informally, two-way contact is probably already well established. Moreover, through briefing sessions managers can keep their staff abreast of the state of business and the implications for their own work group.

One of the benefits of self-managed teams is that these sorts of issues are dealt with between colleagues. Only in a case of policy direction or where differences cannot be reconciled will the supervisor be asked to intervene.

KEEPING AN OPEN MIND

Another characteristic of this mutuality approach, on the part of managers, is being prepared to hear the views of others and keep an open mind. In other words, managers should avoid a natural tendency to pre-decide situations, to know the answer before the question is proposed. It is all too easy for the busy manager to rush to the solution on what they might reasonably believe to be a good knowledge of the facts, instead of stopping to ask. 'I know Claire only wants to work full-time because she can't afford to drop her wages'; 'I know Bill won't do shifts because he's a single parent and can't arrange childcare for evenings or nights'. At least such a supervisor is sensitive to the needs of the staff, but he or she might have the facts wrong. Claire might be feeling that full-time work is too much of a struggle to look after her children and aged mother, and might be quite keen to reduce her working hours now that her partner is in a more secure job; Bill might be in a new relationship that allows him to be more flexible in his working hours than previously.

The same problem occurs in more formal consultative structures. Managers go through the motions of obtaining the views of employee representatives but have already made up their minds. Management thereby gives the impression of involvement without the substance. This may be because managers find it hard to delegate decisions. They wish to avoid losing control over the situation or they believe they know best. They may be pressed for time or events may be outside their control, determined by more senior management. Whatever the reason, employees who sense that they attend meetings only as a matter of form will soon cease to attach much credibility to the process. As we have seen before, such forms of participation will then wither on the vine. Instead, managers need to acknowledge that employees can contribute to decision making. As a Tesco manager involved in the partnership deal reported earlier pointed out: our employee forums 'are there to canvass views, since no one has a monopoly on good ideas' (Involve-

ment and Participation Association, 1998a).

Being open to the possibility of change and taking the trouble to hear your employees' hopes and fears is part of keeping an open mind. The other part is responding positively to what you hear. This means having respect and understanding for the needs of your staff. It may mean seeing the other person's point of view, recognizing that there are two sides to the equation. What you learn may not be what you want to hear. You, the manager, may have devised a neat scheme to meet the cost challenge placed upon you by your own boss. It may involve changing people's working hours and combining tasks. But it may not be within the capacity of your employees to cope with what you propose. Not all may be able to change hours. They may not have the skills to take on the new tasks. You are then faced with a choice: do you drive the change through despite their misgivings and concerns, or do you do your best to take account of them? This could be by giving more notice of the adjustment in hours – so childcare can be rearranged – or by providing more coaching or training to give staff the confidence that they can deal with different tasks. You can choose to alter the work schedules so that you meet most of your objectives, though not all, and help some of your team cope more easily.

This sort of practical give and take might seem normal behaviour to the reader. We hope it is, but fear it is not always the case. There are the horror stories reported in Chapter 6, but there is also the suspicion that such is the pressure on managers to deliver that even the best are forced to cut corners and push for solutions without sufficient regard for the consequences on others.

MANAGEMENT SKILLS

The sort of situation we have described will test the skills of managers. It is an oft-repeated complaint in organizations up and down the country that management skills are not what they should be. For example, if you ask why a performance management system is not working, you may be told that the problem is not with the design but with the operation, and that it is the inability of managers to give time, importance and skill to the task which is the cause. These failings of managers are more often than not attributed to the criteria for promotion – technical ability or successful delivery of results is given a predominant place; interpersonal skills are ignored.

Asking managers to use the model described may test their capabilities. This is especially so because there are some distinctive features about operating in the way we propose that add to the managerial challenge. Managers will face the following issues:

● they have choice in what they decide: they do not have to accept the present situation; they can decide to make changes
● they should be thinking of how the work is best completed, not in terms of the current configuration of jobs
● they need to determine the *real* rationale for any change, that it is not simply following the latest fad or fashion
● they will be required to embrace change: this means opening the mind to new possibilities, assessing risks against benefits and addressing stakeholder needs
● they should aim to tell employees clearly what is expected of them and why there is a need to change, and seek employee consent to any job alteration
● they will have to know when the circumstances are right to trust people, be it in homeworking (when they are out of sight) or flexitime (if it is a self-policing system), and to find ways of ensuring that the trust is reciprocated
● they will have to manage differences in work patterns, contracts or location. This may include managing boundaries across people, such as between a contractor's employees and the organization's own staff
● they will have to oversee the training and development of all those working for them, whatever their employment status
● they will have to be aware of the legal framework within which they are operating
● they will have to know something of the

labour market context, the relative position of supply and demand; terms and conditions that might be tolerated when jobs are scarce may not be in a tight labour market
● they will have to accept not just the legitimacy of the employee point of view, but the worth of their opinions.

These challenges are made all the harder by the rapidity of change within organizations, be it of structure or personnel. The multiplicity of deals done is matched by the number of people doing the deals. Some are clear-cut, as between the manager and the employee. Some are more indirect: between another 'agent' of the organization, for example a recruitment officer, and the employee or his or her (union) representative. Other deals are even more indirect, such as with third-party contractors. This makes consistency hard to achieve and confusion hard to avoid. Agreements made by others may not be explicit or written down. Even at the recruitment stage, when offer and acceptance should be at their clearest, there may be promises made or understood to have been made, which the manager is expected to deliver. For example, a recruit might have requested an early departure on a Friday afternoon to travel to see elderly relatives at the weekend. This message may not have been conveyed to the manager responsible, who may or may not have problems in accommodating this wish. The longer the distance between the principal parties and the greater the number of intervening participants, the greater the risk of misunderstanding.

EMPLOYEE CONTRIBUTION

It should not be assumed that all the responsibilities lie at the feet of management. Employees have a critical role to play if mutual flexibility is to work.

Firstly, employees need to accept the business realities. They need to be informed of what the organizational imperatives are. They need to realize that their future employment depends upon the success of the enterprise. This used to be true only of parts of the private sector, but downsizing and restructuring in the public sector have made the message relevant here too. Understanding of the business realities has to be translated into recognizing that their representatives need support when they secure agreements that entail short-term pain, but longer-term gain. The partnership deals reported earlier frequently make such a balance, where relative job security has been secured in exchange for changes in working practices.

Secondly, employees need to get beyond any anti-flexibility rhetoric and recognize the benefits it can provide. These benefits may be to the advantage of the organization or to themselves – hopefully to both. Employees should understand when the flexible work arrangements have been constructed to meet business needs, and hence see their necessity. They should also be able to spot their value to themselves. For example, on the one hand functional flexibility may present some people with problems in stretching them to learn new skills, but on the other it also allows staff to add to their capabilities, thereby improving their marketability. Thus mutual advantage is obtained.

Thirdly, employees have to accept differentiation, and even value diversity. Employees must accept that they do not always benefit; it may be that other individuals do so because of their own particular circumstances. They have to recognize that a solution to one person's problem or need does not set a precedent for everyone else. Organizations cannot be run on the basis of what happened in Dickens's *Great Expectations* – because Pip got a half day's holiday to visit Mrs Haversham, Orlick, his workmate, claimed one as well: 'Now, master! Sure you're not going to favour only one of us? If Young Pip has a half-holiday, do as much for Old Orlick.... No favouring in this shop. Be a man!' Orlick had a point in equity but not in terms of utility. As Joe, the master, retorted: 'Why, what'll you do with a half-holiday, if you get it?' Nevertheless, Joe was soft or generous enough to concede Orlick's claim. As readers of that story will remember, it all ended in tears, or at least blows, in the argument that ensued

between Joe's wife and Orlick over what she saw as the master's foolishness in wasting wages on 'idle hulkers'. This demonstrates well the difficulty for employers in dealing fairly with their employees, yet at the same time responding to their particular needs – all within the context of running a successful business. If everyone acts like Old Orlick, then managers will tend to be unresponsive however valid the individual request, for fear of stirring up a hornets' nest.

Managers should be in a position to say 'Smith can leave early today to pick up his children from school' or 'Jones can switch day shifts to this week from next to allow his partner to go into hospital' without having to offer the same to one and all. In fact, these examples are the easy ones. In organizations where there are self-managed teams, these sort of decisions are made by the group themselves. What is harder is that in a differentiated workforce some may be on one set of terms and conditions, because they are employed by an employment agency, while others may be employed on a different basis by the provider of an outsourced service. Even within the same organization contracts may vary between those employed on permanent and temporary contracts. So when a bank holiday comes round, some individuals may be off work; some be working at premium rates; and for a third group it may be a normal day's work. It may be hard to say so, but these differences have to be accepted in this flexible world.

Fourthly, much flexibility is predicated on greater employee involvement at work. This might be as part of a self-managed team or in scheduling the workload oneself. This calls for a more active attitude to employment. Some workers have been somewhat passive: it's management's right to manage, and ours to resist if our interests are threatened. This apathy, whether it is related to ideology, lack of interest in the world of work or even lack of self-confidence, will inhibit the success of any changes. If what on offer does genuinely provide mutuality, then it is incumbent on employees to welcome it and make it work. But, by the same token, employers need to encourage employees to participate by demon-strating that it will be worth the effort. Nothing turns people off more than the feeling that having tried to be involved, management ignores the results. The syndrome of a working group's proposals being neglected, or worse rejected, in favour of the management's opinion is the classic example of this situation. But conducting employee opinion surveys and doing nothing with the messages they convey is another. Employees are more likely to take an interest if they see some positive end result. This might be more money (for example, through skill-based pay), greater job security (in exchange for greater flexibility) or better/easier work conditions (for example, homeworking).

Many of these difficulties can be overcome by good communication: for example, manage-ment setting clear terms of reference for a working group or indicating the limits to what impact the results of an attitude survey could have. Some benefits can be achieved through training employees to maximize the benefits of their participation, be it in formal structures such as works councils or in individual discus-sions about flexible work arrangements. But employees must also respond in kind by giving value to any training courses on offer and by recognizing what is and is not possible for managers to do.

GETTING TRADES UNIONS ONSIDE

Just as employees have to adapt to the new sort of employment relationship we describe, so too do trades unions. Many are used to a collectivist and adversarial approach, which is in complete contradiction to the flexibility model suggested. They are used to 'distribu-tive' forms of negotiation, where the parties have opposing interests and find it hard to accept the other side's position. For some this is born of the view that labour relations are an aspect of the class struggle, where labour has to extract the maximum it can from the repre-sentatives of capital. Such people reject whole-heartedly the HRM model that suggests that there is a common purpose to enterprises.

They dislike the individualization of terms and conditions of employment that threatens collectivization. They often object to forms of employee participation, and implicitly forms of mutuality, because they believe that these are attempts by management to undermine the trades union's position and weaken it through divide and rule. Those trades unionists who agree to partnership deals are accused of selling out to management. Geoff Martin of Unison explained this position in a *Guardian* interview at the time of the 1999 TUC Confer-ence:

> It is all this partnership stuff again which ignores the age old conflict between capital and labour. These conflicts don't just get resolved because Blair thinks it would be a good idea for us all to get along. If the Tolpuddle Martyrs had forged a partnership with the Dorset land-owners, then there would be no TUC Congress for Blair to address. What the PM wants is employees and unions which are house trained. When Blair uses the term 'partner-ship' it is code for workers' subser-vience. (*Guardian*, 1999b)

Without necessarily going this far, other trades unionists regard doing deals on flexibility as leading, however inadvertently, towards work intensification, cost-cutting and increased job insecurity.

What we propose is closer to the 'integrative' form of bargaining. This tries to increase the possibility of satisfying both sides. It recognizes the legitimacy of the other point of view and aims for win/win solutions rather than the win/lose results that characterize distributive bargaining. The latter tends to inhibit free communication, exaggerates differences and makes a virtue out of conflict. Integrative bargaining should maximize 'joint welfare' by seeking end results that satisfy both parties sufficiently.

Some trades unions have adopted partner-ship with employers as their preferred position.

This clearly supports the notion of integrative bargaining. The GMB, for example, has produced booklets proclaiming the virtues of partnership deals with management, and its leaders have shared platforms with senior managers jointly to extol the virtues of their approach. The TGWU together with Manpower has hosted a joint conference on temporary workers, to demonstrate that it is not against the use of agency staff. Unison, AEEU, USDAW, MSF and other unions have concluded partnership deals with employers.

However, these 'enlightened' views are not always extended to promoting flexibility at the workplace. Yet it is precisely here that mutual flexibility will succeed or not. We talked of the need for organizations to devolve power and responsibility: trades unions have to do the same if mutual deals are to be satisfactorily concluded. The union leadership can set frameworks and provide encouragement, and this is to be welcomed, but the attitudes of shop stewards, and the like, are critical to the actual employee relations in the workplace.

Union representatives will have to accept the business realities, as the partnership approach makes clear. They need to understand where management is coming from; what the reasons are for any proposed change. They may legitimately and usefully press management to justify their ideas, thereby reducing the risk that these proposals are simply following fad or fashion. In the end they will have to accept the employer's view on the merits of the case, given the environment within which the organization is operating. This may not be easy. As an AEEU convenor at Alstom Gas Turbines explained:

> There was nothing difficult about saying 'no', but it did not get you very far. So when we started down this path [of a partnership approach] it felt risky, but the pay off for our members has been enormous: better job security, higher standards of training and a chance to use our ideas to secure the firm's future.
> (Trades Union Congress, 1999b)

In striking a deal the union along with management will need to recognize the interests of individual employees. This has not always been the case. Both parties have found it convenient to satisfy the majority, and not be too concerned with minority concerns. Trades unions are democratic organizations, so unlike management they do need to take account of their members' views if they are to survive. Nevertheless, unions have tended to argue for uniform arrangements. If Jones is to have his compassionate leave, then so should Smith and Bloggs, even if their cases are different. Management then ends up saying 'no' to Jones for fear of having to say 'yes' to Smith and Bloggs. It is the dead hand of precedent at work. The union approach can also mean satisfying the lowest common denominator. Technicians, trades unions have argued, cannot be paid extra for their added contribution because the money is not available to those without the skills or training. Instead trades union representatives will have to accept differences in the same way as managers and employees. As Patricia Hewitt, then at the Institute for Public Policy Research, put it: 'the challenge to the trades union movement is to find new ways of using their collective strength to achieve benefits which different people will enjoy in different ways at different times of their lives' (Hewitt, 1993).

This is not to say that trades unions should accept discrimination or favouritism. Nor should they stop fighting for equivalent rights across the categories of employment: they have a role to play in preventing exploitation. This is especially true where the power balance clearly favours the employer, either because of the labour market situation or because of the management's relative negotiating skills. There will also be occasions where bargaining will emphasize the divergent interests and a common solution will not be possible. There are inherent tensions in the relationship between employer and employee that are the result of the need to satisfy different requirements. Employees want to increase earnings, while companies strive to raise profits. These differences should not be denied, but equally they should not be overemphasized. Mutual understanding is key. As one union full-time official put it to a company chief executive: 'If you think staff, I'll get my members to think business.' The point about mutuality is that it is based on shared aims: employees can only increase their wages if profits rise, and companies may only become more profitable if they have a committed and motivated workforce.

Any trades union crusade to protect the employee's position should recognize this fact. Moreover, it should not be pursued in a way that prevents individuals meeting their needs in the own way. Just as trades unions are increasingly providing services to their individual members, so should they accept that a 'one size fits all' approach does not serve the interests of employees. And failing to appreciate individual needs not only does their members a disservice, but also can leave the union looking foolish. Union leaders will lose credibility if employees positively respond to a management initiative that they have opposed. One transport company battled for years to get their trades unions to accept new work rotas that would improve productivity and suit employees. After long resistance the unions conceded that if their members wished to voluntarily sign up to the revised patterns that would be acceptable. Forty per cent of employees jumped at the chance to alter their work arrangements, as these fitted in better with their lives at home.

However, it is also possible that trades unionists can play a leading role in enlightening their members to the realities of life and in overcoming deep-seated prejudice. The TUC is keen to promote examples where negotiation with the unions has overcome initial objections from employees. One such occurred in a hospital trust where management wanted to extend the hours of the radiography service. The existing workers did not want to change their hours so, following discussions with the unions, a compromise was agreed: part-timers would be recruited to work the unsociable hours and the regular staff would provide absence cover for the part-timers.

Another example comes from the BMW investment in Rover saga. In 1999, to save the Longbridge plant, the workforce accepted work arrangements that were more flexible. However, when it came to implement the deal at the Land Rover plant at Solihull, some workers objected to the introduction of a Friday night shift because it ate into their weekends. Sporadic industrial action followed. The union leadership backed the management. Tony Woodley, national officer of the TGWU, said that management was entirely within its rights as this was part of the agreement that had been made.

The danger for the trades unions in these circumstances is that they are seen as management stooges, incapable of properly defending their members' interests. Union representatives may have had a say in the implementation of company plans – a good thing in itself – but have had little influence over the direction of change. Most trades unionists can tell tales of done deals being rejected by a membership that concluded that they had been sold out, or of shop stewards being voted out for taking too 'conciliatory' a line with the employers. Sometimes the problem has arisen because neither management nor employee representatives have been able to successfully communicate problems facing them. This may be in part because of confidential knowledge they share that cannot be passed on, or it may be that communication only happens at times of crisis and the workforce is ill-prepared for the facts of life.

So the trades union adjustment to mutual flexibility has to go hand in hand with change in the attitudes of employees. Both need a level of maturity that recognizes the realities of the world while still adhering to their basic principles.

For the unions this has to operate at all representative levels. It is no good if trades union leaders argue the case for partnership deals on public platforms but do not support examples of mutuality in practice. At the other extreme are trades unions that appear to their colleagues in other unions to have gone too far in satisfying the employer. The so-called 'sweetheart' deals with no-strike agreements and single union representation seem to their critics to deny employees their right to challenge management behaviour. So the balance to be struck is between acting as true defenders of employee interests, while at the same time operating in a way that acknowledges the pressures employers are under.

DEVELOPING TRUST

In making mutuality work, management has to develop skills in effecting change successfully. These are essential given the organizational turbulence that exists at present and is unlikely to ease. This means that there will be more and more cases where managers are obliged to find the means to adjust working patterns, flex labour supply still further, externalize activities or alter work duties. It means employees and their representatives will have to understand these pressures.

As my colleagues and I have argued elsewhere (Herriot et al., 1998), to deal with these transitions successfully managers will need to have the trust of its workforce – and vice versa. Management needs to be confident that employees will deliver their side of any bargain. Putting your trust in others makes you exposed to risk, makes you vulnerable to the weaknesses, inadequacies or, even, bad intentions of the other party. But the rewards of such risk may be found, not only in lower transaction costs, but in developing a culture that is not easily transferable or copiable – in other words a source of competitive advantage.

Trust can be secured when the following conditions are met:

- employees believe that managers will fulfil their side of any bargain, and vice versa, at least in so far as it is within their power to do so
- neither side expects the other to deceive them by giving misleading, untruthful, incomplete or partial information
- employees especially, but also managers to a lesser extent, believe that the other party has the competence to deliver
- both parties expect that their needs will be

respected, that they will not be deliberately harmed.

In other words we are talking about reciprocal obligations. Trust from employees in their managers is likely to be stronger if past behaviour suggests that they have been worthy of trust, that is they have delivered what they said they were going to do. It is likely to be more forthcoming if people feel secure in their environment and if they feel they have some control over events rather than being merely victims of them.

Managers will choose to talk to employees and their representatives if they believe they can air ideas without producing an ill-considered reaction; if they can speak confidentially of upcoming initiatives without the risk of finding themselves quoted in the newspaper the following day; if they can pass on bad news without the fear that the messenger will be shot! Managers will then consult at an early stage and test out their initial thoughts, knowing that they will receive a constructive answer.

The circumstances where reciprocal trust is necessary abound in the flexible world. Such trust is the 'social lubricant' that allows organizations to operate properly. In functional flexibility, employees need to trust their employers that breaking down traditional barriers will lead to investment in skill development and not exploitation. Employers want to be assured that such investment will be rewarded by commitment to use new skills. Organizations have to offer training and workers to accept it. Some forms of temporal flexibility require a trusting environment: flexitime is a system that can work well but equally can be misused. Annual hours contracts may be more successful where the management of the rotas is left to the teams themselves. Supervision trusts the teams to discharge this responsibility fairly and the teams repay that trust. Overtime is ripe for abuse if the conditions of trust do not apply.

Home or mobile working is also underpinned by trust. Employers need to be assured that work is being undertaken productively and efficiently, especially where it is not easily measurable. Employees at home want to know that they are getting their fair share of tasks. Where trust is not present this sort of flexibility will not even start to operate. For example, Charles Handy (1995) quotes an interview he had with a journalist in a noisy newsroom. When asked why the discussion could not have taken place somewhere quieter, the journalist replied: 'Because they [the editors] want me where they can see me. They don't trust me.' One cannot see locational flexibility operating for this newspaper!

HR AS A FACILITATOR OF CHANGE

The human resource function has an important role to play in developing mutual flexibility. This may begin by building organizational support for change, by arguing the merits of mutual flexibility. This may either mean convincing management colleagues that there are other better ways of working, or it might mean insisting that getting employee support is a prerequisite for success. Once the broad picture is in place, HR should lay out the context within which the managers and employees do their 'deals'. This might involve specifying 'the rules of the game'. For example, how will trials and pilots work? What will the role of employee representatives be? Next, there needs to be a policy framework within which any agreement must operate. This might include: a premium paid for out-of-hours working; an end-of-contract bonus for fixed-term contractors to ensure their retention for the duration of the contract; or the permissible size of time credit or debit in an annual hours agreement.

Another task for HR is to monitor how well flexibility is working. Some organizations require that any deals are registered with HR so that they can check that there are no policy implications, or breaches of the rules. HR might wish to publicize particular deals as examples of good practice. Monitoring should then go on to consider issues such as:

- are there problems of management inconsistency in policy application?

- are managers getting the advantages they should from the flexible work arrangements on offer?
- are they sufficiently aware of the options they have?
- what are employees' views of policy and practice?
- do trades union or employee representatives have concerns?

This process is immeasurably better if the organization has been clear from the outset on what its objectives are, what it is seeking to achieve. This allows success criteria to be developed so that outcomes can be monitored. All change processes have their costs and benefits: what organizations need to know is whether what was expected beforehand is realized in practice.

A third task for HR is to provide management with high-quality labour market information. This means giving managers data on labour market trends – how tight or loose the labour market is for particular occupational groups in specific locations. This should guide their choices in resourcing, so they are mindful of what may or may not be appropriate.

Finally, HR staff should advise on the legal aspects of flexibility. This means ensuring policy, practice and individual treatment conform with the law. It also requires anticipation of forthcoming legislation to see what adaptation will be necessary to comply with future law. As we saw in Chapter 7, this can be a complex business. The Working Time Regulations and Employment Relations Act are difficult to apply. Interpretation of legislation at UK and European level complicates matters, since it can seemingly extend or restrict the rights of employees. But those organizations that are forward-thinking in sensing the legal direction can gain advantage from being in the vanguard of change.

It should not be supposed that HR has only a passive role to play. In many organizations it is the HR function that is pushing for change against reluctant managers. This may be precisely because HR is aware of the 'big picture', both internal and external. They may know the cost and competitive pressures on the business, but they also can anticipate the implications of forthcoming legislation or realize the requirements to attract and retain staff. HR needs to put these messages across to line managers, who may be more preoccupied in meeting day-to-day targets. This may mean holding workshops to paint the environmental picture, identify options for change and realize where the real obstacles lie.

ENSURING HR POLICY INTEGRATION

A great danger with any form of HR intervention is that it occurs as a stand-alone initiative. Many organizations have found that they have not developed integrated approaches to HR policy. Thus they may have introduced a new reward framework without consideration being given to performance assessment, or a personal development plan concept may have been launched without consideration for the implications for the training resource. The same risks occur with changing the organizational approach to flexibility.

Firstly, there may be an effect on recruitment. If the organization wishes to engage workers through an agency rather than by direct recruitment, then the number of staff engaged in recruitment will fall, but those that remain will need different skills – those of the contract manager. If, instead, these temporary staff are hired directly on short-term contracts, then organizations will have to accept:

- greater recruitment activity, given a higher turnover of staff
- a switch of emphasis in recruitment positioning, less focused on longer-term engagement, more on short-term need
- a possible change in recruitment criteria, less concerned with career attributes, more with job-specific knowledge
- more careful monitoring of the external market because the organization is likely to be tapping into it more frequently
- larger administrative cost because there are more on- and off-payroll entries to be made.

Similarly, if the organization is prepared to offer a wider range of working patterns, in hours or location, then recruitment staff need to be geared up to explain the various permitted permutations of pay and conditions offered, and administrative staff will need systems to keep records of what employees have opted for.

Changing the resourcing approach also can have an impact on the organization's internal labour market. It may be that temporary staff are used where permanent staff were employed before, or these activities may have been contracted out: either way, this may have an effect on career paths. Some organizations have found that they have cut off their supply of labour to more senior positions as a result. Thus maintenance technicians had in the past progressed to supervisory and then often to managerial posts. If the technician role has been contracted out, who is to be the future supervisor? Organizations have sometimes avoided the problem by recruiting graduates at a higher level, but these may lack the shop-floor experience to manage an external contract.

Career development is also likely to be more complex where there is a high level of locational and temporal flexibility. If employees are working non-standard hours and in non-standard places, performance assessment is harder and the decisions on promotion can be tougher. Training and development will also have to adjust, as they would if there were a variety of contractual arrangements.

Selection, appraisal and development of staff will need to recognize the implications of having a flexible workforce. For example, a publishing company with 80 per cent female staff and average employee age of 32 has realized that, in a highly competitive labour market, it has to work hard to attract and retain staff. So, amongst other things, it has decided to recruit and promote people who value diversity (Dench et al., 2000). Organizations might also have to offer management training in the skills necessary to deal with flexibility. Training might aim to encourage staff to appreciate the need for personal adapt-ability and how they can get their home and work lives in balance.

Reward will need to be consistent with the approach to flexibility employed. At a simple level, this might mean being aware of the differentials between categories of worker, so that they do not get out of line. It may mean as a result taking difficult decisions over what terms and conditions to offer to whom. Fixed-term contractors may not be offered pension-able employment, but do they receive any payment in lieu of pension? If agency workers get a 3 per cent pay increase, how does the organization respond with respect to its own employees of the same type? If functional flexibility is sought, it may require supporting the acquisition and use of skills through reward. How will this bear upon the existing form of performance-related pay? Similar decisions may have to be made if there are lots of new homeworkers. Can they be treated in the same way as office workers when it comes to linking performance with pay?

In sum, changing the organization's approach to flexibility should lead to a thorough examination of all HR policies to see whether they remain robust in the new circum-stances. And any change should lead to an integrated response. As we saw in Chapter 7, there is good research evidence that 'bundles' of positive HR policies, rather than single initiatives, are likely to be more effective in maximizing employee performance. Thus gainsharing as a form of reward might be combined with self-managed teams and a proper consultative system to demonstrate that the organization values the employee contribu-tion. One-off exercises, especially where they are not consistent with other messages sent by management, might be seen by the workforce as pseudo-involvement.

The Nottingham City Hospital example of functional flexibility quoted earlier (p. 52) illustrates the power of HR policy integration. Not only was multi-skilling introduced and new roles created that crossed traditional lines of demarcation, but also a new pay and grading system was launched, the manage-ment structure was revised, terms and condi-tions relating especially to overtime were changed and work rotas were amended. The effect of the combination of these measures was to increase productivity and cut absen-teeism and wastage.

LEADERSHIP FROM THE TOP

The final but perhaps most important prere-quisite to success is that top management in any organization supports mutual flexibility. Senior managers can encourage its use, but they can also hinder its development.

A key way in which management can promote flexibility is by creating an environ-ment of trust within which the other players can act. They can do this by:

- gathering the views of all interested parties
- determining the course of action for the organization
- explaining why this route has been chosen
- delivering against this promise or, if this is not possible,
- explaining why changes have been made.

An example of what I mean may help illustrate the point. Faced with a sudden surge in orders, management decides to consult over whether it is better to cover the load with overtime, draft in some extra help by asking an agency to supply temporary staff or engage some perma-nent recruits. Management chooses to cope through a combination of overtime and agency labour. It explains that this decision is based on the expectation that the boost in demand is short term. Management then finds volunteers to work the overtime, adjusting the extra hours to suit individual needs, and responds positively to a few part-time members of staff who offer to work full-time for a short period. The balance in what is required is supplied by the agency, on the basis that the level of help might need adjustment if the number of orders changes. Management then monitors the situa-tion, and on realizing that part of the high demand seems set to last, recruits a few extra staff and reduces overtime and the supply from the agency.

In its response to the business situation, senior management will hopefully have demonstrated that it is competent: it knows what it is doing. It is reliable: it does what it says it will do. It involves the workforce in the decision making at appropriate moments and in appropriate ways, and its solutions take account of the needs of its employees. At the shop-floor level these principles can be realized in an even more mutual way so that flexibility delivers the business objectives, but in a way acceptable to staff.

The key to this process is that senior management is able to communicate what the business situation is and what action will accordingly be taken. The managers then need to demonstrate their own personal commitment to the chosen course of action. As Alan Hooper and John Potter (1999) remark: 'The most effective antidote to the fear of change is a sense of ownership and this will not happen until the reasons for the change are known.' The responsibility for doing this lies at the top. Passing the buck to more junior managers merely sends the signal that the corporate leadership does not care or believe in what is proposed.

There are various ways in which senior management can show its commitment to mutual flexibility. Managers can give speeches. They can be visibly supportive by participating in employee consultative forums. They can genuinely give responsibility to line managers to respond to employee needs. They can show empathy; even if they commit themselves 24 hours a day to their job, they have to demonstrate understanding that not everyone else will be in the same position. So they can encourage certain behaviours and provide policy backing for appropriate initiatives. For example, to show their support for a sensible home/work balance, senior managers have been known to encourage their staff to go home and not stay late working – though the cynical might say that if these managers eased up on their deadlines, people would not have to stay late in the first place. Other managers have gone further in trying to counter a tendency towards a culture of presenteeism that rewards those

who 'work' long hours by remaining at the office. The chief executive at Asda did this by reminding his managers at quarterly meetings of the importance of controlling the working hours of their subordinates (Kodz et al., 1998). If this is then backed up by assessing the performance of these subordinates in the area of people management (as Littlewoods has done – see p. 105), it is more likely that the organization will have moved from exhortation to action.

The phrase 'walking the talk' is used to convey the fact that words are not enough: support for mutual flexibility must be demonstrated by your actually doing something that indicates the value you attach to the concept. The case in point is one such example, as nothing shows greater commitment than paying for your views.

CASE IN POINT

A UK motor manufacturer was concerned about investment by its US parent being diverted to the continent because of the high costs of production in the UK.

Management persuaded the unions to agree to a deal that offered lower pay increases than competitors, greater pay flexibility and more flexibility in working hours, including an annual hours arrangement. The unions accepted that these might have to be the necessary concessions to secure jobs. To demonstrate that he himself was committed to the deal, the managing director announced that he would forgo his annual pay for a year and other senior executives their increases.

The reverse can also happen: management can signal its lack of support for representative structures by not attending meetings or treating them in a cavalier fashion. It can undermine policy plans by rubbishing them in public or undermining them in practice. By their very behaviour senior managers can convey their lack of support for initiatives. A manager who ticks people off for leaving early, however much in jest, demonstrates that he or she is not that keen on trying to make working hours more flexible. If he or she lacks conviction about a policy, this will quickly convey itself to the workforce, which will draw its own conclusions. As an interviewee put it when complaining about the top man in his organization: 'I've never seen you in training sessions like some of the CEOs I've read about. I've never seen you on my floor. The only time I see you is as a "talking head" in some well rehearsed video. These videos never answer the right questions' (Pearce, 1998).

Leaders have to see mutual flexibility work through thick and thin. Often initiatives are launched at times of business crisis: we need to save the plant, so we all have to pull together. However, if mutuality is to be enduring, its value has to be recognized when the context has changed. It is a philosophy and practice for all seasons. Management might obtain employee support to get through a crisis, but, if the benefits of mutuality are to be fully realized, when things are going well in the business there is all the more reason to build upon earlier success – and vice versa. Many organizations have abandoned their consultative mechanisms because of the perceived exigencies of the situation. More often than not this is down to the senior management's forgetting to bring their employees with them, or deliberately ignoring them because they expect them to cause 'trouble'. This may bring short-term success, but it is bought at the price of making employees less likely to believe management the next time they call for a common effort to solve a shared problem.

Leadership has to provide continuity across time, and especially across management succession. Particular chief executives may inspire an organization with a vision of mutuality and employee participation, but this may not be shared by his or her successor.

CHAPTER ELEVEN

The Constraints and the Limits to Flexibility

It should not be assumed through reading this book that there are no problems with introducing flexible work arrangements. There are constraints on what can sensibly be done and there are also examples where matters have gone wrong despite the good intentions of the parties.

In this chapter we will review the problem areas at a general and specific level. The following chapter will consider ways in which mutuality might help solve or mitigate the effects of these difficulties.

GENERAL PROBLEMS

RHETORIC

As I indicated right at the beginning of the book, the concept of flexibility suffers from too much rhetoric, not just from politicians, but also from management and unions. Sometimes management makes the mistake of believing its own rhetoric. At the board meeting you hear the CEO claim: 'our drive towards a new, more flexible and empowered workforce has reaped dividends in lower costs and a more energised workforce.' The truth may be some way distant: employees might have felt the effects of the cost saving through fewer jobs and smaller pay increases. They may see the greater use of temporary staff and more activities outsourced. What they do not see is any *real* transfer of power from managers, only talk. They may regard the use of external labour and greater outsourcing as threats, not opportunities And far from being energized, the employees may feel ever more insecure, prepared only to do what seems necessary to retain a job.

The union response to this situation is to denounce the evil of flexibility, to blame it for all the ills that the workforce is suffering and to call on members to resist its further introduction. So we end up with a verbal bun fight, which does little to address either the needs of the business or those of the individual employees.

LACK OF TRUST

Even if management avoids the rhetoric and gets down to solving the real problems, progress may be slower than expected because employees and their representatives may not trust the motives of their managers. Why might this be so? Some possibilities include:

- management's past track record – they have reneged on previous deals
- managers' fine words are not borne out by their behaviour
- espoused values and formal policies do not translate into how people are actually treated
- managers either do not want to understand employee needs or they are incapable of so doing
- what managers are currently offering in the employment relationship is seen as wholly one-sided
- the rewards for success go disproportionately to the top people; not much trickles down through the organization.

In the absence of trust, it is difficult to obtain honest views from employees and to get them to engage in ways of helping the organization address its future problems. Lack of trust also means that all the i's have to be dotted and the t's crossed whenever there is change, as employees will not have faith in management dealing with them fairly. In the jargon of economics, this means that there will be higher transaction costs in managing change because of the need to spell everything out before people will adjust. Lack of trust is likely to be manifest in antagonistic employee relations. Trades unions may see their role as merely to secure short-term benefits for their members, in which case every additional task performed has to be paid for and every change in working practices is disputed.

Trust is harder to develop if organizational commitment varies substantially among a body of workers. Will a temporary employee have the same feeling of trust as a permanent member of staff? Where do the loyalties of the employee of an IT contractor lie? Managers have to work hard if the energies of such a disparate group are to be harnessed under one organizational banner.

This lack of trust was evident in interviews carried out by Marchington (1998), which demonstrated how trades union representatives saw management as pursuing their own agenda under a veneer of collaboration. They complained of management as 'secretive' and 'devious', 'seeking to undermine the unions wherever possible'. Whether this was the result of business pressures causing managers to cut corners, or whether they were pursuing a covert anti-union campaign, it bred on the union side a real cynicism about the reality of partnership. This prompted comments like: 'information sharing meetings are when management tell us what they will do'. Or: 'Management is very supportive of our role – provided our suggestions are to the company's benefit.' So in this situation the lack of trust has infected what should be a more mutual approach to employee relations, making it harder to achieve successful change.

DIFFERENT PERSPECTIVES

Even if there is a trusting relationship, it is naive to assume that both parties will always see eye to eye over the same set of circumstances. This was illustrated by a dispute between what was then BIFU (the Banking, Insurance and Finance Union) and bank employers over the use of 'employment registers' of the sort described in Chapter 3. Management set these up to provide short-

term cover from former employees who wished to work occasionally. The union believed that these arrangements were exploitative by denying those on the register regular work and pay, as they had no guaranteed hours or income. Instead, the union argued that permanent employees should be recruited to do this work. The banks denied the claims of exploitation by pointing out that those on the register were not seeking regular work, and were free to accept or refuse the offer of work as they wished. Furthermore, management claimed to use such people only for short-term cover, not for the regular work for which permanent staff would be used: 'They are rather like plumbers, they are people to call on in emergencies to meet peaks and troughs in demand', said Alan Grant of Barclays (Overell, 1997a).

Part of the difficulty in these situations is naturally that the parties have distinct constituencies to serve: the trades unions are concerned to protect their members' interests, while management must look after the needs of shareholders. This may manifest itself in arguing about the division of the spoils: what proportion of profit should go to shareholders and what to workers? Sometimes these differences in perspective result from divergent time horizons – senior management is concerned with the long-term viability of the organization; employees are focused on the here and now. For example, a pharmaceutical company realized that future profits would dip as the patent expired on one of its best-selling products. To anticipate this situation, management commenced a change programme that sought to generate a new climate in employee relations and make changes to the way people worked. To the employees this was hard to accept given the apparent success of the organization.

Another difficulty is that employees are more likely to enter into the spirit of change if they feel their livelihoods are secure. However, change by its very nature disturbs the status quo from which many people take comfort. Thus, management might see the value or necessity in new, flexible work arrangements, while employees resist their efforts from fear of losing their jobs, or, if these are not under threat, from the dislike of having to alter their work patterns. These may be practical difficulties (changing working hours may make childcare difficult); emotional concerns (such as being separated from liked work colleagues); status worries (no longer being the 'expert' in an activity); fears regarding competence ('can I learn these new skills'); and so on.

UNION OPPOSITION

Trades unions have both general and specific complaints about flexibility. The general objections partly stem from the fact that new flexible work arrangements have often been introduced by organizations at the same time as job cuts. So functional flexibility may have arisen out of the need to cover work with fewer people. Temporary contracts have been used in place of permanent ones, and part-time staff have replaced those on full-time contracts. The heightened insecurity that downsizing brings is not conducive to ready acceptance of flexible work patterns. Indeed, anxieties frequently breed antipathy. These concerns have been stoked by the rhetoric of full-time union officials and shop stewards. They have perceived flexibility as engendering further insecurity and leading to diminished terms and conditions, and objected to any kind of innovation in contractual form for this reason. They may resist any other changes that smack of work intensification.

More specifically, trades unions have disliked functional flexibility. They object to the blurring of boundaries that multi-skilling brings, because it cuts across demarcations that segregate the skilled from the unskilled. Such a distinction has been a feature of historical trades unionism and is reflected in union organization. Skilled workers were separated by their trade and distinguished from general workers. Trades unionists also frequently dislike forms of flexibility that decentralize responsibility to teams to organize their rosters and workloads. The disadvantage for the unions is that their place as representatives of employees can be usurped in this way. Unions prefer centralized bargaining with corporate HR, rather than issues being devolved to line managers in the field, as they find it harder to deal with the latter. Similarly, annual hours contracts give managers the freedom to manage and remove the union's role in seeking to control overtime on behalf of their members.

Unions have objected to fixed-term contracts because they have seen them as insecure and exploitative. They have resisted the use of agency workers and rejected outsourcing. Partly this view is born of self-interest – the consequence of loss of members – but it also stems from the fundamental conception that these are 'atypical', that is non-standard work arrangements. We will discuss later that managers are capable of stereotyping flexible workers (p. 127), and so are some trades unionists. They have had an aversion to part-time work and variable hours contracts, even where they have met the needs of employees, because they do not fit their norm of what constitutes typical working. As Simon Petch of the Society of Telecom Executives said at the 1997 TUC Conference, 'we have to conquer one of our traditional prejudices, that in some way, permanent, full time work is better than anything else'.

UNFRIENDLY FLEXIBILITY

Nevertheless, there are employees coerced into working arrangements that they do not care for. As was pointed out in Chapter 6, there are many examples of people forced into flexible work arrangements who suffer exploitation. Less serious but still important is the inadvertent distress that can be caused to employees. This can happen across the range of flexible options. Functional flexibility can be introduced without sufficient training or explanation. Homeworking might be encouraged without paying due attention to domestic working conditions. People may be hired on fixed-term contracts without any clear indication as to whether this might be a precursor to permanent employment or not. Split shifts may be used to the detriment of the individual's domestic life. Short-time working with all its uncertainties may be used rather than annual hours contracts, which seem to be a better means of regulating working time.

Lack of appreciation of the impact of new flexible work arrangements on employees can come from employers' failing to realize that employment is a social as well as an economic activity. An example reported in the personnel press, and shown in the following case in point, well illustrates this point.

CASE IN POINT

A senior manager of an engineering maintenance company called in a consultant after the engineers started leaving work 'in tears and tantrums'. This was because the company had changed the engineers' work rotas without consultation and introduced a computerized scheduling system. This prevented employees from managing their own time, as it was now imposed by the system which only considered how best to maximize efficiency. The employers acted in good faith but had only a narrow and one-sided view of work dynamics (People Management, 1999a).

MANAGEMENT SKILLS AND ORGANIZATION

We talked in the previous chapter about the organization of decision making and the management skills that are necessary to make mutual flexibility work. There might be the problem that power has not been devolved to front-line managers or that HR staff insist on determining every variation to standard practice. It may be difficult to free up the time required to make the process work, especially if employee representatives are antagonistic or staff are suspicious.

We reported earlier that some organizations are bent on flexibility on ideological grounds. As a consequence, they sometimes force flexibility on the organization even when it is not suited to the pattern of work demand or the labour supply. For example, an IT company insisted on recruiting all its staff on fixed-term contracts, including its graduate

intake. These were highly marketable people. They were prepared to accept the initial fixed-term contract because having the company name on their CV was good for their career, but as the contract drew towards an end, they all looked elsewhere for another job, which was not difficult to find, or they insisted on having a permanent contract. To justify its behaviour the company could only claim that the fixed-term contract worked as a trial period of employment, thereby allowing them to avoid permanent recruitment of sub-standard staff. If their performance management processes were any good, they could have come to that conclusion anyway in the first couple of years of service, and dismissed unsatisfactory employees without difficulty.

There are organizations that make the opposite mistake. They ignore or deny the benefits of flexibility. This may be due to a lack of sophistication in resource management, such that flexible work arrangements are not considered even though they might offer a solution to their problems (see case in point).

CASE IN POINT

A clothing company with significant seasonal variations in demand used overtime to deal with the peaks and short-time working to cope with the troughs. This meant that the employees' wages and hours fluctuated with the workload. This they intensely disliked. It was a situation ripe for annual hours contracts, but it was never considered (Casey et al., 1997).

They may fail to choose flexible solutions out of prejudice, or possibly jaundiced experience. One financial services company was so convinced that temporary staff made poor workers that it limited their use to only 5 per cent of the workforce across the whole organization. This was despite the fact that certain of their operational areas had very variable workloads that would have benefited from using temporary staff.

Managers themselves may be resistant to the

whole notion of flexibility. For them, it may be a threat to their role, job security and status. Variable hours working may make it harder to allocate work or manage tasks. There is evidence that a lack of accommodation in working hours is the principal reason why females who have returned from maternity leave then drop out of work (Wilson, 2000). In one case reported in a BBC *Panorama* programme an employer objected to a 15-minute adjustment in start time. Self-managed teams deny the right of supervision to determine shift rosters or task flexibility. Multi-skilling may leave managers unsure of whether they themselves have the competence to supervise a variety of skills. They may be under threat from the emergence of super-technicians. Homeworking leaves managers without face-to-face methods of control. Moreover, they may not like the mutuality approach, preferring a more traditional command and control method. They themselves may not have the skills to involve individuals in decisions about their work. Instead, they dismiss the whole notion as 'marshmallow management' – soft and insubstantial.

STEREOTYPING

Managers may not seize the opportunities of change because they have a rather narrow conception about how work might be discharged and by whom. They may have prejudices about non-standard workers. This may manifest itself in gender stereotyping, which at the extreme sees the woman's place to be in the home or at least restricted to certain occupations. Managers may not be entirely at ease with women returning to work after childbirth. An Institute of Directors survey in 1998 (Lea, 1999) found that 50 per cent of respondents would think twice about employing women of childbearing age. Similarly, the Equal Opportunities Commission found 'men reluctant to promote women in case they became pregnant' (*Attitudes to Equal Pay*, 1999). Managers may see long hours as associated with commitment and necessary to get the job done, which may make them antagonistic to some forms of temporal flexibility.

They may also have set notions of where work should be carried out, thereby rejecting homeworking. They may have fixed ideas on standard patterns of work arrangements or ways of working, making them cautious about functional flexibility. They may not have the skills to deal with diversity and difference, or they may simply have stereotypes in their mind when they think of work and workers. This may be the product of their own experience as employees themselves, used to a conventional career as a full-time, regular member of staff. Anything else is therefore seen as an aberration. This may not be because managers are actually discriminatory in their views, just that they are set in their ways. As Vroom and Jago (1998) suggest: 'Behaviour can become a matter of habit rather than choice. Most managers have been making decisions for such long periods of time that the processes can become automatic'.

One transport company had particular problems because managers had a very stereotyped view of what flexibility meant and who was involved. They tended to view certain jobs as 'men's work', and this meant certain patterns were natural (full-time) or suitable (shift); others were seen as only fit for women – part-time or variable hours. This sort of stereotyping also limits functional flexibility because some boundaries are seen as rightly separating groups of workers. In this view, there are clear demarcations between what skilled people can be expected to do compared with unskilled employees, especially where this distinction is reinforced by gender. This is illustrated by the way female secretaries are sometimes treated by their male managers. The women are expected to get the drinks, answer the phone, do the photocopying, even type the manager's e-mails, as this is seen as women's work. The man gets on with the real work of making decisions. The polite term for the role the secretary plays is that of office wife!

Besides gender differences, there are assumptions about the sort of work that can be done by part-time or temporary staff. Some managers think that part-time staff are never around when needed, so important tasks are given to full-timers. One manager described a common perception of temporary workers as 'low quality people for low quality work needing low quality attention' (Corfield Wright, 1996). This is reinforced by the feeling that if such people were any good they would have obtained regular employment. Similarly, those who have reduced hours for personal reasons get accused of 'committing career suicide', demonstrating lack of commitment or proving that they 'can't hack it'.

It is certainly easy in some organizations to form the impression that flexible workers are distinctly different from permanent staff. The very words used convey this meaning: 'regular' employees compared with 'atypical' or 'casual' workers. As Table 11.1 suggests, flexible workers may be seen as a stereotype, but this is only a partial view.

The difficulty with this kind of stereotyping is that there may be a grain of truth to it. More women are in atypical forms of employment than men – a much higher proportion of women work part-time; there are more females in temporary employment and more female outworkers. By the nature of their work, many atypical workers are in poorly paid jobs with only a brief exposure to any particular organization. Some no doubt have little attachment to their work, have few skills and offer their employer little commitment or

Table 11.1 Stereotypes of flexible workers and alternative views

Stereotype	Alternative view
casual	as committed to a career as any
low skill	as skilled as any
poor quality	as capable as any
short term	having a range of service
disposable	having their own rights
uncommitted	just as motivated
female	of both genders
poorly paid	having a range of income

Adapted from Reilly (1997a)

quality. But there is plenty of contrary evidence. Lloyds TSB found flexibility is attractive not just to female, clerical staff (Treanor, 1999). In the initial response to the offer of flexible working hours, 30 per cent of applicants were managers and 22 per cent were male, in line with their employment profile. There are also plenty of highly paid fixed-term contractors about. Part-time employment for many women is a matter of choice, and within their hours, there is evidence that they work at least as hard as their full-time equivalents. In the past atypical workers have been seen as easy to dispose of, but now employers increasingly are having to face up to legal equivalence in the rights of temporary workers. The problem is that, if organizations believe these workers to be different, then they will feel different. If they are treated as poor cousins, then their commitment is likely to suffer. In other words, there is the danger of creating a self-fulfilling prophecy. There is research evidence to support this view: work by Guest and Conway (1997, 1998) for the IPD suggests that the working relationship between the employer and employee is more important than the contractual form, as temporary workers are at least as committed as those on regular contracts.

Stereotyping may also be fostered by permanent employees for job protection reasons, and by trades union representatives. As we have said before, some union leaders have embraced the concept of a flexible labour force; others still regard it with suspicion. This is certainly the position of ETUC, the European trades union umbrella organization. It seeks to marginalize temporary contracts as much as possible on the grounds that they are intrinsically inferior to regular contracts. It is not too far a step, for those less sophisticated union members, to see those who hold temporary contracts as inferior people.

Finally, the suggestion that this group is 'atypical' is not borne out by the statistics. Full-time males on regular contracts represent just 45 per cent of the employed workforce. The standard employment type is therefore now a minority.

SEGMENTATION

A particular problem faced by 'flexible' organizations is how to handle the variety of employment relationships (outsourced, agency, temporary, fixed-term contractor, regular) that may have arisen. On the one hand, does the organization segment the workforce by employment category on the justifiable grounds that their employment 'deals' vary a lot, or, on the other hand, does the organization treat them as one group working towards common goals? Most organizations try to have their cake and eat it. They want both segmentation and harmonization, but regrettably they often choke because this is an indigestible mixture. While it is desirable to conceive of all those who work at an establishment as being part of one big happy family, the difficulty is that they do not all share common interests or common terms and conditions. Those that work for third-party employers must have ultimate loyalty to them. A chef employed by a catering firm knows that his or her career rests with his or her employers, not the temporary client. A maintenance technician working for an agency may have an extended spell with a particular organization, knowing he or she will at some point move to another company. The irony is that both the client and the third-party employer want to see integration because it is the means through which the best service is likely to be delivered. What clients must realize, though, is that there are limits to this teamwork. A trivial example from my own experience concerned invitations to the Christmas dance. One year only our own employees were invited, but this caused complaints because of the exclusion of contractor co-workers. The next year everyone associated with the site was invited, but this lack of exclusivity also brought complaints from others who thought there was insufficient discrimination between company employees and others.

As one security contractor bitterly told me:

Clients cosy up to *our* employees most of the time and want them to be part of the team. Then we have difficulties because managers start giving them holidays they are not entitled to or altering their working times to suit their individual needs; they even try to give them bonuses from their own company's scheme. But once there is an issue, they do not want to know them. The managers say that is your problem, you deal with it. If it is a disciplinary matter, all they want to see is the person off the premises double quick, fast.

The ambivalence that organizations have to those not directly employed is evidenced by badging. Some organizations adopt a transparent approach: contractors may wear their own company overalls (for example, ticket collectors for Connex South Central trains in ADI uniforms) or they may have different coloured badges or swipe cards. Trivial though this might be there is a symbolism of difference and a desire not to mislead. The contrary approach is taken by organizations that make no such distinctions – badges, uniforms, vehicle and so on are all in the corporate livery: this is to demonstrate to all concerned that this is a single indivisible operation.

Whether badged or not, those employed by third parties may be clearly distinguishable from employees, but not always in the right way. Inflexibility may result from too clear a demarcation. The case in point is an example of this. Not having labour that is interchange-

CASE IN POINT

A manufacturing company used an increasing number of secretarial temps brought in from an agency. This irritated the 'permanent' secretaries because the temporary staff were not permitted to handle money or any company confidential documentation. The regular staff had to keep covering them, and thereby getting overstretched, leaving the temporary staff relatively underemployed.

able, irrespective of employment or contractual status, can cause not only frustrations for workers, but problematic resource management for supervision.

The boundaries between those employed by the organization and those brought in from a third party may be clear enough. What can be more problematic are the distinctions within the workforce. We have talked of the drive towards functional flexibility which breaks down barriers and aims for interchangeability of resource. We have suggested that there is a tendency for broader roles to replace narrowly conceived jobs. While this is true, there is a countervailing tendency to segment activities. So, in a bank there may be increased task flexibility at the branch level, but very specific duties undertaken at a call centre. When these activities are separated by a hundred miles, then perhaps the segmentation is not an issue. If, however, both narrow and broad jobs are performed in the same place there may be greater difficulties. The management of the two types of work is necessarily very different, and probably different terms and conditions are required. The danger is that if these groups are treated such that one is clearly favoured over the other then jealousies may result. Or, as Charles Handy (1995) has warned: 'If a trust based organisation means trust for some and the old instrumental contract for the less able, then trust will become a dirty word, a synonym for selfishness.' The result may be that those who are in the favoured circle provide the contribution that is required, but those on the outside see little point in performing beyond that which is necessary to secure the monthly pay cheque.

COMPLEXITY

Another problem to be recognized is that this sort of complexity that has to be managed has a price. This might be in terms of:

- information systems – communication is harder if there are a number of different communities. Does everyone get invited to hear everything or are certain messages to be directed only to particular groups?

- management time – dealing with a multiplicity of relationships takes up a lot of time, especially if the rules are not laid down
- absence of group cohesion – how do you get everyone pulling in the same direction when their commitment and connection to the organization vary so widely?
- new inflexibilities – the organization can lose flexibility because what the organization can ask of a long-serving regular, it might not be able to ask of a part-time agency temporary (see the case in point on p. 129). One also cannot assume that a 'flexible' worker is going to demonstrate flexible attitudes or behaviour
- boundary management – managers may have to give attention to boundary disputes if the segmentation is too rigid and one group will not stray into the work territory of another, especially if they are employed by different organizations
- 'horses for courses' – recognition that some jobs require a high degree of task flexibility, while others should have a narrow focus. The former allows easy job mobility; the latter suggests more continuity
- danger of false economies – the organization may save money through outsourcing or using agency workers, but then spend the savings dealing with the management of this complexity. It has its own price in terms of bureaucracy and management effort.

Complexity may result from management's attempts to control resourcing. One organization laid down a series of rules for the engagement of temporary staff in terms of authorization and use of preferred suppliers. Line managers found this so onerous that they used various tricks to circumvent the regulations, for example using contracts for service instead of contracts for labour or bringing in self-employed consultants. The situation reached such a pitch of duplicity that the chief executive called an amnesty to encourage managers to own up to the resources that they used. It was discovered that significantly more people were working for the organization than were formally employed by it. A similar tale comes from another company that thought it was spending £2.6 million per annum on 'complementary work services' found that in reality it was spending £11.3 million (Corfield and Wright, 1996).

There is also a requirement for decision making to be flexible not rigid. A single model of flexibility should not be imposed on the organization. Flexibility for some staff does not mean flexibility for everybody. Organizations do not want many people to become 'jacks of all trades'; they need to be master of something at least. Similarly, while some jobs may be filled by fixed-term contractors that does not mean that this is appropriate for every job.

ENSURING A TRAINED WORKFORCE

Successful flexibility is also likely to be dependent on the investment in training. But the same problems occur: who gives it and who receives it? It may be clear-cut, one would hope, on some issues, such as safety induction – especially on a production or construction site. Yet, as the case in point shows, even this is not always true.

CASE IN POINT

An investigation in an explosion in a chemical works found that the principal cause was that the maintenance contractors were unfamiliar with working in such a dangerous environment, and had not had a proper safety induction. They failed to isolate a plant properly before commencing work – hence the explosion.

It may be straightforward in very specific job-related training, but even here clients may make the assumption that they are taking on a fully trained worker, whereas the contractor expects the client to get the person up to speed. Much more contentious are broader issues of skill development and awareness. Are those only temporarily working for the organization to be given sessions in, say, quality management or customer sensitivity? Better commitment and contribution are likely to

follow if they are so trained, but the benefit may be only short lived and therefore costly.

Previously, many smaller organizations could rely on the larger ones to provide basic training. British Steel's apprenticeship programme, it is said, provided many companies with well-trained craftsmen. The BBC offered an industry-wide standard in many broadcasting related skills. These organizations are no longer in a position to train other people's workforces. This puts even greater pressure on the contractors to train, but competitive pressures limit what they can do without the support of their clients.

This is borne out by the statistics. One study based on data to the mid-1990s found that men in temporary contracts were 16 per cent less likely to be trained compared with their regular contract counterparts. For women the figure was 12 per cent. The percentage differences were less for part-timers at 7 per cent and 9 per cent, male and female respectively (Arulampalam and Booth, 1998). A recent study for the DfEE (Rix et al., 1999) had similar findings, albeit they reported a better position for fixed-term contractors; see Table 11.2.

The research supports earlier work (White, 1996) that suggests that those in professional positions receive good access to training. However, perhaps not surprisingly, flexible workers tend to receive task-specific training, and suffer by comparison with permanent employees when it comes to developing their skills and encouraging more job responsibility and discretion.

Table 11.2 Proportion of workers receiving training in previous 13 weeks

Full-time permanent employees	29%
Part-time permanent employees	21%
Fixed-term contractors	34%
Casually employed workers	24%
Self-employed	12%
Agency workers	19%
Homeworkers	38%

Source: Office for National Statistics (1999a)

THE LEGAL MINEFIELD

The law is in a constant state of flux. Not only is there new legislation but frequent changes in case law. So over the last couple of years in the UK there have been restriction in the number of hours worked, changes in rules concerning part-time and fixed-term contracts, and the introduction of various laws affecting consultation and communication with employees. The labyrinthine nature of law relating to business transfers as it has emerged from the decisions of the courts merits a book in its own right. The definition of employment status is quite often problematic. This can be seen in zero hours contracts: is the worker an employee obliged to accept work or actually in effect self-employed and able to refuse? Similarly, is a consultant truly working for him/herself or in fact an employee because he or she works almost exclusively for the same firm? There is also the difficulty of establishing the correct contractual relationship between employment agencies, workers and hiring organizations. Sometimes the worker is an employee of the agency, supplied under a contract to the hiring company. On other occasions the agency introduces the worker to the hiring company, which may be used as a self-employed contractor. Alternatively, the worker may be on the agency's books, but free to accept or reject work. Here the employment relationship can be very unclear. (See Aikin, 1999.)

SPECIFIC CONSTRAINTS

FUNCTIONAL FLEXIBILITY

One has to start with the recognition that many employees merely want to be told what to do and to be left to do it. They want clear boundaries to their work, and they want these to be fixed. Functional flexibility challenges this notion because it can profoundly alter the boundaries and suggest that they might be movable. To a mechanical craftsman who expected to carry out a known range of tasks for which he had training and experience, it might come as a profound shock to discover

that he is now expected to deal with electrical and instrument problems, and even learn how to run a process plant. So in many instances functional flexibility is greeted with employee or union resistance. Even if this is absent, or can be overcome, there are costs to be met.

Firstly, there is almost certainly the investment to be made in training. This comes from having to widen and develop employees' skills in new areas. This cost is naturally greater if the skills or knowledge to be imparted are very different in nature from the employees' current skills. In these circumstances, resistance to learning is likely to be more of a problem and there is the potential danger of errors occurring due to inexperience. The fear of such mistakes is one often shared both by supervision and employees.

To avoid this problem, or reduce its likelihood, it is important to rotate staff so that they get exposed to all the facets of the job equally. Naturally, this has to be organized, which is another cost. The hope is that the standards are raised in each area to at least better than acceptable. The risk is, however, that the employees' skills deteriorate in their prime discipline without their ever becoming fully competent in the newly learnt skills. An example of these problems is given in the case in point at the top of p. 133. It is easier if those recruited are aware of the demands being placed upon them or they are selected for their aptitude to work cross-functionally, but pushing existing employees too hard towards multi-skilling may be self-defeating.

In some organizations technology may give rise to another investment cost in facilitating flexibility. Having computers on every desk programmed with the information necessary to deal with all possible customer queries is certainly not an expenditure to be taken lightly. If the training cost is added, the size of the investment is all the greater.

Cost can also come from having expensively trained staff performing menial jobs. Some production processes need cleaning up before and after use. Employing fully flexible operators to do this costs more than deputing cheaper lower-skilled staff to do these tasks.

CASE IN POINT

A manufacturing company decided upon a multi-functional, multi-skilled workforce. Production and maintenance employees were trained with the aim that they would become interchangeable.

The employees, however, did not like the fact that they were becoming jacks of all trades and masters of none. They felt that their skill in their principal trade was deteriorating and that there was no compensation in learning other work areas because they never felt confident that they knew what they were doing. This was particularly true for the most complex areas in instrument engineering, and it occurred despite extensive training.

Employees also did not like the rota system that required them to move between disciplines. It made arranging holidays all the more difficult, especially since the management rightly suspected that the employees manoeuvred to be absent on the shifts where they were expected to use their new skills.

Their complaints went unheeded by management, so they approached the trades unions for help.

TEMPORARY STAFF

Survey evidence (Atkinson, et al., 1996) suggests that most, but not all organizations, report disadvantages in using temporary or agency labour. The following complaints about temporary staff were identified, listed in order of importance. Compared with permanent staff, they:

- were less reliable
- produced a higher training cost
- were less productive
- suffered from higher turnover.

Many of these points interlink. In a tight labour market, it will be hard to attract good-quality labour to these contracts, except for specific occupational groups. The same labour market conditions are likely to induce higher turnover among the temporary staff. This will mean a higher training load as the number of starters rises. Investing in their skill development may seem a waste of money and effort if there is only a short payback period. Even trained temporary staff may lack familiarity with systems or work methods. They may not adjust to the culture. They may see themselves merely as short-term members of staff with little future in the organization and work strictly to rule and to hours. They may spend their time worrying about the next job rather than the present one (see case in point below). They may then be seen by their managers as untrustworthy, not to be given sensitive or important work. Thus organizations may find themselves in a cycle where temporary staff rotate through with little commitment, poor work rates and low quality levels. In addition, for those brought in via an agency, there is also the latter's fee to be paid.

CASE IN POINT

'TV is getting more fragmented all the time and the personal toll is very high... Such a freelance culture seems to mean no one concentrates on what they are actually doing – they are always sorting out the next thing – the next project ... I think it is all rather depressing and I'd like to work elsewhere' (Dex et al., 1998).

These difficulties may cause resentment among regular employees expected to train and support these frequent new starters. An example from a secretarial population is shown in the case in point on p. 134.

Different people seem to react to temporary work in different ways. Some seem motivated by the prospect of doing a good job with the possibility of being offered a permanent position, or they simply value any form of work, having been unemployed. Others

CASE IN POINT

In this company, the proportion of fixed-term contractors at secretarial grades rose from 3 per cent to 22 per cent between 1992 and 1996; 98 per cent of those who joined at these grades in 1997 were fixed-term contractors, not regulars. This 'policy' has not been well received by the secretaries. They complained of the extra work in training the new staff. They doubted the merit of the approach in terms of the:

- loss of continuity because of higher turnover
- lack of commitment and quality
- absence of company-specific knowledge (systems, people, organization, culture)
- loss of career development

- opportunities.

While they acknowledged that agency staff might be cheaper, and the use of temporary staff might give resourcing flexibility, they questioned the real long-term cost/benefit to the company. These criticisms were stronger for agency temporary staff than for fixed-term contractors.

---

demonstrate less interest, perhaps because they feel that the organization does not see a future in them. They feel the insecurity of their situation, with contract renewal outside their hands and a fear of being left without a job. Even those who are more confident of their prospects may treat their employer with suspicion. In the IT industry there is evidence (Patch et al., 2000) of knowledge hoarding – IT contractors not being prepared to pass on information that ensures their own market value.

Whether the individual is committed to the organization or not may also be a question of time: the longer the individual is a temporary worker with an organization, the more dissatisfied he or she may be with his or her status. This is what Sainsbury's and Tesco discovered. Nigel Broome, Sainsbury's operations director, told a House of Commons Select Committee: 'We found that people were left on temporary contracts too long. That was affecting customer service because their motivation was poor. So we made thousands of temporary colleagues permanent' (Pickard, 1998).

Of course, some employees find themselves in jobs they would rather not have. Figures from the UK Labour Force Survey (Office for National Statistics, 1999a) indicate the number of those who did not want temporary work varied with the state of the labour market. The proportion of temporary workers who were seeking but could not find a permanent job amounted to 35 per cent in spring 1999. This compared with 43 per cent in 1995, as the country came out of recession, but was higher than the 30 per cent in 1990. In other words, it seems that around a third of those in temporary employment are not entirely satisfied with their lot.

If temporary staff are used for the purpose of numerical flexibility, especially if the organization subscribes to the core/periphery model, then the expectation would be that the number of temporary workers would be reduced before permanent staff are threatened with redundancy. In practice, some organizations have found that fixed-term contractors or agency temporary staff are better performers than those on permanent contracts. They may have more skills (because of exposure to other more advanced companies) or better work attitudes (if they are seeking permanent employment from the organization). If this is the case, either the organization loses some of its better workers and sticks to its resourcing principles, or it retains temporary staff in place of regular employees, in which case the intended flexibility turns out to be illusory.

A similar fate befalls those organizations that become dependent upon their temporary staff. They find that instead of using them to give themselves flexibility, the opposite is the case. They become locked into an arrangement over which they have little control. Take, for example, a financial services company that

Outputs are then easier to measure and monitor. The exception may be those autonomous jobs with a lot of work discretion and responsibility, which are not particularly dependent on the work of others and where concentration is especially necessary.

Growing computer and communication sophistication offers more possibilities for some types of activity, but these have to be paid for. So the savings made on office overheads may then be spent on installing home computers. With a greenfield operation the balance may be in favour of the home workstation, but where there are existing premises the benefits are less obvious.

In terms of cost, there is the initial computer hardware and software kit, all the forms of telephony, and possibly furniture and even physical adaptation of the home to be included. There is the continuing maintenance and support of these facilities. Various allowances may have to be paid to the employee, as in the agreement between an insurance company and the Manufacturing, Science and Finance Union (Incomes Data Services, 1994). The deal gave employees an allowance of up to £400 to purchase suitable office furniture and a one-off taxable allowance of £200 towards upgrading the workstation, payable after three years. All stationery was supplied and postage costs reimbursed by the employer. Interestingly, employees also retained their arrangements for lunch expenses, and their location allowances.

Oxfordshire County Council staff are compensated for the extra expense involved in working from home by a maximum payment of £50 per month plus telephone costs. These are dealt with through the use of a phone-card charging work-related calls directly to the council (Industrial Relations Services, 1999).

If the employer is not so generous as these, employees will have to foot the bill for additional heating, electricity and lighting costs. There may be extra insurance to pay on computer equipment. Telephone bills will be higher. Office-type furniture may have to be bought and the house adapted. Against these costs, staff can set their savings on commuting and the use for non-work purposes of facilities that have been acquired.

Next, there are regulatory concerns that

Table 11.3 Solutions and risks in using flexible work arrangements

Drivers for flexibility	Possible solution	Potential problems/risks
reducing costs	outsourcing variable hours patterns temps/agency labour remote working	contract monitoring complex administration questionable commitment problematic communication
improving quality/service	outsourcing variable hours patterns cross-functional working	loss of control complex administration lack of real expertise
increasing productivity	multi-skilling variable hours patterns	loss of knowledge/skill complex administration
hedging against change	outsourcing temps/agency/contractors	cost of early contract-termination higher staff turnover
meeting supply needs	variable hours patterns remote working temping	complex management questionable productivity questionable loyalty

Adapted from Reilly (1997c)

took on some employees to solve the millennium bug problem. It had no capacity to deal with this itself as it had lost all its own staff with 'legacy' skills (knowledge gained from having operated older software) in an earlier downsizing exercise. The contractors having done a good job were rewarded with further work, to the point where they were engaged in routine maintenance of the computer operations. This work should really have gone to permanent employees, but, because of the excellence of the contractors, problems with recruitment and difficulties retraining the company's own staff, the contractors were kept on. However, the company was paying a premium for these services, and an exasperated finance director told the IT manager that he would sanction no more extensions to the contract beyond the next six months.

The danger that an organization faces is a similar one to that posed by outsourcing. Figure 11.1 shows that an organization that cuts its workforce by outsourcing or using contract labour risks losing the expertise to innovate, or, as in the example, to maintain operations. Support for this argument is to be found in the television industry, where a third of respondents to a BFI survey said that being on a short-term contract made them cautious about using new ideas in their work (British Film Institute, 1999).

OUTSOURCING

Despite its increased popularity, outsourcing has not been without its problems. These include:

- contractual (legal) difficulties
- service problems
- lack of technical expertise to manage contractors
- employee relations issues, for example over the terms of the transfer, selection, consultation and negotiation
- unexpected costs
- bureaucracy and cost of monitoring contractor performance
- limited management skills to deal with external service provision
- poor communication between the contracting parties.

Some of these issues have been avoided by careful attention to the process setting up the contract, particularly the legal issues, and then in the transition to the new arrangements. But there are more fundamental concerns about outsourcing, certainly if it involves any mainstream activities. Firstly, there is the fear that competitive advantage will be lost if knowledge is not retained within the company but transferred to a contractor. The organization's capacity to innovate will be reduced. Secondly, the worry is that business performance will suffer through the client's loss of control over operations and the difficulty of remedying this situation if one is locked into an inflexible contract. Finally, critics point to the basic difference of outlook between the contractor (wishing to maximize profit) and the client (aiming to minimize cost) which imperils the whole venture. To avoid these problems, the theory is that organizations should not outsource their vital interests. If expertise is needed, it can be bought in as required. The difficulty is having the foresight to know what will be vital in the future, and to be certain that lost skills can be replaced at a reasonable price. The millennium bug showed

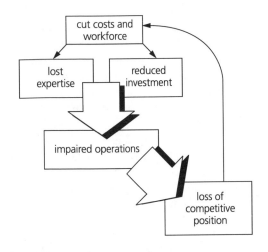

Figure 11.1 Possible consequences of relying on an external workforce (source: Reilly and Tamkin, 1997)

that organizations neglected the centrality of IT systems until this was painfully brought home to them, and the labour market was such that those with the necessary skills could demand a high price for their labour.

Practical difficulties may manifest themselves in cost over-runs or poorer service. With cost-plus contracts there is a tendency for contractors to try to over-staff to maximize their profits, whereas the opposite happens with fixed-price contracts. Similarly, contractors may try to exploit every opportunity in cost-plus contracts to 'gild the lily'. With fixed-price contracts there may be a tendency to skimp on the service as much as possible. These fears are borne out in the Workplace Employee Relations Survey (1998). There were very mixed views on whether outsourcing had saved money, despite the fact that nearly half the organizations outsourced for this reason. Only a third of respondents reported that costs had fallen. Similarly, the University of Sheffield found that a quarter of the more than 500 manufacturing companies responding to its survey said that outsourcing had failed to meet its objectives, and only one third were really positive about the benefits (quoted in Lonsdale and Cox, 1998).

VARIABLE WORKING HOURS

Difficulties with the variable working hours patterns tend to be practical ones:

- administrative and inefficiency costs
- poorer production or quality standards
- employee relations problems.

There are administrative costs in having diverse work schedules from flexitime to part-time working. Some require complex organizing, such as annual hours contracts and some shift systems. There are often frequent handovers to negotiate (between shifts or job sharers), which can lead to inefficiency. By and large more people have to be recruited when working patterns are varied, leading to higher recruitment bills. Thus there are costs attached to the management of complexity, but more serious costs arise from badly managed arrangements. Annual hours contracts

sometimes suffer call-in problems. If there is no incentive to respond to cover absent colleagues, then individuals may try to avoid coming in, especially if it disrupts domestic (for example, childcare) arrangements. Flexitime, too, will fail if during non-core hours there is poor coverage provided by staff. Likewise, the non-availability of staff because of flexible working hours can lead to inefficiency. Work by Forth et al. (1997) on family-friendly practices found the administrative burden and employee absence were the principal difficulties faced by employers.

Overtime can cause the opposite difficulty in that some employees are reluctant to go home if they can maximize their earnings by working on. People may work unproductively to fill up the hours until overtime begins. MD Foods recognized that productivity fell towards the end of the week as employees slowed their work in order to build up their wages through overtime (Arkin, 1998). This problem can be exacerbated if premium rates are applied to overtime or if the basic pay rates are so low that employees use overtime to boost earnings to a reasonable level. In this they are sometimes aided and abetted by their supervisors. The result may be that overtime adds cost but does little to satisfy work demands. Moreover, tiredness through long hours at work may lead to deteriorating production or quality levels, with the customer bearing the brunt of the problem. In certain occupations (drivers, health workers and so on) and in certain sectors (for example, manufacturing) there may be more significant health and safety implications. Some shift patterns, too, can be very stressful both at home and work. They may be very disruptive of family life, requiring all members of the household to adapt to unfamiliar rhythms of life. The shift worker may for instance sleep during the evening when children expect to see their parent, and certainly do not expect to have to creep about the house. Problems at home may then manifest themselves at work.

Poorer standards of quality and production may also come from using part-time workers in place of full-time staff. The same criticisms

are sometimes made of part-timers as of temporary workers, that they lack commitment and demonstrate limited loyalty. It is true that the job tenure of part-timers is often shorter than that of full-timers (a mean of 67 months versus 99 months), but naturally longer than for temporary staff. However, the accusation that part-timers offer poorer contribution than full-timers seems altogether too sweeping, particularly given that the vast majority of those working part-time choose to do so, unlike temporaries. The number of those who would rather not work on a part-time basis also varies with the state of the labour market and especially by gender. So in spring 1999 only around 8 per cent of women worked part-time because they could not get a full-time job – a proportion which ranged in the 1990s from a low of 5 per cent in 1990 to a high of 11 per cent in 1995. Involuntary part-time working is much higher for men at over 21 per cent, but the number of people involved is small (Office for National Statistics, 1999a).

Employee relations problems may be encountered over questions of internal inequity when flexible work arrangements are being introduced. Some employees may be paid overtime, others not. Some employees might enjoy premiums for working shifts or annual hours that are denied to others who are jealous of their colleagues' favourable treatment. Flexitime may be offered to one group rather than another because flexibility may be possible for some employees where it is impossible for others. Though this may be a valid argument to managers, it can cause resentment among employees. At a manufacturing site I know, it came to be summarized as which 'side of the wire' you were on: production workers in the protected area were excluded, office workers were allowed flexitime. This can also have practical implications. Office workers, or especially laboratory staff, might be unavailable when required because of the flexitime system. Indeed, this is the reason why an organization interviewed by Industrial Relations Services abandoned their scheme (Industrial Relations Services, 1996a).

LOCATIONAL FLEXIBILITY

While locational flexibility can give employers increased flexibility and reduced costs, particularly in terms of overheads, there may be a reluctance to allow employees too much freedom through homeworking, and perhaps a wish to conduct important business face to face. There is the fear that an attitude of 'out of sight, out of mind' will take over. There are indeed risks that staff become separated from the organizational culture in general and managers lose touch with what precisely they are doing, especially in jobs with wide discretion. This makes both performance assessment and development more difficult. For employees, despite complaints about commuting, they too may feel the need for the social interaction of work, and find their productivity and effectiveness decline if they do not have the stimulation of a place of work to go to. Some individuals just do not adapt to the self-discipline necessary to work productively from home; they are too easily distracted or drawn into domestic routines. Others fear that promotional opportunities will be denied them if they work away from the office. Their career choice will be narrowed; they will get stuck in one particular rut.

Some organizations, managers and staff, find moving to a world of remote communication extremely difficult. They find the adaptation to electronic messaging as the predominant mode of communication hard to come to terms with, especially if it is combined with remote and mobile working. Those that are used to direct, physical interaction have to become used to the reality of leaving messages by e-mail or answering machine, with the response coming some time later.

There is also the potential limitation that not all processes can be easily or affordably transformed into packages of work that can be done at home. Outworking, for example, has to be restricted to simple, light, non-capital-intensive activities. Work where there are clear outputs to the efforts expended seems to be better suited to using locational flexibility than those that rely on high inputs of time and energy.

have to be faced, especially with respect to health and safety. Employers retain a statutory responsibility for ensuring the health and safety of their employees wherever they are at work. Since 1993, for example, regulations have been in force in the UK concerning employers' responsibility in relation to the health and safety of users of visual display terminals (VDTs). These regulations impose a duty to ensure safe working conditions for people who habitually use display screens for a significant part of their normal work, and they apply in the same way to homeworkers as to office workers. The difficulty is the remoteness of the homeworker, which makes it harder to comply with the regulations. This is especially true with respect to the requirement to conduct risk assessments of workstations and to plan periodic breaks or changes of activity. As the London Borough of Enfield discovered, their home-based clerical

workers had workstations set up in conservatories, in attics and under the stairs, which posed real health and safety concerns (Incomes Data Services, 1994).

Those employers that seek to save costs by using teleworking must also be mindful of the equal-pay-for-equal-work principles, as women may form the majority of teleworkers in an organization. If they can prove that they are paid less than their conventionally employed predominantly male counterparts, then a claim of sexual discrimination can be lodged. This is especially tricky since the mode of payment for the two groups may differ – a monthly salary for those at the office or factory, payment based on output for the homeworker.

SUMMARY

The sort of problems that the various forms of flexibility create are summarized in Table 11.3.

CHAPTER TWELVE

How Mutual Flexibility Can Help

We should not be deluded into thinking that all the above obstacles can be overcome, even if flexible work arrangements are introduced in a mutual manner. Nevertheless, some difficulties can be dealt with and problems eased.

SOLUTIONS TO GENERAL PROBLEMS

Many of the ways of dealing with the general problems we have already covered in the prerequisites to mutual flexibility in Chapter 10. We have frequently complained that rhetoric has got in the way of progress. Managers would be better off talking less and listening more. They would do well to ignore fads and fashions and get down to discovering what would make for an energized and committed workforce. Similarly, on the trades union side, representatives should avoid taking fixed positions based on ignorance and prejudice, and make their judgements on the merits of the case. If both sides approach flexibility in this manner, it should go some way to nullify the lack of trust in organizations that we have also reported.

It may be a long, slow road but mutuality can be developed over time. Management awareness of the human implications of its plans will limit the risk of unfriendly flexibility. Mutual understanding should help reduce the risk of employers' failing to see problems through the eyes of their employees, and vice versa. Success in following this approach should hopefully marginalize opponents to flexibility, because it will have been introduced in a way that brings benefits to all.

Senior management especially can signal that it intends to tackle some of the obstacles to successful flexible work arrangements. It can invest in training and development of its managers. Courses, workshops, events can be used to help handle a diverse workforce, show how to avoid stereotyping people and deal with managing complexity. It can demonstrate the pitfalls of flexibility and the benefits to be obtained. Training can go further and address these issues for the workforce as a whole, ideally co-sponsored by employee representatives.

Organizations that are sensitive to the needs of flexible workers can reach out and include them in training. They can adjust timings to suit part-time workers or choose a medium that makes it easier for remote workers. The proportion of homeworkers receiving training reported on p. 131 is particularly noteworthy, given that the DfEE project found that distant workers often find it hard to participate in training events. It demonstrates the efforts of some employers to use new training technology to ensure that home- or outworkers are included in appropriate exercises.

Thus the philosophy of mutuality and its practical manifestation in the way that problems are approached and the process by which they are solved will help ease many of the difficulties we reported in the last chapter. There are, though, specific issues still to be tackled.

HELP WITH THE SPECIFIC PROBLEMS

MULTI-SKILLING

The main cause of problems in functional flexibility is organizational overambition. Companies ask too much of their employees, too quickly. The latter then, as the case in point at the top of p. 133 showed, may react negatively. Instead, organizations should proceed slowly, gaining support as they go. Management does not need to wait for a crisis before acting, and then trying to deliver instant success. Involving employees can help allay their fears, and, importantly, discover their training requirements and get their views of what will work well or less well. How many clever blueprints of reorganization designed by management consultants have been found wanting in their execution? And why? Because nobody remembered, or chose to ask, those who are most familiar with work arrangements, namely the workers themselves.

Again, in a climate of mutual trust employees will not exaggerate the difficulties of change, nor will management delude themselves or their staff about the benefits.

One reason why employees may be reluctant to widen their job scope is the fear that they may be putting a colleague out of work. If all the operators can do maintenance, what future is there for the existing craftsmen? One way that this can be dealt with is to address the question of insecurity head on. Blue Circle Cement found this was the way forward for them. To improve productivity, there needed to be greater work flexibility. With an offer of job security, employees were prepared to learn new work areas and take on new tasks. As a shop steward put it: 'this (agreement) creates an atmosphere where you can get commitment without fear' (Involvement and Participation Association, 1997).

A number of organizations, especially those that have been successful without the need for radical change in employee behaviour, have recognized that fear of change is a severe inhibitor to the organization's taking the measures it feels necessary to deal with future competitive pressures. This is particularly true among older, more traditional workers, who say: 'Why do you want to do it that way? We always managed in the past to do it this way!' The Blue Circle Cement agreement confronts the job security fear and helps with the reluctance to change argument. Other organizations have decided not to force the pace with long-serving staff. Staveley Chemicals, for example, realized that not all older serving craftsmen would be able to cross-skill, so they concentrated instead on selecting apprentices with the right capability (Involvement and Participation Association, 1995). Change may come more slowly that way but it will be less threatening to the workforce.

While it is sensible to give attention to those who are fearful of change, it should also be acknowledged that there are others in the increasingly educated workforce who want more interest and variety in their work. Functional flexibility can build upon earlier experiments in job enrichment, enlargement and rotation that have sought more satisfying work for employees. Similarly, giving employees more responsibility over how they do their tasks should make for a more productive and engaged workforce. A mutual approach recognizes that there are gains for employees in adding skills and making work more interesting, as well as for organizations in greater efficiency and output.

TEMPING

The problems we saw in the last chapter over using temporary workers concerned the reliability, productivity and commitment of such people, and the difficulties in ensuring that they are fully trained.

Organizations can first of all obviate some of these problems by choosing a reputable company to supply its agency labour. Next it can seek to ensure that good-quality labour is supplied. One way of making this happen is by paying for it. This may be done by insisting on minimum pay and benefit levels for all agency staff at an appropriate level, taking account of comparisons with internal rates. This can be properly structured. For example, one organization became very concerned about the debate over what terms and conditions should apply to its agency workers (managers were spending too much time dealing with minor issues such as entitlement to eye tests or compassionate leave) and with the plethora of emerging custom and practice, such as company bonuses, among its labour suppliers. So it decided to act. Firstly the company limited the number of contractors supplying staff, and then it required the agencies to work to a common framework. The latter addressed the issue of the tension between being temporarily part of one team, with its rules, and at the same time still employed by another, with its own policies and practices. See the case in point at the top of p. 142.

Another solution to problems with

CASE IN POINT

An IT company concluded its deal with three suppliers of agency workers. Its aims were to assign responsibilities and to monitor actions. Its definition of company responsibilities highlighted three themes:

- managers had to provide the agency with full job descriptions
- managers should not subvert the employment relationship between the agency and the worker by discussing terms and

conditions, involving themselves in disciplinary matters or any other HR issue
- managers should ensure full legal compliance, especially with respect to health and safety.

The agency's responsibilities included:

- recruitment to the job specification
- engagement of workers on proper contracts
- legal compliance

- payment in line with market rates
- the obligation to conduct performance assessment
- proper management and communication with the workers.

The parties to the agreement held regular monitoring meetings and established a change process whereby any changes to the agency workers' terms and conditions had to be agreed.

temporary staff may be found through investment in their training and development. Some organizations have insisted on receiving fully trained staff from agency suppliers. They have accepted that they have to pay for this, usually via an initially higher charge-out rate, but they believe it is worth it. All organizations have the right to expect a minimum level of capability from agency employees on arrival, but development should be continued once the person is at work. Not only can the organization ensure that staff have the skills necessary to complete the work, but it may also generate higher motivation from its temporary workers if they are included in training events. And, if there is a route to recruitment as a regular employee through temporary work, this gives a further incentive for temporary staff to contribute as much as possible.

NatWest Retail tried to develop a closer partnership relationship with an agency supplier to improve the training of those involved. It used a preferred agency to supply staff for its cheque-clearance work. The agency replicated the bank's own systems so that it could send ready-trained people to NatWest when required. The difficulty for both parties to this arrangement is that it is commercially based, and therefore the contractor is liable to be changed – as indeed has happened in this case (Purcell and Purcell, 1998).

Adopting this approach will cost money, but the principal reason for using temporary staff is the quick and easy adjustment of the quantum of labour, not saving money through paying lower wages or avoiding training. Moreover, rather than exploiting the temporary staff, if the organization demonstrates its commitment to their welfare it should receive reciprocal commitment in terms of better productivity and effectiveness.

CASE IN POINT

A catering company, Beeton Rumford, values its temporary workers as much as its permanent employees: 'Whether they are a cook, a bottlewasher, a manager or a student seeking two weeks' work, they will undergo an ongoing structured training programme which includes recognition of individual achievements. The MD is so determined that part-time and temporary workers should be valued as much as full-timers that he has even banned the term "casual".' (Pickard, 1995)

Another way of addressing the reported problems with agency workers is to bring resourcing in-house, where the balance between worker, customer and supplier can be more easily achieved in a mutual fashion.

The same principles apply that we have discussed above: investment in training and development is necessary, as are fair terms and conditions. Recruiting temporary staff directly also has the advantage that the organization can ensure an appropriate selection process takes place and that those hired have the attributes sought. If a register of ex-employees is used, there is even greater certainty that the organization gets what it seeks. Moreover, those on the register are likely to have positively adopted temporary work as a matter of choice, rather than being forced into it. There is consequently a more mutual relationship, where benefits are achieved for both employment parties.

We have already seen the examples of NatWest and Cable and Wireless (pp. 31 and 53). The North East Wales Institute for Higher Education also used a register of contacts to employ people for temporary cover or assignment purposes (Grethé, 1998). After the frustrations it had with agency temporary staff, it felt that this more intimate arrangement (there were only 20 people on the list) created a special team feeling and ensured high quality standards. Individuals were free to refuse work. They were given a preferential opportunity to take up permanent positions should they become available, and their terms and conditions were equal to their permanent counterparts.

OUTSOURCING

Outsourcing often fails because organizations do not conduct a proper cost–benefit evaluation that takes account of the risks involved against the alternative external and internal options. This evaluation should give attention to the employee implications of such a move. This is not just a question of getting transfer of undertakings right in legal terms, but also of considering the impact of outsourcing on the ability of the organization to meet its business objectives through people. This requires an evaluation in terms of skills and culture.

Where outsourcing is clearly ideologically driven such an evaluation may not take place. Moreover, implementation may be executed in a closed and secretive manner. In these circumstances, employee interests are likely to be neglected. The consequence will be that employees will not trust the integrity of the decision to contract out, however appropriate that might be.

The alternative approach is to recognize the importance of employees and value their contribution. If communication is done in an open and participative way, it is likely to yield significant benefits at a later stage. As Kessler et al. (1999) found in a study of outsourcing in local government, the way in which employees discovered information about their new employers was 'crucial in shaping perceptions'. By this means employee concerns are likely to be brought to the surface, their needs taken into account and, wherever possible, solutions found to problems identified. The benefit of taking this approach will be realized in gaining employee understanding and support to the outcome, should the outsourcing process go ahead.

A US company, 3Com, told its employees of the outsourcing plan nine months ahead of the scheduled move and found that the process benefited from that openness (Waterman et al., 1994). The local authority in the Kessler case created an employee committee that concentrated on employee concerns – it was even given a small budget to fund legal advice on the trickier transfer issues. Another employer went so far as to rule out certain potential contractors because they were not seen to be good employers. In a recent deal between local authority employers, contractors and trades unions, local authorities are specifically allowed in awarding contracts to take account of the track record of contractors with respect to health and safety, training and development, equal opportunities and working conditions (Welch, 1999). In the same deal, local authorities, contractors and trades unions agreed that local government employees moving to private firms under transfer of undertakings would be able to remain in their original pension scheme or to transfer to a mirror employer scheme. This is not currently a legal right – transfer of undertakings law excludes occupational pension schemes from its regulations – but the intention of permitting pension protection was to remove an area of conflict from the transfer process.

This demonstrates that mutuality is possible in terms of the process used. Organisations can inform and involve staff recognizing the legitimacy of their interests, even if management reserves the ultimate right to decide what to do in-house, what to buy in and to whom work might be contracted. The advantage of an approach which respects employee interests is that the final outcome is likely to be better for all parties. The opposite approach may meet the vendor's need to dispose of an activity in a way that maximizes return on the investment of their shareholders, but may leave their ex-employees fearful and suspicious. The consequences of this environment are picked up initially by the contractor, but then returned to the client because it may well be that the same people are involved. As one IT manager put it: 'all we did was transfer our weaker staff and then we had to deal with them all over again' (quoted in Earl, 1996).

VARIABLE HOURS WORKING

Temporal flexibility, as we saw in the last chapter, can suffer from administrative complexity and costs if work patterns are unduly complicated. Employers, though, do not always acknowledge the savings they may be making on recruitment and training that usually more than offset the administrative burden. Moreover, some of this cost derives from management's need to control employee behaviour. There is a lack of trust in what employees will get up to if they are not monitored and checked up on. And as we saw in Chapter 6 (case in point 5, p. 76), there is evidence to support this case. There is, however, evidence the other way. Giving employees some choice over their working pattern has proved beneficial. Informal team decisions to allow individuals to vary their start/finish times, or to select their preferred shift schedule, may ameliorate some of the negative side-effects that are found in certain shift patterns. As the MD Foods example from p. 105 showed, teams

can successfully be given responsibility for managing annual hours rotas, securing better attendance and less wastage. This gives the lie to the other accusations made in Chapter 11 that variable hours working produces poorer production or quality standards, and leads to employee relations problems.

What is critical to the success of any work arrangement that gives employees this sort of trust is that they understand and recognize the business need. As some flexitime systems emphasize, 'work comes first'. The essence of mutual flexibility is that there is a balance struck between the interests of the employer on the one hand and the employee on the other. Both parties need to feel confident that each will behave as promised. Rules can be used, for example, in a flexitime system to ensure there is minimum cover and a range of skills available throughout the working day. Nevertheless, with a degree of trust it is easier for management to contemplate genuine empowerment and less supervision of the operation of variable hours contracts.

Mutuality can also be demonstrated in the way the benefits of success are apportioned. How this is handled will in large part determine the nature of employee relations. MD Foods, for example, took the view that some of the savings from the introduction of annual hours contracts should be ploughed back into employees' wages, as well as invested in new technology. Taking such an approach will go a long way to securing staff support for any change. As the TGWU official involved in these negotiations said:

> If employers want to use annual hours to take costs out of the system, then my view is that the scheme will fail. But if they want to increase productivity and flexibility on the back of an annualized hours scheme and build the money on an average basis back into the scheme, then it's more likely to succeed. (Arkin, 1998)

Black and Decker took a similar approach to annual hours contracts. They increased basic pensionable wages by 40–50 per cent in order to provide a more stable income for their employees (Involvement and Participation Association, 1999a).

Recognizing domestic needs is at the heart of many forms of temporal flexibility that offer a real chance of mutuality. Work arrangements can help keep at work those with caring responsibilities, or allow a well-managed transition from employment to retirement. If this is done well, both the employer and employee derive benefits. A financial services company, for example, offered women returnees from maternity leave a step-by-step return to full-time working. This helped retention for the employer and child rearing for the employee (Rajan et al., 1997). As another example, organizations may ease people into retirement by scaling down their working hours as they approach their leaving date, but without compromising their pension entitlement. Mutuality can also be seen in job sharing, if it is well constructed, as in the case in point. The job sharers can benefit from time off for domestic, educative or leisure reasons. The employer can see the virtue in having two minds applied to a job rather than one.

REMOTE WORKING

Done in the right way, offering homeworking can be seen as a positive signal to employees by demonstrating that the organization recognizes that their staff, no matter how long or how short their contractual hours, have lives outside work, and that these lives impact upon their contribution at work.

As we observed earlier, home or mobile working is not to everybody's taste, nor does it suit all types of job. Organizations should concentrate remote working where activities are individually driven, require minimal supervision or instruction, do not need to be performed at set times and can produce measurable outputs. As to employees, some like the personal flexibility remote working gives. Others dislike the social isolation. So if remote working is to succeed it has to be voluntary: no one should be press-ganged into it. If this flexibility is forced, then there will be many unhappy people, who will vote with their feet given half a chance.

Homeworking need not be an all-or-nothing decision. Surveys suggest that a substantial number of people would like to work from home, but in combination with being at the office or factory. Partial homeworking may therefore suit employees, while mitigating for management some of the potential disadvantages of fully fledged homeworking, especially the loss of contact with staff.

Preparing for the switch to remote working

CASE IN POINT

When a job was advertised in the personnel office of a civil service department, two women who were looking at the possibility of job sharing decided to put in a joint bid. They were interested in part-time work because of childcare responsibilities, but at their level very few part-time positions existed. The appointing personnel manager had not thought of job sharing as an option, but mindful of the departmental policy of encouraging women to remain in employment, he was prepared to give it a go.

In practice, it has worked out well. This may be because it is a policy position and so does not suffer the problems of operational pressure. The job sharers are very mindful of the need to ensure consistency and to communicate frequently, and so they have built in a day in the week when they are in the office together. They see disadvantages in not always being able to follow things through to the end and in feeling guilty in not having completed things themselves, but in other ways the job has benefited. There is 20 per cent more input due to the shared day, there are two people to generate ideas, and a discussion partner is available to test out thoughts. And for the projects that arise frequently, there is a choice in who carries out the work.

needs to be fully thought through. Research (Huws, 1994) suggests that the transfer to a teleworking culture is much easier when asynchronous (where there is a lag between question and response) and electronic communication have preceded the switch to distant working. People should have the chance to get used to this world before they also have to cope with being out of the office.

Care is still needed, even if there is no pressure on individuals to nominate themselves, that those selected to work from home or in a peripatetic manner are able to cope. Questions an organization might ask include whether the individual:

- has self-discipline
- can cope with isolation
- is able to motivate him/herself
- can separate home and work life successfully (physically and emotionally)
- is good at time and work management
- is a good communicator.

For those who do volunteer and are suitable, management should be sensitive to their needs. This means ensuring they are included in any training and development. This might be achieved by compulsory on-site initial training or regular attendance at work for learning purposes. Content should include dealing with issues arising from remote working. This applies both to those working away from the office and those giving support to remote colleagues. Specific attention might have to be given to basic skills training – so much knowledge is acquired by tacit learning, through sitting with Nellie, which is difficult if Nellie is miles away. Different mechanisms may have to be used to reach these people, for example through multimedia methods, or through the allocation of a buddy or mentor. While away from work, remote or mobile employees need to be kept informed. This means they should be included in any circulated communications, and mechanisms should be found to keep them in contact with fellow workers, including via training events.

Employers, in the way that they manage mobile or homeworkers, can acknowledge that their employees have outside lives and social needs which bear upon work. Mobile workers can find their own ways of easing their social isolation. They can meet up for an 'espresso and Danish' near a convenient motorway junction, as did those reported in the study of mobile workers by Laurier and Philo (1999). Employers should recognize and understand these responses, and support their employees' need to deal with isolation, rather than see it as a threat to productivity.

CASE IN POINT

Being out of sight does not necessarily mean out of mind. A charity demonstrated how to send a positive signal to a teleworker, who was working from home following the birth of a child. She said: 'The on-site staff make you feel part of the team. I had been teleworking for only two months and they laid on a cream tea for my birthday. It makes all the difference' (quoted in Huws, 1998).

At the practical level, employers can give support by addressing questions on the reasonable costs incurred in working from home. They should also ensure that working conditions and equipment are safe. Organizations need to protect their security and ensure that the workers are productive, but there are different ways of achieving this end. If there is limited trust, there may be unannounced flying visits from supervisors to check up on people, or 'spy' cameras installed to keep an eye on work activities; key-depression or telephone checks can be also used to monitor those engaged in this sort of work. In a more trusting environment these sort of methods are eschewed in favour of judging employees by their actual output, not how this is produced. Confirming that working conditions are safe and secure can be done through pre-arranged visits rather than in a way that casts doubt on an individual's integrity.

Thus if remote working is carefully selected, if the right people are chosen and if account is taken of their needs, then remote workers can be highly productive and the organization may become more efficient. And, as the 1999 BT annual review argues, there are advantages for employees too:

> Communications technology gives us more choice – choice of when, how and where to work, for example. It also gives us the chance to achieve a better balance in life – balance between work and home. It gives us the freedom to work differently, to run our lives differently, and to do what we want, when we want to do it. We are in control of the technology – it serves us, not the other way around.

CHAPTER THIRTEEN

Conclusion

As the writing of this book drew to a close my belief in its thesis was encouraged by two pieces of information, both of which confirm the existence of a rhetorical dispute over flexibility and its impact at work. The battle that continues to be played out between those fundamentally opposed to the notion of flexibility and those who see it as a necessary precondition to business success was illustrated by a polemic from Steve Fleetwood of Lancaster University (Fleetwood, 1999). This poured scorn on the benefits of a flexible labour market. Instead, he saw high levels of unemployment, increased insecurity and long hours – 'working conditions reminiscent of the 19th century'. He claimed that the workforce was being offered a 'Hobson's choice: workers can either have an insecure, stressful, badly paid job or no job at all'. Since Fleetwood aimed his argument at those about to attend the TUC conference, it was clear that he wanted to embolden their resistance to the flexibility agenda being pursued by government and employers.

A few weeks before, I had heard of the effects of such rhetoric. A personnel manager wearily told me of the difficulties his organization was having in updating the service it offered to customers to make it more attuned to their needs. He complained that flexibility was a dirty word in the eyes of the trades unions, and he said that it was hard to debate with them changes to working patterns because of this mental block – and even if the union leadership were convinced of the merits of change, antagonistic employees still had to be persuaded.

These examples reinforce the argument of this book that there is a war of words over the concept of flexibility, which stems from two quite different conceptions of the employment relationship. This has created a climate of exaggerated claims and ill-informed objections.

If the opposing parties merely stand in their own corners yelling across the divide, little progress will be made. What I argue instead is that progress can be made: if the warring factions were to stop and listen to each other they might discover that both sides can derive benefits from flexibility. I argue for balanced flexibility that recognizes the needs of both the employer and employee, and aims to satisfy them both.

To achieve this position much work has to be done. At the national level there needs to be a continuing recognition that:

- regulation does not necessarily herald unemployment or severely hamper business activity
- many of the benefits to employers in terms of adjustment to changing business requirements that come from flexible work arrangements are not endangered by regulation
- sensible regulation is necessary to protect employee rights as a matter of principle
- making employees more confident in their job security is likely to bring beneficial economic consequences to the wider society and, if they are more satisfied with their work, better productivity to their employers
- cowboy operators need to be stopped from abusing vulnerable workers
- the State should not have to pick up the tab for those who under-pay or mistreat their staff.

Support for these ideas comes from what might be regarded as unlikely sources. For example, here is a CBI statement:

> The CBI believes that labour market flexibility is a key concept, but views are too often polarised. We believe flexibility is essential to improving competitiveness and raising employ-

ment levels; but to others flexibility is synonymous with low paid and insecure part-time and temporary jobs. The challenge is to go beyond the slogans and identify which aspects of flexibility are vital and how they can be achieved. (Confederation of British Industry, 1997)

The company secretary of the UK arm of Manpower, the vast agency for temporary staff, has given his views:

So the balance that governments and trades unions have to strive to help establish is between a sufficiently deregulated business environment to encourage the investment and entrepreneurial activity that creates the long-term growth in employment, while building in sufficient protection for the individual to ensure that short-term, shareholder driven strategies to create competitive advantage do not, by exploiting the vulnerability of individual workers, have the opposite effect. (Keith Faulkner at the Temporary and Agency Worker conference in 1999)

Clive Mather, at the time personnel and administration director of Shell UK, spoke about the wider benefits of family-friendly flexibility: 'For both men and women the flexibility to juggle work and family commitments is a precious benefit. Individuals, families, neighbourhoods and communities all gain and the relational base [of society] is strengthened' (Mather, 1996).

So from the heights of British industry we have arguments in favour of flexibility, that it can benefit both employer and employee, but within a protected environment that recognizes the risks to the vulnerable – and to society as a whole – of unfettered capitalism.

Assuming that the macro-policies are in place, there remains much to be done at the organizational level:

● getting beyond ill-informed rhetoric, fads

and fashions to finding the right answers to business needs
● applying flexible solutions appropriately with proper cost–benefit analysis
● giving line managers real responsibility for people management, but in ways that mean that they respond to individual needs in a fair, sympathetic but also business-conscious way
● obliging HR departments to facilitate mutual flexibility at policy and practice levels
● encouraging employees and their representatives to understand the organization's needs and respond positively to them, while protecting their right to decent terms and conditions
● requiring senior management to demonstrate leadership in support of mutual flexibility by what they say and, above all, do.

Through these means trust should be (re)established at work, a balanced view taken of the needs of the various stakeholders and the implicit contract between the employer and employee restored in a way that is based on mutual understanding and respect. It is a flexibility that assumes that there can be win/win deals, rather than zero-sum outcomes. This argues for the high road to flexibility based on a strategic and self-conscious approach rather than a series of ad hoc solutions to short-term problems.

There are still those that object to these views. Those that come from the political left would say that this is a typical liberal, soft-hearted and -headed book, full of woolly thinking and unrealistic aspirations. Concepts like mutuality, partnership, and balanced flexibility are just sophisticated variants of HRM. The aim is still to seduce workers into seeing only the management view of the world and to co-opt them, and their representatives, to the employers' side.

My argument to these objections is this: do the employees or trades unions actually have a choice? They can stand and boo from the sidelines or they can engage. In the former case they can retain the purity of their position, but while their virtue may remain intact, jobs will be lost and employee insecurity will rise with climbing unemployment. If they engage, they may come to acknowledge the business pressures employers are under and recognize the need for change, however difficult that might be to stomach. There are undoubtedly risks to this approach – that they will be taken for a ride, their goodwill abused. But the rewards are that they may be able to influence decisions and affect how they will be implemented. Downright opposition will only reinforce employer perception of the negativity of trades unions. It will create further reluctance to engage employee representatives in the debate about the future.

Critics from the right would advance surprisingly similar arguments. They would be equally dismissive of these left-wing efforts to restrain the right of managers to manage. They would argue that this book is overly idealistic in its attempts to bring harmony to employee relations. They would contend that neither managers nor the managed can stand in the way of global capitalism. The business imperative must rule, ok!

I would advance a similar response to the one I gave those on the left. Do employers really have a choice, at least in the long run? They can decide whether to manage people as economic units to be dispensed with when no longer needed, or they can recognize the potential in their workforce. To be successful in the 21st century organizations should surely opt for the latter. Do they not need to capture the hearts and minds of the workforce? As we have seen from the research evidence, this should bring rewards in having more committed people, and that will translate ultimately into profits. People who are not engaged in their work are less likely to take responsibility for their actions. A cowering, insecure workforce is unlikely to delight the customer or maximize quality production.

The argument of this book is that there are economic reasons to adopt mutual flexibility, and, implicitly, there are moral reasons to do so. We can argue on the basis of utilitarianism – that a balanced approach to flexibility maximizes the benefits for one and all – or even more narrowly it provides advantages for specific organizations. But I would also want to argue on the basis of broader social values. These recognize that employees have a right to be heard; they have a stake in the organization; they have legitimate interests to be met; they should be able to affect the way they do their job and they should have some control over their own destiny.

Jeremy Pfeffer (1998) captures the mixture of the moral and economic imperatives in his book *The Human Equation*. His challenge to bosses is: 'Do you, like so many people, see people as labour costs to be reduced or eliminated; implicit contracts for careers and job security as constraints to be negated; and mutual trust and respect as luxuries not affordable under competitive conditions?'

Pfeffer argues that this view of people is morally flawed but equally poor business. He claims, with much supporting evidence, that business solutions like mergers and acquisitions, downsizing and outsourcing, have failed to deliver results, and that instead organizations should put people first.

If there are still any doubters who need to be convinced of the business case for mutual flexibility, they should look at the external pressures that will continue to bear upon employers from the labour market, the government and the EU.

The UK labour market is currently tighter than it was during the recession and its immediate aftermath. There is likely to be an increasing demand for a skilled and educated workforce that the labour supply will find hard to meet. At the same time, the demographic profile of the labour force is shifting and becoming more diverse. The needs and wants of such a workforce will be different from the past. It is alleged that 'Generation X', for example, is more interested in getting the right balance between work and life than the workaholic baby boomers have been. If this is true, working patterns will have to respond if employees are to be attracted, retained and motivated. This will push employers even further in the direction of discovering the needs of individual members of staff.

There will be pressure for involvement too from the trades unions. Some are beginning to flex their muscles, encouraged by the new legal framework and labour market conditions. There was a record 75 union recognition deals in the first ten months of 1999 (TUC, 2000), and union membership rose that year for the first time since 1980. Others genuinely wishing to follow the partnership route want to engage employers in debate on how best to respond to employee requirements at the same time as responding to business imperatives. Either way, employee interests cannot be neglected in these circumstances.

If the Labour government remains in power for two terms, the climate within which business operates may gradually shift further towards one that will allow mutuality to flourish. Family-friendly initiatives will be encouraged. The rhetoric of workplace partnership will continue. Legislative action may be limited, but where it happens it will tend to give support to flexible work arrangements that benefit both parties, and to outlaw practices that facilitate exploitation.

The European Union will lend its hand in support of these developments. As we saw in Chapter 7, there is not much at present in the legislative pipeline to trouble the equanimity of business people, but the arrival of the euro means that there is a greater likelihood of labour market harmonization across the Union. European convergence may be at a halfway house in regulatory terms based upon some notion of minimum standards. This would suggest that a continental European model, albeit a modified one, will be become more influential on the UK than will its US counterpart.

This of course is speculation. However, I believe it is certain that organizations, whether because of external pressures or internal rewards, cannot fail to see the benefits of forms of flexibility that are balanced, inclusive and mutual.

Bibliography

Abraham, K.G. and Housman, S.S. (1993), 'Does employment protection inhibit labour market flexibility? Lessons from Germany, France and Belgium', Cambridge, Mass.: National Bureau of Economic Research, no. 4390, June.

Ackroyd, S. and Procter, S. (1998), 'British manufacturing organisation and workplace industrial relations: some attributes of the new flexible firm', *British Journal of Industrial Relations*, 36, June.

Aikin, O. (1999), 'Change agencies', *People Management*, 19 August.

Allen, M. (1998), 'All inclusive', *People Management*, 11 June.

Anderton, B. and Mayhew, K. (1994), 'A comparative analysis of the UK labour market', in R. Barrell (ed.), *The UK Labour Market: Comparative Aspects and Institutional Developments*, Cambridge: Cambridge University Press.

Arkin, A. (1997), 'No place like work', *People Management*, 18 December.

Arkin, A. (1998), 'Cream of the crop', *People Management*, 12 November.

Armitage, B. (1998), 'British labour force projections', *Labour Market Trends*, June.

Arthur, J. (1994), 'Effects of human resource systems on manufacturing performance and turnover', *Academy of Management Journal*, 37.

Arulampalam, W. and Booth, A.C. (1998), 'Training and labour market flexibility: is there a trade off?', *British Journal of Industrial Relations*, 36 (4), December.

Atkinson, J. (1984), 'Flexibility, uncertainty and manpower management', Brighton: Institute of Manpower Studies, *Report* 89.

Atkinson, J. and Meager, N. (1986), 'New forms of work organisation', Brighton: Institute of Manpower Studies, *Report* 121.

Atkinson, J., Morris, S., Rick, J. and Williams, M. (1996), 'Temporary work and the labour market', Brighton: Institute for Employment Studies, *Report* 311.

Atkinson, M. (1999), 'New Deal gets young into work', *The Guardian*, 18 February.

Bakkenist Management Consultants (1998), *Temporary Work Business in the Countries of the European Union*, Brussels: CIET.

Barber, L., Hayday, S. and Bevan S. (1999), 'From people to profits', Brighton: Institute for Employment Studies, *Report* 355.

Barney, J. (1991), 'Firm resources and sustained competitive advantage', *Journal of Management*, 17 (1).

Barrell, R. (ed.) (1994), *The UK Labour Market: Comparative Aspects and Institutional Developments*, Cambridge: Cambridge University Press.

Bassett, P. and Cave, A. (1993), 'Time to take the unions to market', *New Statesman and Society*, September.

Beardwell, I. (1998), 'Voices on', *People Management*, 28 May.

Beatson, M. (1995), 'Labour market flexibility', London: Department of Employment Research Series, *Report* 48.

Benardy, A. (1999), 'Why firms are bringing humanity into work', *The Guardian*, 31 July.

Benson, J. (1996), 'Management strategy and labour market flexibility in Japanese manufacturing enterprises', *Human Resource Management Journal*, 6 (2).

Bettis, R.A., Bradley, S.P. and Hamel, H. (1992), 'Outsourcing and industrial decline', *Academy of Management Executive*, 8.

Bevan, S. (1996), 'Are you ready to downshift?', *The Independent*, 3 May.

Bevan, S., Robinson, D. and Barber, L. (1997), 'Keeping the best: a practical guide to retaining key employees', Brighton: Institute for Employment Studies, *Report* 337.

Bigwood, S. (1996), 'The advantages of a caring approach', *People Management*, 16 May.

Billot, H. (1996), 'Business alloys', *People Management*, 10 October.

Black, S. and Lynch, L. (1997), 'How to compete: the impact of workplace practices and information technology on productivity', Cambridge, Mass.: National Bureau of Economic Research, *Working Paper* 6120.

Blank, R.M. and Freeman, R. (1994), 'Evaluating the connection between social protection and economic flexibility', in R.M. Blank (ed.), *Social Protection and Economic Flexibility*, Chicago: University of Chicago Press.

Boyer, R. (1988), *The Search for Labour Market Flexibility*, Oxford: Clarendon.

Brannen, J., Meszaros, G. and Moss, P. (1994), 'Employment and family life: a review of research in the UK', Sheffield: Employment Department Research Series, *Report* 41.

Bresnen, M. and Fowler, C. (1994), 'The organizational correlates and consequences of subcontracting: evidence from a survey of South Wales businesses', *Journal of Management Studies*, 31 (6).

Brewster, C. (1993), *Flexible Working Patterns in Europe*, London: IPD.

Brewster, C. and Hegewisch, A. (1994), *Policy and Practice in European Human Resource Management*, London: Routledge.

Brewster, C., Mayne, L., Tregaskis, O., Parsons, D. and Atterbury, S. (1996), *Working Time and Contract Flexibility in Europe*, Cranfield: Cranfield School of Management.

Bridges, W. (1994a), *Jobshift: How to Prosper in a World Without Jobs*, Wokingham: Addison-Wesley.

Bridges, W. (1994b), 'The end of the job', *Fortune*, September 14.

British Film Institute (1999), *Industrial Tracking Study: Third Report*, London.

Burchell, B.J. et al. (1999), *Job Insecurity and Work Intensification*, York: Joseph Rowntree Foundation.

Business Strategies Ltd (1998), *Occupations in the Future*, London.

Buxton, J. (1999), 'Balancing work life and personal life', *The Guardian*, 6 January.

Caffman, C. and Harter, J. (1998), *A Hard Look at Soft Numbers*, London: Gallup.

Callaghan, G.S. (1997), *Flexibility, Mobility and the Labour Market*, Aldershot: Ashgate.

Casey, B., Metcalf, H. and Millward, N. (1997), *Employers' Use of Flexible Labour*, London: Policy Studies Institute.

Christy, D. (1998), 'Downsizing to disaster,' *The Guardian*, 5 November.

Claydon, T. (1998), 'Problematising Partnership', in P. Sparrow and M. Marchington (eds), *Human Resource Management: The New Agenda*, London: Pitman Financial Times.

Commission of the European Communities (1995), *Social Europe: Flexibility and Work Organisation*, Brussels.

Commission of the European Communities (1997), *Partnership for a New Organisation of Work*, Brussels.

Commission of the European Communities (1998a), *Managing Change*, Brussels.

Commission of the European Communities (1998b), *Modernising the Organisation of Work: A Positive Approach to Change*, Brussels.

Commission of the European Communities (1999), *Employment in Europe*, Brussels.

Commission on Social Justice (1994), *Social Justice: Strategies for National Renewal*, London: Vintage.

Commission on Wealth Creation and Social Cohesion (1995).

Confederation of British Industry (1997), *Labour Market Flexibility: Getting Beyond the Slogans*, London.

Corfield Wright (1996), *Flexible Work Means Business*, Manpower: London.

Coupar, W. (1999), 'Partnership under fire', *IPA Magazine*, August.

Crace, J. (1999), 'A million workers make a night of it', *The Guardian*, 2 October.

Cross, S. (1999), 'Mixed reaction to call for labour law talks', *European Voice*, 25 March.

Davis, R. (1999), 'Smoother operators', *People Management*, 6 May.

Daycare Trust (1998), *Families that Work*, London.

Demos (1994), *Generation X and the New Work Ethic*, London.

Dench, S., Bevan, S. and Tamkin, P. (2000), 'Family-friendly employment: its importance to small and medium enterprises', *Labour Market Trends*, March.

Department for Trade and Industry (1994), *Competitiveness: Helping Business to Win*, London.

Department for Trade and Industry (1997a), *Competitiveness through Partnerships with People*, London.

Department for Trade and Industry (1997b), *Competitiveness UK: Our Partnership with Business*, London

Department for Trade and Industry (1998), *Working for the Future: the Changing Face of Work Patterns*, London.

Department for Trade and Industry (1999), 'Foundations laid for new culture of fairness at work' (press release), London, 28 January.

Dex, S. and McCulloch, A. (1997), *Flexible Employment: The Future of Britain's Jobs*, Basingstoke: Macmillan.

Dex, S., Willis, J., Paterson, R. and Sheppard, E. (1998), *Workers Strategies in Uncertain Labour Markets: An Analysis of Casualisation in the TV Industry*, Cambridge: Judge Institute.

Diamantopoulou, A. (2000), 'Europe must get to work', *People Management*, 2 March.

Dyer, C. (1998), 'Train driver mother wins landmark sex bias case', *The Guardian*, 1 June.

Earl, M.J. (1996), 'The risks of outsourcing IT', *Sloan Management Review*, Spring.

Eclipse (1999), 'Flexible working', *Eclipse*, 4 (6), September.

Elliot, L. (1999a), 'Oskar falls, capital moves on', *The Guardian*, 15 March.

Elliot, L. (1999b), 'Labour through the class ceiling', *The Guardian*, 24 May.

Employment Policy Institute (1997), 'Anglo-Saxon Economics and Jobs', Economic Report 11 (1), February.

Faulkner, K. (1999), 'Dutiful people', *People Management*, 11 February.

Felstead, A. (1996), 'Homeworking in Britain: the national picture in the mid 1990s', *Industrial Relations Journal*, 27 (3).

Felstead, A. and Jewson, N. (1996), *Homeworkers in Britain*, London: Department for Education and Employment and Department for Trade and Industry, HMSO.

Felstead, A. and Jewson, N. (1999), 'Domestic product', *People Management*, 16 December.

Fleetwood, S. (1999), 'Less unemployment, but more bad employment', *The Guardian*, September 13.

Flood, P.C. (1996), 'Is HRM dead? What will happen to human resource management when traditional methods are gone?', ESRC Workshop *HRM In Crisis*, Manchester Business School.

Flood, P.C., Gannon, M.J. and Pauwe, J. (1995), *Managing Without Traditional Methods: International Innovations in Human Resource Management*, Wokingham: Addison-Wesley.

Forth, J., Lissenburgh, S., Callender, C. and Millward, N. (1997), 'Family friendly arrangements in Britain, 1996', Sheffield: DfEE, *Research Report* 16.

Foster, J. (1996), 'Home alone', *People Management*, 26 September.

Fowler, A. (1996), 'How to benefit from teleworking', *People Management*, 7 March.

Gallie, D. and White, M. (1993), *Employee Commitment and the Skills Revolution*, London: Policy Studies Institute.

Gallie, D., White, M., Cheng, Y. and Tomlinson, M. (1998), *Restructuring the Employment Relationship*, Oxford: Oxford University Press.

Gasteen, A. and Sewell, J. (1994), 'The Aberdeen Offshore Oil Industry: Core and Periphery', in J. Rubbery and F. Wilkinson (eds), *Employer Strategy and the Labour Market*, Oxford: Oxford University Press.

Gibbs, G. (1999), 'Night shift nurses win tribunal ruling', *The Guardian*, 15 January.

Goss, D. and Bridson, J. (1998), 'Understanding interim management', *Human Resource Management Journal*, 8 (4).

Gregoriadis, L. (1999), 'Single mother wins case

over 16-hour shifts', *The Guardian*, 3 August.

Grethé, C. (1998), 'Pool position', *People Management*, 26 November.

Grønning, T. (1998), 'Whither the Japanese employment system? The position of the Japanese Employers' Federation', *Industrial Relations Journal*, 29 (4).

Grubb, D. and Wells, W. (1993), 'Employment regulations and patterns of work in EC countries', *OECD Economic Studies*, 21.

Guardian (1999a), 'Two views of leader's challenge', 14 September.

Guardian (1999b), 'Can we be friends?', 15 September.

Guest, D. (1989), 'Personnel and human resource management: can you tell the difference?', *Personnel Management*, October.

Guest, D. and Conway, N. (1997), *Employee Motivation and the Psychological Contract*, London: IPD.

Guest, D. and Conway, N. (1998), *Fairness at Work and the Psychological Contract*, London: IPD.

Guest, D. and Conway, N. (1999), *How Dissatisfied are the British Workers? A Survey of Surveys*, London: IPD.

Guest, D. and Peccei, R. (1998), *The Partnership Company*, London: IPA.

Handy, C. (1995), 'Trust and the virtual company', *Harvard Business Review*, 73 (3), May–June.

Hart, R. (1987), *Working Time and Employment*, London: Allen and Unwin.

Heller, F., Pusic, E., Strauss, G. and Wilpert, B. (1998), *Organisational Participation: Myth and Reality*, Oxford: Oxford University Press.

Herriot, P. (1996), 'Applying the psychological contract', *ESRC Conference*, Manchester.

Herriot, P. and Pemberton, C. (1995), 'A new deal for middle managers', *People Management*, 15 June.

Herriot, P. and Pemberton, C. (1996), 'Contracting careers', *Human Relations*, 49 (6).

Herriot, P. and Pemberton, C. (1997), 'Facilitating new deals', *Human Resource Management Journal*, 7 (1).

Herriot, P., Hirsh, W. and Reilly, P. (1998), *Trust and Transition: Managing the Future Employment Relationship*, Chichester: Wiley.

Hewitt, P. (1993), *About Time: the Revolution in Work and Family Life*, London: Institute for Public Policy Research.

Hillage, J. and Morale, J. (1996), 'Return on investors', Brighton: Institute for Employment Studies, *Report* 314.

Hillage, J. and Pollard, E. (1998), 'Employability: developing a framework for policy analysis', Nottingham: DfEE, *Research Report* 85.

HM Treasury (1991), *Competing for Quality*, London: HMSO.

Hooper, A. and Potter, J. (1999), 'Take it from the top', *People Management*, 19 August.

House of Commons Education and Employment Select Committee (1999), *Second Report on Part Time Work*, London.

Hunter, L., McGregor, A., MacInnes, J. and Sproull, A. (1993), 'The flexible firm: strategy and segmentation', *British Journal of Industrial Relations*, 31 (3), September.

Huselid, M. (1995), 'The impact of human resources management practices on turnover, productivity and corporate financial performance', *Academy of Management Journal*, 38.

Hutchinson, S. and Brewster, C. (1994), *Flexibility at Work in Europe*, London: IPD.

Hutton, W. (1995), *The State We're In*, London: Jonathan Cape.

Huws, U. (1994), 'Teleworking in Britain', Sheffield: Employment Department, *Employment Department Research Series* 18.

Huws, U. (1996), *Teleworking and Rural Development*, Salisbury: Rural Development Commission.

Huws, U. (1997), 'Teleworking: guidelines for good practice', Brighton: Institute for Employment Studies, *Report* 329.

Huws, U. (1998), 'In from the cold', *People Management*, 24 December.

Huws, U. (1999), *Teleworking and Local Government: Assessing the Cost and Benefits*, London: LGMB.

Huws, U., Podro, S., Gunnarsson, E., Weijers, T., Arvanitaki, K. and Trova, V. (1996), 'Teleworking and gender', Brighton: Institute for Employment Studies, *Report* 317.

Huws, U., Jagger, N. and O'Regan, S. (1999), 'Teleworking and globalisation', Brighton: Institute for Employment Studies, *Report* 358.

Incomes Data Services (1994), 'Teleworking', London, *Study* 551, April.

Incomes Data Services (1998), 'Public sector labour market survey', London, *Report* 775, December.

Industrial Relations Services (1994), 'Non standard working under review', *Employment Trends Report* 565, August, London.

Industrial Relations Services (1996a), 'Still a flexible friend? A survey of flexitime', London, *Employment Trends Report* 603, March.

Industrial Relations Services (1996b), 'Flexible workers on call at Tesco', London, *Employment Trends Report* 620, November.

Industrial Relations Services (1999), 'The state of telework', London, *Employment Trends Report* 673, February.

Industrial Society (1998), 'Flexible work patterns', London, *Managing Best Practice: Report* 46.

Institute for Economic Research (1999), *Review of the Economy and Employment 1998/9*, Warwick.

Institute of Management (1997), *The Quality of Working Life*, London.

International Herald Tribune (1999), 26 August.

International Monetary Fund (1997), *World Economic Outlook*, Washington.

Involvement and Participation Association (1995), *Towards Industrial Partnership: Putting it into Practice*, 2, London.

Involvement and Participation Association (1997), *Towards Industrial Partnership: New Ways of Working in British Companies*, London.

Involvement and Participation Association (1998a), *IPA Magazine*, July.

Involvement and Participation Association (1998b), *IPA Magazine*, October.

Involvement and Participation Association (1998c), *Sharing the Challenge: Employee Consultation, a Guide to Good Practice*, London.

Involvement and Participation Association (1999a), *IPA Magazine*, February.

Involvement and Participation Association (1999b), *IPA Magazine*, May.

Involvement and Participation Association (1999c), *IPA Magazine*, August.

Iziren, A. (1999), 'Age concerns', *People Management*, 20 May.

Johnson, G. (1987), *Strategic Change and the Management Process*, Oxford: Blackwell.

Johnson, R. (1999a), 'Family values', *People Management*, 11 March.

Johnson, R. (1999b), 'Constructive surgery', *People Management*, 11 November.

Jones, C. and Stredwick, J. (1998), 'Cracking services', *People Management*, 3 September.

Kent, S. (1996), 'Time difference', *Personnel Today*, 22 October.

Kessler, S. and Bayliss, F. (1992), *Contemporary British Industrial Relations*, Basingstoke: Macmillan Press.

Kessler, I. and Undy, R. (1996), *The New Employment Relationship: Examining the Psychological Contract*, London: IPD.

Kessler, I., Coyle-Shapiro, J. and Purcell, J. (1999), 'Outsourcing and the employee perspective', *Human Resource Management Journal*, 9 (2).

Kodz, J., Kersley, B., Strebler, M.T. and O'Regan, S. (1998), 'Breaking the long hours culture', Brighton: Institute for Employment Studies, *Report* 352.

Labbs, J.J. (1993), 'Why HR is turning to outsourcing', *Personnel Journal*, September.

Labour Party (1996), *Road to the Manifesto: Building Prosperity – Flexibility, Efficiency and Fairness at Work*, London.

Lacity, M.C. and Hirscheim, R. (1993a), *Beyond the Information Systems/Outsourcing Bandwagon*, Chichester: Wiley.

Lacity, M.C. and Hirscheim, R. (1993b), *Information Systems Outsourcing: Rights, Metaphors and Realities*, Chichester: Wiley.

Lacity, M.C., Hirschheim, R. and Willcocks, L.

(1994), 'Realizing outsourcing expectations', *Information Systems Management*, Fall.

Lacity, M.C., Willcocks, L.P. and Feeny, D.F. (1995), 'IT outsourcing: maximize flexibility and control', *Harvard Business Review*, May–June.

Lacity, M.C., Willcocks, L.P. and Feeny, D.F. (1996), 'The value of selective outsourcing', *Sloan Management Review*, 37, Spring.

Laurier, E. and Philo, C. (1999), *Meet You at Junction 17: a Socio-Technical Study of the Mobile Office*, London: ESRC.

Lawler, E.E. (1994), 'From job based to competency based organisations', *Journal of Organisational Behaviour*, 15.

Lawler, E.E. (1996), 'Far from the fad in-crowd', *People Management*, 24 October.

Lawler, E.E., Mohrman, S. and Ledford, G. (1995), *Creating High Performance Organisations*, San Francisco: Jossey Bass.

Lea, R. (1999), 'How do we strike the right balance with work', *IPA Magazine*, February.

Legge, K. (1998), 'Flexibility: the gift wrapping of degradation', in P. Sparrow and M. Marchington, (eds), *Human Resource Management: The New Agenda*, London: Pitman Financial Times.

Leigh, A. (1999), 'Don't be a fashion victim', *People Management*, 28 January.

Leighton, P. and Syrett, M. (1989), *New Work Patterns: Putting Policy into Practice*, London: Pitman.

Lester, T. (1995a), 'Flexibility: myths and realities', *Human Resources*, September/October.

Lester, T. (1995b), 'The art of clock watching', *Human Resources*, September/October.

Lewis, S. and Lewis, J. (eds) (1996), *The Work Family Challenge*, London: Sage.

Locke, R., Kochan, T. and Priore, M. (eds) (1995), *Employee Relations in a Changing World Economy*, Cambridge, Mass.: MIT.

Lonsdale, C. and Cox, A. (1998), 'Falling in with the out crowd', *People Management*, 15 October.

Low Pay Unit (1998), *Response to Fairness at Work White Paper*, London.

MacLeod, D. (1999), 'Part-timers hit back', *The Guardian*, 5 October.

Marchington, M. (1998), 'Partnership in Context: Towards a European Model', in P. Sparrow and M. Marchington (eds), *Human Resource Management: The New Agenda*, London: Pitman Financial Times.

Mather, C. (1996), 'Developing corporate responsibility', in N. Baker (ed.), *Building a Relational Society: New Priorities for Public Policy*, London: Arena.

McLean Parks, J. and Kidder, D.L. (1994), 'Till death do us part: changing work relationships in the 1990s', in C. Cooper and D. Rousseau (eds), *Trends in Organisational Behaviour*, vol. 1, Chichester: Wiley.

Michie, J. and Sheehan, M. (1999), 'Human resource management practices: research and development expenditure and innovative investment: evidence from the UK's 1990 Workplace Industrial Relations Survey, *Industrial and Corporate Change*, 8 (2).

Milne, S. (1996), 'Victory for part-timers', *The Guardian*, 11 October.

Milward, N., Steven, M., Smart, D. and Hawes, W.R. (1992), *Workplace Industrial Relations in Transition*, Aldershot: Gower.

Mintzberg, H. (1994), *The Rise and Fall of Strategic Planning*, New Jersey: Prentice Hall.

Monks, J. (1996a), 'British industry: a genuine partnership', *The House Periodical*, London Parliamentary Communications, 4 November.

Monks, J. (1996b), 'Stakeholders in the workplace', in N. Baker (ed.), *Building a Relational Society: New Priorities for Public Policy*, London: Arena.

Monks, J. (1999), 'Ready, willing and able', *People Management*, 20 May.

Murphy, E. (1996), *Flexible Work*, London: Director Books.

Murphy, P. (2000), 'The internet's spine tingler', *The Guardian*, 12 February.

National Association of Citizens' Advice Bureaux (1997), *Flexibility Abused*, London.

Navarro, B. (1996), *Temporary Fault: a Report on the Terms and Conditions of Workers Employed through Employment Agencies or*

Employment Businesses, Manchester: Greater Manchester Low Pay Unit.

Neathey, F. and Hurstfield, J. (1995), *Flexibility in Practice: Women's Employment and Pay in Retail and Finance*, London: Industrial Relations Services.

New Ways to Work (1993), *Changing Times: A Guide to Flexible Work Patterns for Human Resource Managers*, London.

Nickell, S. (1997), 'Unemployment and labour market rigidities: Europe versus North America', *Journal of Economic Perspectives*, 11 (3), Summer.

North, S.-J. (1996), 'Part time parity', *Personnel Today*, 13 February.

Office for National Statistics (1996), *Labour Force Survey*, London.

Office for National Statistics (1997), *Social Trends*, London: The Stationery Office.

Office for National Statistics (1998), *Labour Force Survey*, London.

Office for National Statistics (1999a), *Labour Force Survey*, London, Spring.

Office for National Statistics (1999b), *New Earnings Survey*, London.

Office for National Statistics (1999c), *Social Trends*, London: The Stationery Office

Organization for Economic Cooperation and Development (1994), *Jobs Study*, Paris.

Organization for Economic Cooperation and Development (1995), *The OECD Jobs Study: Implementing the Strategy*, Paris.

Organization for Economic Cooperation and Development (1996a), *Economic Outlook*, Paris.

Organization for Economic Cooperation and Development (1996b), *Economic Survey of the UK*, Paris.

Organization for Economic Cooperation and Development (1999), *Economic Outlook*, Paris.

Ostroff, C. (1995), 'Human resource management: ideas and trends in personnel', June 21, Issue No. 356, CCH Incorporated.

O'Reilly, J. (1992), 'Where do you draw the line?', *Work, Employment and Society*, no. 6.

Overell, S. (1997a), 'Banks attacked over zero hours contracts', *People Management*, 11 September.

Overell, S. (1997b), 'Germany staggers as UK flexes its markets', *People Management*, 20 November.

Overell, S. (1998), 'Confusion reigns as France shortens its working week', *People Management*, 28 May.

Patch, A., Guest, D., Mackenzie Davey, K. and Kidd, J. (2000), 'What will encourage employees to acquire and share knowledge at work?', *Paper to Occupational Psychology Conference of the British Psychological Society*, 6 January.

Patterson, M.G., West, M.A., Lawthom, R. and Nickell, S. (1997), *Impact of People Management Practices on Business Performance*, London: IPD.

Pearce, J.L. (1998), 'Job security is important but not for the reasons you might think: the example of contingent workers', in C. Cooper and D. Rousseau (eds), *Trends in Organisational Behaviour*, vol. 5, Chichester: Wiley.

People Management (1999a), 'Engineers in breakdown over change', 14 January.

People Management (1999b), 'Council set to put check on overtime', 11 March.

Perry M. (1992), 'Flexible production, externalisation and the interpretation of business service growth', *Service Industries Journal*, 12 (1), January.

Personnel Today (1996), 'Ebb and flow', 13 February.

Pettinger, R. (1998), *Managing the Flexible Workforce*, London: Cassell.

Pfeffer, J. (1994), *Competitive Advantage Through People: Unleashing the Power of the Work Force*, Harvard: Harvard Business Press.

Pfeffer, J. (1998), *The Human Equation: Building Profits by Putting People First*, Harvard: Harvard Business School Press.

Pickard, J. (1998), 'Retail giants view temping as past its sell by date', *People Management*, 11 June.

Pickard, J. (1995), 'Food for thought', *People Management*, 30 October.

Pilger, J. (1999), 'What did you do during the dock strike?', *The Guardian*, 13 July.

Pollert, A. (ed.) (1991), *Farewell to Flexibility?*, Oxford: Basil Blackwell.

Pollock, L. (2000), 'Ground force', *People Management*, 20 January.

Poole, M. and Jenkins G. (1996), *Back to the Line? A Survey of Managers' Attitudes to Human Resource Management*, London: Institute of Management.

Portillo, M. (1994), *Clear Blue Water*, London: Conservative Way Forward.

Proctor, S., Rowlinson, M., McArdle, L., Hassard, J. and Forrester, P. (1994), 'Flexibility, politics and strategy', *Work, Employment and Society*, no. 8.

Prodi, R. (2000), 'European Revolution', *The Guardian*, 21 March.

PTC Inland Revenue (1996), *Alternative Working Patterns and You*, London.

Purcell, J. (1997), 'A good question', *People Management*, 17 April.

Purcell, K. and Purcell, J. (1998), 'Insourcing, outsourcing and the growth of contingent labour as evidence of flexible employment strategies', *European Journal of Work and Organisational Psychology*, 7 (1).

Rajan, A. and van Eupen, P. (1998), *Tomorrow's People*, Southborough: Create.

Rajan, A., van Eupen, P. and Jaspers, A. (1997), *Flexible Labour Markets*, Southborough: Create.

Rana, E. (1999), 'Social partnership is no panacea warns GMB chief', *People Management*, 17 June.

Reich, R. (1997), 'New deal and a fair deal', *The Guardian*, 14 July.

Reilly, P. (1997a), 'Balancing the flexibility scorecard', in Arthur Andersen, HR Director, London.

Reilly, P. (1997b), 'Fixed term or regular contract: do you make a choice?', *Croner's Recruitment, Selection and Induction Briefing*, no. 2, 12 August.

Reilly, P. (1997c), 'Flexible work arrangements in a growing business', in R. Willsher and A. Jolly (eds), *Growing Business Handbook*, London: Confederation of British Industry, Kogan Page.

Reilly, P. (1998), 'Balancing flexibility: meeting the interests of employer and employee', *European Journal of Work and Organisational Psychology*, 7 (1).

Reilly, P. and Tamkin, P. (1997), 'Outsourcing: a flexible option for the future?', Brighton: Institute for Employment Studies, *Report* 320.

Rix, A., Davies, K., Gaunt, R., Hare, A. and Cobbold, S. (1999), 'The training and development of flexible workers', *Labour Market Trends*, October.

Robinson, D., Buchan, J. and Hayday, S. (1999), 'On the agenda: changing nurses' careers', Brighton: Institute for Employment Studies, *Report* 360.

Rousseau, D. (1995), *The Psychological Contract in Organisations*, London: Sage.

Rousseau, D. (1997), 'Organizational behavior in the new organizational era', *Annual Review of Psychology*, no. 48.

Rubbery, J. and Wilkinson, F. (eds) (1994), *Employer Strategy and the Labour Market*, Oxford: Oxford University Press.

Rucci, A.J., Kirn, S.P. and Quinn, R.T. (1998), 'The employee-customer profit chain at Sears', *Harvard Business Review*, January–February.

Sako, M. and Sato, H. (eds), (1997), *Japanese Labour and Management in Transition*, London: Routledge.

Sen, A. (1997), 'Inequality, unemployment and contemporary Europe', *International Labour Review*, 136 (2).

Simmons, S. (1996), *Flexible Working*, London: Kogan Page.

Smith, D. (1997), *Job Insecurity Versus Labour Market Flexibility*, London: Social Market Foundation.

Solomon, C.M. (1996), 'Flexibility comes out of the blue', *Personnel Journal*, June.

Sparrow, P. (1997), 'Job based flexibility: changing times for human resource management', *Flexible Working*, July.

Sparrow, P. and Marchington, M. (eds) (1998) *Human Resource Management: The New Agenda*, London: Pitman Financial Times.

Stevens, J. (1999), 'Northern exposure', *People Management*, 25 February.

Storey, J. (ed.) (1989), *New Perspectives on Human Resource Management*, London: Routledge.

Stredwick, J. and Ellis, S. (1998), *Flexible Work Practices*, London: IPD.

Taylor, M. (1999), 'Saxons v Anglo-Saxons', *The Guardian*, 6 December.

Thomas, R. (1996), 'Fears for job security "unfounded"', *The Guardian*, 12 June.

Thompson, M. (1993), 'Pay and performance: the employee experience', Brighton: Institute of Manpower Studies, *Report* 258.

Thurlow, L. (1994), 'The global company', *RSA Journal*, November.

Trades Union Congress (1998a), *Britain and the Netherlands: Polls Apart*, London.

Trades Union Congress (1998b), *Flexible Friends: Case Studies of Positive Workplace Flexibility*, London.

Trades Union Congress (1998c), *The Time of Our Lives: a TUC Report on Working Hours and Flexibility*, London.

Trades Union Congress (1999a), *Jobs in Europe: What the Eurosceptics Don't Tell You*, London.

Trades Union Congress (1999b), *Partners for Progress*, London.

Trades Union Congress (2000), *Focus on Recognition: Trade Union Trends Survey*, London.

Treanor, J. (1998), 'Corporate financiers toast record year for mergers', *The Guardian*, 11 December.

Treanor, J. (1999), 'Lloyds TSB ends 9 to 5', *The Guardian*, 6 May.

Tremlett, N. and Collins, D. (1999), 'The temporary employee survey', *Labour Market Trends*, October.

Tsui, A.S., Jone, L.P., Porter, L.W. and Tripoli, A.M. (1997), 'Alternative approaches to the employee/organisation relationship: does investment in employees pay off?', *Academy of Management Journal*, no. 40.

Tully, S. (1993), 'The modular corporation', *Fortune*, 8 February.

Tyler, T.R. and Bies, R.J. (1990), 'Interpersonal aspects in procedural justice', in J. S. Carol (ed.), *Applied Social Psychology in Business Settings*, Hillsdale, New Jersey: Lawrence Erlbaum.

Vliet, A. van der (1996), 'What women want', *Human Resources*, July/August.

Vroom, V.H. and Jago, A.G. (1998), 'Managing participation: a critical dimension of leadership', *Journal of Management Development*, 7 (5).

Walker, L. (1996), 'Instant staff for a temporary future', *People Management*, 25 January.

Walker, M. (1999), 'There's no need to vote, the fix is in', *The Guardian*, 14 June.

Walsh, J. (1999a), 'Bristol fashions a flexible hours scheme to please all', *People Management*, 30 June.

Walsh, J. (1999b), 'Surprise choice for top job in new look commission', *People Management*, 29 July.

Ward, L. (2000), 'PM challenged over drive to give parents more time off', *The Guardian*, 10 March.

Waterman, R.H., Waterman, J.A. and Collard, B.A. (1994), 'Towards a career resilient workforce', *Harvard Business Review*, July–August.

Welch, J. (1999), 'TUPE changes to give staff a fairer deal', *People Management*, 25 February.

Wheatley, M. (1999), 'Rover reborn', *Human Resources*, September.

White, M. (1996), 'Flexible response', *People Management*, 21 March.

Whitehead, M. (1998), 'The elastic bandwagon', *People Management*, 8 January.

Whitehead, M. (1999a), 'Nat West to put all branch staff on annualised hours', *People Management*, 28 January.

Whitehead, M. (1999b), 'Tribunal supports nurses' rights to put families first', *People Management*, 28 January.

Whitehead, M. (1999c), 'Watch your work-loads, firms told', *People Management*, 15 July.

Whitehead, M. (1999d), 'Rover's return', *People Management*, 16 September.

Whittaker, D.H. (1998), 'Labour unions and industrial relations in Japan: crumbling pillar or forging a third way?', *Industrial Relations Journal*, 29 (4).

Wickens, P. (1987), *The Road to Nissan: Flexibility, Quality, Teamwork*, Basingstoke: Macmillan.

Williams, A. (1993), *Human Resource Management and Labour Market Flexibility*, Aldershot: Avebury.

Williams, E. (1999), 'A serious side to pulling pints', *The Guardian*, 30 November.

Williamson, O.E. (1973), 'Markets and hierarchies: some elementary considerations', *American Economic Review*, 63.

Williamson, O.E. (1975), *Markets and Hierarchies: Analysis and Antitrust Implications*, New York: Free Press.

Williamson, O.E. (1979), 'Transaction-cost economics: the governance of contractual relations', *Journal of Law and Economics*, 22 (2).

Wilsher, P. (1996), 'Flexible workers or spare bodies', *Human Resources*, July–August.

Wilson, A., Holton, V. and Handy, L. (1994), *The Ashridge Management Index*, Ashridge: Ashridge Business School.

Wilson, J. (2000), 'One third of mothers forced out of full-time working', *The Guardian*, 24 January.

Workplace Employee Relations Survey (1998), Department of Trade and Industry, ESRC/Essex University Data Archive.

Index

Assessment and Development Centres

Iain Ballantyne and Nigel Povah

Assessment and development centres have been established for some years as an effective method for selecting and developing people. Recent dramatic growth has led to increased demand for guidance on how to run them. This book, by two of the UK's leading specialists in the field, will go a long way towards meeting that need.

It looks at the entire process, from the underlying concepts to the most effective methods of validation - not forgetting the organizational politics involved. The main objectives of the book are:

- to establish a thorough understanding of the principles and practice of assessment centres
- to provide sufficient knowledge to enable practitioners to run their own events in a professional manner
- to help readers to recognize when they may need to call on outside expertise
- to equip readers to ask pertinent questions of any prospective advisers.

Assessment and Development Centres represents a practical approach which is sure of a warm welcome from HR professionals.

Gower

Designing and Using Organizational Surveys

Allan H Church and Janine Waclawski

Organizational surveys are widely recognized as a powerful tool for measuring and improving employee commitment. If poorly designed and administered, however, they can create disappointment and even disaster.

There are many excellent books on sampling methodology and statistical analysis, but little has been written so far for those responsible for designing and implementing surveys in organizations. Now Allan H Church and Janine Waclawski have drawn on their extensive experience in this field to develop a seven-step model covering the entire process, from initiation to final evaluation. They explain in detail how to devise and administer different types of organizational surveys, leading the reader systematically through the various stages involved. Their text is supported throughout by examples, specimen documentation, work sheets and case studies from a variety of organizational settings. They pay particular attention to the political and human sensitivities concerned and show how to surmount the many potential barriers to a successful outcome.

Designing and Using Organizational Surveys is a highly practical guide to one of the most effective methods available for organizational diagnosis and change.

Gower

Developing Your Business Through Investors in People

Second Edition

Norrie Gilliland

- What does Investors in People involve and how would it benefit my organization?
- How can I make sure that our training and development activities will help achieve our business objectives?
- How can I encourage employees to 'take ownership'?
- How do I prepare for IIP assessment?

These questions and many others are addressed in this revised edition of Norrie Gilliland's highly acclaimed book. Drawing on experience acquired working on Investors in People with more than 50 organizations, the author describes the business benefits of developing employees through systematic communication, involvement and training.

He examines the IIP national standard in detail and suggests numerous ways of meeting it, showing how to align training and development with business objectives, how to assess individual development needs and what should be the role of managers in the process. For this new edition the text has been enlarged and improved to reflect the revisions to the national standard introduced in 1997.

For managers in every kind of business, for HRD specialists and for consultants, Norrie Gilliland's book will continue to be the best available source of reference and guidance in its field.

Gower

How to Resolve Conflict in the Workplace

Hoda Lacey

In the world of work, conflict is never far away. It can arise between boss and subordinate, between peers, between departments. You may be directly involved as a party to the dispute, or indirectly as a referee or mediator. Whatever the circumstances, conflict is probably the most common cause of stress in the workplace, affecting motivation, teamwork, productivity and ultimately profit. Indeed, unmanaged conflict is probably the largest reducible cost in organizations today. Hence the wise manager will ensure that he or she is equipped with the strategies and techniques of conflict resolution.

Rooted firmly in the philosophy of win/win, Hoda Lacey's book will enable you to use conflict in ways that actually benefit both yourself and your organization. And by encouraging you to become aware of your own behaviour it will also give you a basis for avoiding conflict in the future. Drawing on the approach pioneered by the Conflict Resolution Network, it provides a step-by-step method of tackling the problem. Part I sets the scene and Part II introduces the skills involved, including creating empathy, using assertiveness, dealing with emotions (your own and other people's) and overcoming reluctance. Finally, Part III presents some practical conflict resolution tools. The text is reinforced throughout by examples, illustrations and real-life case histories, and there is an appendix containing details of useful contacts and organizations.

Anyone who works with other people will find this book helpful. But it will be of special value to managers, supervisors, consultants and counsellors.

Gower

Manual of Remote Working

Kevin Curran and Geoff Williams

Remote working - sometimes known as teleworking - is transforming the organizational world. With the aid of modern technology more and more operations are moving out of the office and into the home or neighbourhood telecentres.

But how do you decide whether this is a suitable route for your own company? What are the potential pitfalls and how can you avoid them? How do you recruit suitable people? How can you monitor - and motivate - staff you can't even see? What are the legal and contractual problems?

These are the kinds of question you will need to address if you are using, or thinking of introducing, remote working. And these are the kinds of question the *Manual* is designed to help you answer. Drawing both on their own experience of running a company where all the personnel are remote workers and on best practice from around the world, the authors provide not just detailed advice on the key issues but actual procedures and documentation that you can adapt to suit your own circumstances.

The *Manual* will be an invaluable aid for senior managers, and particularly for those concerned with personnel and HR matters. It certainly represents the most comprehensive practical guide available to the planning and management of remote working.

Gower

Motivation Management

Sheila Ritchie and Peter Martin

Experienced managers have always known that what galvanizes John may leave Sally unmoved. But how do you decide which type of reward or incentive will produce the maximum effect in each case? This groundbreaking book provides some of the answers.

Over a period of many years Sheila and Peter separately carried out research into motivation in the workplace. Both of them field-tested Sheila's motivation profiles with more than 1400 managers around the world. The outcome was a unique set of insights into what makes people work with a will.

The findings are presented here for the first time, identifying 12 forces that drive people at work, including not only obvious factors, like money and recognition, but also equally powerful drives, like variety or the scope to be creative. For each individual there is a combination of factors that will encourage optimum performance, and the manager who understands what is required will inspire outstanding effort. He or she will also avoid the disappointment that can arise from, for example, granting someone more autonomy when their primary need is for structure.

The book starts with a questionnaire designed to produce a 'motivation to work' profile. It then shows how, by understanding our own needs and those of others, we can significantly improve the way we motivate people. Finally, it explains how, on the basis of such understanding, we can work more effectively with our staff in areas such as stress management, training and development, teamworking and culture change.

Motivation Management has the power to transform organizations. Managers, team leaders and HRD specialists will all benefit enormously from what it has to offer.

Gower

Powering Up Performance Management

An Integrated Approach to Getting the Best from Your People

Richard Hale and Peter Whitlam

In *Powering Up Performance Management* Richard Hale and Dr Peter Whitlam provide a refreshing approach to the subject of performance management. This will be of practical value to human resource managers and organizational development specialists or other senior managers concerned with getting the best from people in their organization. Structured around an integrated model of performance management this book is rich with tools and case studies, which are valuable contributions to understanding the use of behavioural competencies for the purpose of selection, target setting, appraisal and coaching.

Inside this book the authors:

• present a structured model of performance management;
• provide practical materials including questionnaires and case studies;
• outline a dynamic approach supported by pragmatic experience within international organizations; and
• put forward material based upon leading edge research.

The book is essential reading for anyone interested in understanding how to maximize the contribution from people within their organization.

Gower

Profiting from Multiple Intelligences in the Workplace

Joyce Martin

Economic competitiveness depends on having the smartest workforce possible. Old-style selection and assessment tools which are narrow in focus and inflexible in application will doom their corporations to the same fate as the dinosaurs. Organizations who want to survive and grow need to be open to new ways of uncovering and developing their people's abilities.

Profiting from Multiple Intelligences in the Workplace turns Howard Gardner's revolutionary theory of multiple intelligences into user-friendly tools for understanding and assessing success in everyone from CEOs to cleaners. It provides a complete system for:

- the examination of staff needs
- matching applicants and job specifications
- successful interviewing and induction
- effective supervision
- focused training and development.

The results not only allow the identification of individual skills but also uncover the mosaic of skills needed for multiskilling, multitasking and efficient teamwork.

No other book provides a method of translating the theory of multiple intelligences into workplace practice and, unlike other books which centre on only one intelligence (for example emotional intelligence), the inventories presented here work towards a balance between traditional skills, general competencies and social skills.

Gower

Structured Employment Interviewing

Paul J Taylor and Michael P O'Driscoll

Research shows that structured interviews are markedly superior to the traditional approach found in so many organizations. They produce selection and promotion decisions that are fairer and more consistent, and as a predictor of future job performance they have much greater validity.

This book describes and illustrates the two main approaches to structured interviewing: the behavioural description interview and the situational interview. It explains:

- how to plan the interview
- how to develop suitable questions
- how to conduct the interview
- how to evaluate candidates.

The text is supported by specimen forms, job analyses and interview questions. Also included are complete structured interview guides covering three different jobs.

For personnel professionals - and indeed all managers anxious to improve the quality of decision-making in this key area - *Structured Employment Interviewing* represents an invaluable resource.

Gower